# SOLEMN MOMENTS OF REMEMBRANCE

# Solemn Moments
## of
## Remembrance

*Exhortations by*

DENNIS GILLETT

THE CHRISTADELPHIAN
404 Shaftmoor Lane
Hall Green
Birmingham B28 8SZ
England

First Edition 2005

Other exhortational studies by the same author
available from the publisher:

*May you know it to be True*
(currently out of print)
*The Genius of Discipleship*
*He Healeth all Thy Diseases*
*Words and Weights*

ISBN 0 85189 167 5

Cover picture: Rosebery Reservoir near Edinburgh, Scotland
Photograph and calligraphy courtesy of  Paul Wasson

*Printed in England by:*
THE CROMWELL PRESS
Trowbridge
Wiltshire BA14 0XB

# FOREWORD

WITH this compilation, the publication of exhortations by Brother Dennis Gillett is completed. The first book, *May you know it to be True*, contained 23, and now this offering brings the total to 60.

This is a wonderful legacy from a brother who painstakingly typed out all his talks in full before delivering them at various ecclesias around the world. This has made the task of preserving his thoughts very easy. One might wonder why a brother of such knowledge and experience found it necessary to have every word before him. The answer is perhaps supplied by his daughter, Sister Lois Bradshaw. She says of her Father:

> "He was always anxious to illuminate the events and concepts recorded in the Bible in such a way as to evoke a response in the hearts of the hearers. To this end he used language very thoughtfully, believing the right word could make a difference to our understanding and ability to remember what was said. A thesaurus was his constant companion!"

For those who heard him, just reading these thoughts will revive many memories of the man himself. The soft Oxfordshire brogue, the thoughtful rubbing of the chin, the soothing words of comfort that were so often contrasted with blunt calls to duty.

For Brother Dennis, those memorial moments around the emblems of our Lord's sacrifice, those moments when spiritual awareness was at its height, were indeed solemn moments of sober reflection. Solemnity is the prevailing characteristic of these thoughts. The moment of bread breaking is frequently described as an intensely personal time:

> "The God of Jacob is our refuge. Is there a better moment to realise this than in this moment ... when we are *alone* with the One who is superlatively the refuge, the river and the rock?"

"In this solemn moment when we are *alone* with our Redeemer ... as we bow our heads and hush our spirits ..."

"With solemn hearts and hushed spirits ... when every third party is excluded and we are *alone* with the Redeemer, let us renew our faith."

"What a holy and solemn thing this memorial service is."

"In this solemn moment, let us bow the knee to his throne and kiss his sceptre and place ourselves unreservedly under his authority".

"So in the solemn moment of bread breaking in memory of his life-giving sacrifice, when we have the opportunity to open our hearts *in private* to God, let us give thanks with hushed spirits for this man of Nazareth, the virgin-born, the ever-living, the guarantor of our redemption".

So the quotations could be added to, but the point is made. These words of exhortation are designed to touch individuals, that each may make a personal assessment of his or her relationship to the Lord God and His Christ.

As with the previous book, the exhortations are ordered by the chapters of scripture on which they are primarily based and may perhaps be used for a personal memorial service based on the Daily Readings.

Brother Dennis fell asleep in Christ during November 1992. With his passing, a spiritual mentor was lost to the Brotherhood. How fortunate it is that his words can live on while those who remain await the Master's healing touch. May these words help to keep alive the deepest yearnings for the Kingdom of God in men and women of faith.

"The world travails waiting for the manifestation of the sons of God. That is you. Say it not boastfully but tenderly, reverently, gladly. You for whom the white robe has been woven without seam by the Lamb's striving. For you it is rousing, invigorating, exciting. It is the realisation of all your longing, the issue of all your striving. You are coming to the morning without clouds, to the city where no night is; where tears are wiped away and all harm is excluded."

COLIN WALTON
BIRMINGHAM 2005

# CONTENTS

# 1

## "WHO WILL SHEW US ANY GOOD?"
### (PSALM 4)

THIS little exhortation is concerned with an idea which emerges from Psalm 4. It could be helpful to us today because it could have the effect of confirming our faith and fortifying our resolution as we go into a new year.

One of the things which make the psalms so attractive is the way in which the writers seem able to touch on things and conditions which are utterly apposite to modern life, notwithstanding that the words were written so long ago. Although the great stream of human life has experienced many changes over the centuries – changes in manners and customs, changes in living conditions and working experience, nevertheless when looked at carefully the changes are mostly on the surface. It seems that underneath the same old forces remain unaltered. The same old human nature is there just as ever it was. The same questions are asked, the same amazement is manifested. The same problems emerge. They may have different names but in substance they are as old as man is old. Solomon was right. In some ways there is nothing new under the sun.

In this way Psalm 4 is so interesting today. Notice verse 6: "Who will shew us any good". In the writer's day he says that there were many making that enquiry. We can say truthfully there still are many making it. It is the cry of the man who looking back is dissatisfied. A man looking around him is full of cynicism and looking onward is full of pessimism. It is the language of restlessness and hopelessness. Is it not strange that it was being asked in the day of king David and there is no soul in this house today who is not acutely aware that it is the dominating question of this restless age in which we live – "Who will shew us any good?" What makes it so interesting today is the fact that it is being asked by people in quite opposite circumstances. On the one hand, there are people who are replete in every way – satiated with every earthly blessing – overfull and glutted. They come to a point when at last they are compelled to cry in their gratification "Who will shew us any good?" On the other hand there are men who are hungry, men feeling the pinch of want, men in the pang of poverty. Men gaunt and desperate and in their desperation they cry: "Who will shew us any good?" Successful men who never seem to fail in any particular nor at any level – and men who never seem able to succeed – effort after effort but always beaten. Both say at last: "Who will shew us any good?" Now when those who are so opposite are asking the same question, does it not suggest that they are expressing an underlying malady which is independent of their particular circumstances? The psalmist's answer confirms it. It is as old as the enquiry:

"There be many that say, Who will shew us any good? LORD, lift thou up the light of thy countenance upon us. Thou hast put gladness in my heart, more than in the time that their corn and their wine increased. I will both lay me down in peace, and sleep: for thou, LORD, only makest me dwell in safety."                                          (Psalm 4:6–8)

Mark what the writer is doing. In reply to the question about who will shew us any good he recounts his own experience of good through his relationship with God. "Thou hast put gladness in mine heart, more than they have when their corn and their wine is increased". In other words the gladness which comes from God is more and better than the gladness which comes from materialism, received on the one hand or coveted on the other. The result of the goodness which comes from God is peace and security. "I will both lay me down in peace, and sleep: for thou, LORD, only makest me dwell in safety". It is the lack of peace and security which causes men to cry: "Who will shew us any good?" It is restlessness and fever which wrings this cry from the human heart.

**God's Creation**

Now notice carefully what the psalmist is saying. He is saying that he and all those who share his faith find goodness where God finds it. If I may use the past tense for a moment in order to further the exposition. He found goodness where God found it. Where did God find it? Where in the Bible do you find the declaration that God found it was good? Your minds have already travelled over the pages to the book of Genesis and the record of Creation. All the things which God created He found good. The stars, the flowers, the birds of the air, the fish of the sea, the great creatures upon the earth and man – He said about it: "It is good". And He rested content with that goodness.

Rising above the actual items of creation, the picture which emerges is one of perfect fellowship, of perfect cooperation and therefore of perfect restfulness. I shall not need to take time proving to this audience that the perfect fellowship was soon marred. Everything remained good, but man proved to be vile. The contentment of God was soon disturbed. His rest was soon ended. The Bible tells us that God was not resting, instead He was rising early and sending His prophets. He was at work to repair the ravages made by sin. At last it came to the condition where men were living in the midst of all the good things of God and they were saying in cynical desperation: "Who will shew us any good?" In a world full of goodness there was one centre of pollution and evil. In a world of perfect symmetry there was one manifestation of awful dislocation. The beauty of God was spoiled and, dare I say it, even with reverence – the heart of God grieved, the restfulness of God unsettled, and the contentment of God hindered. The purpose of God was wounded by man's apostasy.

You do not have to be a genius to discern that men failed to find goodness because they had lost their consciousness of God. When men are hot and restless and without anchorage it is because they have no true knowledge of God. There are men and women in this world today who investigate the creation of God and analyse it and seek to conserve it and they deny the God who made it. They rejoice in the means and forget the One who provided the means. They marvel at the beauty of the world and ignore the One who made it beautiful. Put positively, the man or woman who by grace has come into true fellowship with the God of David, says with him: "Thou hast put gladness in my heart".

**Humanity Perfected**

Thinking then of the good things of God spoiled by man's sin and the contentment of God hindered – come on now to Matthew chapter 3:

"Then cometh Jesus from Galilee to Jordan unto John, to be baptized of him. But John forbad him, saying, I have need to be baptized of thee, and comest thou to me? And Jesus answering said unto him, Suffer it to be so now: for thus it becometh us to fulfil all righteousness. Then he suffered him. And Jesus, when he was baptized, went up straightway out of the water: and, lo, the heavens were opened unto him, and he saw the Spirit of God descending like a dove, and lighting upon him: and lo a voice from heaven, saying, This is my beloved Son, in whom I am well pleased." (verses 13–17)

Do you catch the contentment of God in that sentence: "In whom I am well pleased". The creation of God lacking perfect

3

goodness through the spoiling made by men, is restored in the perfection of the Son. What man did to disturb the rest of God, Jesus restored and gave God rest and contentment. You can hear it in the voice if you are attuned with the spiritual: "In whom I am well pleased".

Remember when the earth was made it was made in such a way that man, created to have dominion, would develop it and make it blossom into perfect fullness. No one who lived in Eden ever said: "Who will shew us any good?" The garden was a picture of fellowship and co-operation, designed to unlock the secrets of the creation and unveil all its wonderful possibilities. At first there was no restlessness, no fever, no disappointment – *until*. The tragedy is encapsulated in that word "until", and out of it comes this sad enquiry: "Who will shew us any good?" Man out of harmony with God has lost the key to goodness. Now the contentment in the voice of God: "In whom I am well pleased", is teaching us that the man of Nazareth has realised the first intention of God. In him the lost goodness of Eden is discovered. God found the lost goodness in the one lonely concentric man of the seamless robe. As you watch him at work you see the perfect man mastering the secrets of nature. His miracles attest his goodness. It is sometimes said that his miracles controlling the forces of nature and interfering with the laws of the universe attest his divinity – that is true in a certain way but I want to put it to you in another way. His miracles are an attestation of his perfect humanity. He is the archetypal man – the realised idea of what God meant when he said: "Let us make man in our image and after our likeness". He has dominion because he is truly man.

Listen to this by word of the psalmist: "What is man, that thou art mindful of him?" And the answer is this: "Thou hast made him a little lower than the angels, and hast crowned him with glory and honour. Thou madest him to have dominion over the work of thy hands: thou hast put all things under his feet" (Psalm 8:4–6). That is never true until you come to the man of Nazareth. The Hebrew man quotes the psalm and says: "We see not yet all things put under him. But we see Jesus, who was made a little lower than the angels for the suffering of death, crowned with glory and honour" (Hebrews 2:8,9).

That is why I say that his perfect humanity is proven by his miracles. God made him *man* to have dominion over the work of His hands. This then was where God found goodness and finding goodness found contentment. This is why men cannot find goodness and not finding it cry out: "Who will shew us any good?" The only place to find goodness is where God found it and finds it – in the perfection of His own child Jesus. This is true of you who have been called, blood-sprinkled and chosen. God has lifted up His countenance upon you and has put gladness in your heart.

**Coming Short of His Glory**

If ever you should come to cry in some measure: "Who will shew me any good?" it will be because you have in some way or another neglected His blessed Truth. You have let some other thing interfere with your loyalty to His cause. You have ceased to give His service the leading place in your daily affairs. You have nursed things in your life which ought to be repudiated and denied. You have given your time and your substance and your energy to the forces which dishonour His name. In the words of Psalm 4 – you have sought after vanity and falsehood. There is a sense in which everyone of us has come short of His glory.

I am compelled to linger on that thought when I think of the end of his life and the cross of shame. The men who mauled him and murdered him were saying in their way: "Who will shew us any good?" They had lost their vision through their own selfishness. They could see no beauty that they should desire him. It was not that the beauty was absent but that they were too blind to see it. So he was bruised and broken. On God's side was the profoundest act of love – on man's side the darkest deed of hatred. But the suffering is not the last word. Notice this about the two men who were crucified with him – it is said they reviled him. They were saying: "Who will shew us any good?" Life had brought them fever, disappointment and death. Then one of them came to think that this man of Nazareth had the secret of goodness. From lips paling in death he said: "Lord, remember me when thou comest into thy kingdom". The answer is a revelation: "I say unto thee, To day shalt thou be with me in paradise" (Luke 23:42,43).

Paradise, the garden of God, the Eden where perfect goodness was first established. Where goodness was spoiled and rest was lost. The dying man will find the goodness at last for which he cries and he will find it in the place where it first was created and will at last be re-created through the perfection of the Son. The tragedy is being dealt with now. "Thou hast put gladness in my heart … I will both lay me down in peace … thou, LORD, only makest me dwell in safety". So as we look at the created things, every one is good.

There is delight and rest in the very world where men are soured and restless. All the things of earth are full of His glory.

As the New Year begins let us reassure ourselves of the great truth of Psalm 4; that we shall never satisfy the claimant cry for goodness which comes singing up through our hearts and minds – save as we are mastered and impulsed by our love of Christ the Redeemer. So, at this moment, while the exhorting brother is uttering His last word, in this solemn moment of bread breaking in memory of the saviour, let us resolve to ask, as we step out into a new year, that God will lift up His countenance upon us, every one, and put gladness in our hearts – so that we may rejoice in that return to Him which means perfect rest.

# 2

## "THE LORD OF HOSTS IS WITH US"
### (PSALM 46)

ONE of the outstanding features of these old Hebrew songwriters, these psalmists, is that underlying all their music is the unalterable conviction that God is there and will not be moved and is utterly dependable. Notwithstanding all the reverses and the hardships and the perplexities there is this unswerving and unabated confidence in God. This is the rock foundation upon which they base their words and their faith.

In Psalm 46 the expression of this confidence is most startling and convicting. Verses 2 and 3 show that it matters not that the earth may be moved or the mountains lifted into the sea or the great deep may boil or that the land may quake – because in the midst of the turmoil there is one place which is tranquil. In the midst of the upheaval there is one place which is stable; in the midst of the faltering and flux there is one place unmovable; in the midst of the shaking there is one place which is unshakable. That one place is the City of God and it is ummovable and utterly safe because in that city is the holy place and in that holy place is the God of the elect. The mountains may topple, the heathen may rage, the nations may roar but it matters not – God is in his Holy place and He will be exalted. All this we have heard the singer sing today.

Now notice that in this song in Psalm 46, the confidence which we have just sought to describe is focussed most sharply in one sentence which occurs twice in the psalm in verses 7 and 11: "The LORD of Hosts is with us; the God of Jacob is our refuge". More accurately: "Yahweh of Hosts is with us; the God of Jacob is our refuge". Here we are touching something central in the life of God towards His people. First "He is with us"; second "He is our Refuge". In this little consideration we are to ponder this twofold declaration.

What I want to interest you in especially at this stage is the word "Hosts". "The LORD of Hosts". According to *Young's Concordance* the word means strength, army, force – but that will not help us very much just by itself. The best thing to do is to see how the word is used in the Old Testament, because by that method we shall discover what is intended in its various applications. So let us now engage in a little exegesis on this word "hosts".

First of all it is a word used about and applied to stars. In Genesis we read: "Thus the heavens and the earth were finished, and all the host of them" (2:1). In the prophecy of Isaiah: "Lift up your eyes on high, and behold who hath created these things, that bringeth out their host by number: he calleth them all by names by the greatness of his might, for that he is strong in power; not one faileth" (40:26). In the Psalms: "By the word of the LORD were the heavens made; and all the host of them by the breath of his mouth" (33:6). So it is used of stars.

Second the word "hosts" is used of angels. In 1 Kings we read this: "I saw the LORD sitting upon his throne, and all the host of heaven standing by him on his right hand and upon his left" (22:19). And in the song that sounded over Bethlehem so long ago when earth was waiting spent and restless: "There was a multitude of the heavenly host praising God, and saying, Glory to God in the highest, and on earth peace, good will toward men" (Luke 2:13). So the word "hosts" is used of angels, the ministers of God in heaven and on earth.

Thirdly it is used of men. In Exodus the great company led out of Egypt are called "the hosts of Yahweh" (Exodus 12:41). In Daniel chapter 8 verse 10 the expression "host of heaven" is used of the people of God.

So bring these things together and notice that the word is used of stars in the heavens; of angels the ministers of God in heaven, who are beyond our vision and for the most part outside our knowledge, and then of companies of people who march across the earth and dwell upon its surface. Stars and seraphim and saints. Hosts of stars, hosts of angels, hosts of men.

**The Vast Universe**

Now with that in mind come back to this phrase in Psalm 46. "The LORD of hosts". Notice what it is telling us. It is telling us that God is superior to all these forces which are compressed in this word "hosts". He is pre-eminently and absolutely far above all these things; He is Lord of all these things – sufficient and superior in every way. Think of it reverently. He is Lord of the heavens; He knows all the host of the heavens and marshals them at His will.

Let me detain you for a moment to ask you to think about the enormity of the universe over which He is Lord. It is really beyond our comprehension but here is one measurement. If you go out and look into the north part of the heaven and fix your eyes on Polaris, the Pole star – the light you see is 800 years old. It has taken that time to reach us travelling at the speed of light (186,000 miles per second) because it is that far away. We are looking at something which first came into existence at say the time of the Crusades or when King John signed Magna Carta and tonight will have reached us through the universe. If you were to sit down and make a plan of the heavens and allowed two inches for the 93 million miles between the earth and the Sun and then wanted to fix the next nearest star on the same scale you would need a piece of paper 7 miles long in order to do it. This gives us some idea of the enormity of the universe, where the stars have been set. He is Lord of all this and controls it with infinite wisdom.

**Lord of Angels and Men**

Then He is Lord of all the angelic hosts. In Psalm 103 verse 20: "Bless the LORD, ye his angels, that excel in strength, that do his commandments, hearkening unto the voice of his word".

And he is Lord of the world of men. He ruleth in the kingdoms of men. Not a hair of my head and yours has escaped His numbering; not a sparrow falls to the ground without His knowledge. The universe of matter; the universe of spirit: the universe of mind; He controls and marshals all in infinite wisdom and unchallenged might.

So in the phrase "Lord of hosts" we are reminded of the absolute power and majesty and might and wisdom of the great God of heaven. In other words we are given a vision of one side of the great Sustainer and Creator of life, here and everywhere.

So here is the thing to marvel at. In this short sentence in Psalm 46 suddenly we are given another view of the same great God of heaven. "Lord of Hosts" and then suddenly, daringly, startlingly – The God of Jacob. Think where we were. We were amid the great cosmic conception of the invisible Creator; amid the eternal expanse of His realm, with the angels who could blind us with their glory and baffle us with their power; among the stellar spaces of the universe. Then suddenly without warning we move from that to this – the God of Jacob. The stars grow dim, the angel hosts fade and suddenly we are on one small planet, in one small

9

country looking into the face of one lonely man: Jacob, the heel-catcher. And here is the thing to understand. The psalmist is telling us for our salvation, that the God who is Lord of the universe, Lord of all the heavenly hosts, cosmic and angelic – the Creator of the stellar spaces and the Creator of the angelic intelligences, is the God of that speck of humanity, that one lonely man called Jacob and just as positively He is committed to that man as much as He is committed to all the order of the infinite universe.

**The God of Jacob**

In the Bible every word is important so let us notice that He said "Jacob" – that is Jacob the supplanter. I do not know what you think about Jacob. I know that some people think he was a hard man; a mean man, self-sufficient and astute. Well if you think Jacob was mean, there is one man in the Bible who is meaner and that one man is Laban. Of all the hard, astute, hard-driving mean men, Laban is pre-eminent. It gives me some satisfaction to realise that Jacob was able to manage the meanness of Laban. Whatever you may think of Jacob, this is the thing to fix on now. Whatever he was, God cared for him, nurtured him, watched over him, kept his covenant with him, defeated him at Jabbok. In the defeat, he made him to triumph and re-named him with a wonderful name, Israel, which means God-governed. Yes, challenge it if you like, but that is what it means – God-governed.

So this is the mystery: the Lord is the God of Jacob. All through the years, in spite of the deception, notwithstanding whatever he did, God enwrapped him with His care, told him where to rest his head, and gave him a vision of covenanted love at Bethel. And when this Jacob was filled with fear as he left Paran to meet his brother Esau, full of foreboding over what Esau would do, filled with perhaps forty years of brooding and resentment about the way he had been supplanted, at last God made even Esau's anger to be turned to love and instead of wrath he greeted Jacob with a kiss. This then is the revelation. Yahweh of Hosts, infinite in majesty is the God of Jacob, infinite in mercy. Yahweh of hosts, stupendous in power, upholding all things by His commanding word; is the God of Jacob sublime in His pity. Here is the wonder of it; when you think of the stellar spaces, the light years, the galaxies; when you think of the myriads of angels, the cherubim and the seraphim; Yahweh of Hosts of necessity seems so far away and so far beyond us; the eternal order amid the stars and amid the angels – it is

10

wonderful and awful – but it is so far away. We see just a glimpse of His glory on a starry night, but so far away.

**God is Near**

But we are wrong, He is not far away. The psalmist says He is with Jacob, and because he is with Jacob he is with you and me. So it is not in immensity only that God is great; it is in the smallness of things as well. Notwithstanding the failure; notwithstanding the inconsistency; despite the great gulf between what God intended and what man has done, He is there. In spite of the fact that life has been blighted and humanity ravaged by the dwarfing influences of man's selfishness – never mind. These words are there for all the ages. The God of Jacob, this Yahweh, has created man and made him for one purpose: to give glory to his creator. And the creature has brought shame and degradation into the world and has broken all the holy laws by which he was supposed to live. But still He is the God of Jacob; still He broods over him tenderly, carefully, lovingly – his folly notwithstanding.

With all this upon our hearts, come back to verse 7: "The Lord of hosts is with us; the God of Jacob is our refuge". Notice what it means then in the light of the exegesis we have attempted. The Lord of Hosts is with us. That is, the God of the stars; the God of the angels; the God of men in multitude – He is with us. And He is with us for the making of Jacob and therefore for the making of you and me.

**Wrestling Jacob**

If we are to understand it better we must think of Genesis 32 and the mysterious account of Jacob wrestling with the man through the night. God met Jacob at Jabbok and Jacob was never the same again. Remember that during the course of the conflict Jacob said to the man of God: "I will not let thee go, except thou bless me" (verse 26). I wonder how he said it? It often helps to know the tone of voice. A whole lot of emotion is revealed in the cadence of the cry. There are two ways of saying "I love you", and one is better than the other. If only we knew how Jacob spoke: "I will not let thee go, except thou bless me". Did he say it stridently I wonder? Was it strong like it seems to sound? If only we knew the tone of voice we should know something about wrestling Jacob.

Here is a wonder. Long years afterwards the revelation came when a prophet let slip the tone of Jacob's voice. Look at Hosea chapter 12 verses 1 to 4:

11

"Ephraim feedeth on wind, and followeth after the east wind: he daily increaseth lies and desolation; and they do make a covenant with the Assyrians, and oil is carried into Egypt. The LORD hath also a controversy with Judah, and will punish Jacob according to his ways; according to his doings will he recompense him. He took his brother by the heel in the womb, and by his strength he had power with God: yea, he had power over the angel, and prevailed: he wept, and made supplication unto him: he found him in Bethel, and there he spake with us."

So it was with a voice choked with tears; it was the last sob of a defeated man. He is going down in the last agony of despair beneath the pressure of this mysterious man from God. Here is the contradiction; he triumphed when he was beaten. He was remade when he was broken. He was made whole when he was crippled. A man cannot defeat God but a man comes to victory when God masters him. When a man yields he wins. That is why he is called Israel: God-governed or God-mastered. A man is exalted to be a prince when he is humbled and submits. This is what happened to Jacob. He was blessed, then crippled.

So he tells his friends when he limps up on the other side of Jabbok: I am not anymore Jacob the supplanter but I am Israel the God-governed. I am mastered so that I may have power with God. It is written there in Genesis 32 about Jacob: "As he passed over Penuel the sun rose upon him, and he halted upon his thigh". Some words of the old prophet come to mind: "I will save her that halteth, and gather her that was driven out" (Zephaniah 3:19). Now is this what the singer meant by refuge? The God of Jacob is our refuge.

There may be people here today who understand it well. They are going grey as I am going grey. They are people perhaps upon whom God has put His hand as He did on Jacob, and in the experience they have learned something about God as a refuge. In some sense they have been crippled, but in the crippling found new strength hitherto unsuspected. They came to Marah and the waters were bitter – then trustingly went on to Elim and found rest. Who can tell it properly, this refuge, save those who have known it by experience? They will never be the same again. Mostly the revelation will come out of circumstances of stress and strain: an hour of overwhelming disappointment; a sorrow, a sadness, a failure, a personal affliction, a struggle merging into brokenness, a conflict which brought crippling. Which of us has not been aware in the secret part of our life that we need some healing touch; some eternal medicine which will end the fever and the failure?

Now today, the psalmist for our salvation is telling us that the Lord of Hosts will be a refuge for all who are in need of succour and healing. To the tempest tossed He is a mighty covert. To the weary and broken He is a river of pure water. To the wanderer in the trackless wilderness He is a great rock in a weary land. And at the basis of this confidence is how God treated Jacob. In spite of all the circumstances, God cared for him, loved him and saved him magnificently.

The Lord of Hosts is with us, the God of Jacob is our refuge. Is there a better moment to realise it than in this moment of bread breaking – when we are alone with the one who is superlatively the refuge, the river and the rock?

Let us pray that now as we commemorate this feast, and in the oncoming days, we may in our deepest heart feel it to be true.

# 3

## "CAST THY BURDEN UPON THE LORD"
### (PSALM 55)

I KNEW a brother now fallen asleep in Christ who had a simple and serene contemplation of the purpose of God. Once he said to me: "There are some magnificent promises in the Bible about God's care and compassion for His people, but sometimes when you speaking brethren are explaining them, when you have analysed them, dissected them and put them together again, we are left with a bag of bones. That which began as magnificent finishes up being almost commonplace. That which seemed at first wonderful, when it is explained turns out to be ordinary".

Now whether his criticism was justified I know not and I am not concerned with it now, except to say that we must strive at all costs not to leave you with a bag of bones. We do not want to emaciate the Word of God – only to expose it. We have come to affirm without equivocation that God *will* sustain His people and He will give them peace and we have not come to explain it away. So let us proceed in the spirit of sanctified optimism. We must not diminish the promises one whit but we must not invest them with meanings they do not have. What we need, as ever, is the truth.

### Burdens

Think then of verse 22 of Psalm 55: "Cast thy burden upon the LORD, and he shall sustain thee: he shall never suffer the righteous to be moved". Dwell first on the idea of burdens. This burden is not the burden of responsibility, personal responsibility before God which no man or woman can share or cast upon another and about which Paul says: "Every man shall bear his own burden" (Galatians 6:5). It is the other kind of burden which Paul says can be shared and eased: "Bear ye one another's burdens ..." (verse 2) – in other words the burden of life. It may be pain, worry, fear, hardship, infirmity, disappointment or sorrow. There are so many things which men and women carry as a result of their tempest-tossed experience of life and so they become restless, weary and heavy laden.

14

But there is another division which has to be made. It is the division between burdens which are false and those which are true. There are false burdens; these are the things which men carry which they have bound upon themselves and which they could shed. Just as surely they may bring worry, fear, disappointment or sorrow, but they are false because they are futile. The false burdens which people outside the Truth carry are not likely to be your problems. Planning, toiling, sweating, straining to acquire money, fame, pleasure, ambition, ease. The burden of living for self. Sometimes we say a man is self-satisfied, but if we could get into his inner life we should probably find that he is uneasy about his reputation, or his bank balance, or the market or his friendships and he is never at rest or never really satisfied. He worships his own desires and in a sense becomes an idolater. If you read Isaiah 46 you will discover that idols when they are created have to be carried. Remember: "Bel boweth down, Nebo stoopeth ... your carriages are heavy laden; they are a burden to the weary beast" (verse 1). What Isaiah is saying is that idols have to be carried and at last they will crush you. The burden is not only heavy, it is false. It is futile and by it men are deceived, self-deceived. "Bread of deceit is sweet to a man; but afterwards his mouth shall be filled with gravel" (Proverbs 20:17). No – because you are wise with the wisdom of God's word you will not be deceived by false burdens of this kind – burdens which we take upon ourselves which are really weights which we ought to shed and we could shed, but which for some reason we are tempted to keep and carry.

So as we come individually to think of casting our burden on the Lord, we ought first to ask ourselves whether it is a true burden which we have to carry and cannot evade, or one which we have bound upon ourselves and which to some extent therefore is futile. What I ask is this – has it come to us because of some way of life which we know in our deepest heart is not wholly in harmony with the will of God? Is it something we are loth to shed because there is some desire claimant in our heart, which if we shed the burden we could not satisfy? If it exists, you will know what it is if you give yourselves five minutes of honesty. Some relationship, some undertaking, some ambition, something which we hold with tight hands which ought to be held with light hands. If we bring this kind of burden to the Lord, I do not think He will sustain us so that we may go on and carry it – He will ask us to repudiate it and shed it. The King will not sustain his people in the very things which sap their spiritual strength. But supposing it is a true burden. Something that has come to us by way of faithfulness which we would gladly shed if we could, but which in truthfulness we cannot. I do not know what it is, but each heart will know its own burden. Some continuing adversity to which there seems no end; some disability for which there seems no visible remedy; some pain which cannot be alleviated; some wound which no human physician can heal; some opposition which mars our happiness and steals our joy; some doubt which saps our serenity; some hot turbulent protest which keeps us from contentment; some temptation which we long to master but which too often masters us; some weakness which brings us nigh to fainting; some sorrow deep in the recesses of our daily life.

Think of the man who wrote Psalm 55. His burden was that he had been brought into jeopardy and adversity by the treachery of a friend. The agony had been doubled by the fact that the one who should have shared his burden was the very one who had caused it. A friend is essentially one who bears the burdens of his brother friend – it is the very nature of true friendship. So the Psalmist's sorrow was intensified. He confesses that at one time in the midst of his trouble he was sighing for wings: "Oh that I had wings like a dove! for then would I fly away, and be at rest" (verse 6). But wings do not bring rest. Changing your address does not move the burden – at least not as a rule.

**Sigh of Relief**

Too much sighing means overwrought nerves and leads to ill-health. Jesus sighed only twice – when he healed the man who was deaf and dumb and when the Pharisees were trying to tempt him. It is a revelation. He sighed over the powers of life unused and over the powers of life misused. The man in Psalm 55 gave up sighing for wings and found at last the sigh of relief. He tells us how he came to it: "Cast thy burden on the LORD and he shall sustain thee". The word "cast" is interesting. He could have said place, or put or take. But he said "cast" because the meaning is "to let go altogether". Moses on the mountain cast down the tables of stone – it is the very same word *shalak*. It outlaws the idea of being partial in abandoning the burden. It demands a faith which will renounce all control and will trust God wholly in pursuit of a solution. Sometimes we are loth to do this – we want somehow to keep control and retain some regulation. May I remind you of an old story of the man with a burden who thought it might be eased by riding in the cart behind the donkey. His mistake was to keep the burden strapped to his back!

The condition should be clear then. It means come to the Lord God and in utter faith cast your burden upon Him. In the face of that condition the promise is categoric and emphatic: "He will sustain thee". What does it mean? Does it mean that God will remove the burden altogether? I have no authority to say He will not nor can I affirm positively that He will. The only thing to do is to look to see how He has dealt with those who have cast their burden upon Him hitherto. It will show us how He works and how He may deal with us. So let us come to some examples.

**Hannah's Faith**

Think of 1 Samuel chapter 1 and Hannah the wife of Elkanah. She had a burden and it was breaking her heart. She was childless and the other wife had borne sons and daughters. Peninnah was a cruel woman and provoked Hannah sore and made her fret. Elkanah was a good man. For a good woman there is no grief like domestic grief. It was no good explaining to Hannah that the laws of nature are immutable and changeless – she took her burden to God. She asked for a man child. Perhaps they said she was mad but there is a madness which rightly named is the sublimest sanity. Hannah returned at last to give thanks for Samuel. But here is the wonder of it. After she had prayed to God and went back to Shiloh her countenance was no more sad. Whatever the issue and whatever the outcome, she had cast her burden on the Lord. And it is well worth noticing that she had done it strictly in harmony with the meaning of the word "cast" which we marked earlier. She had let the burden go altogether. That is why she was no more sad or fretful. In this case the Lord removed the burden altogether and Hannah became the mother of a great prophet. Blessed are the boys that have such mothers. So let us take notice again – God removed the burden altogether because of Hannah's faith.

**Asa's Prayer**

Come to 2 Chronicles 14 and King Asa of Judah. He was a good king and everything was going well – the religion and the land prospered exceedingly. Then suddenly they were in dead trouble. A great host of Ethiopians was ready to overwhelm Judah and humanly speaking defeat was inevitable. Zerah had a million men. Think of the awful burden on Asa. Hemmed in on every side he cast his burden on the Lord. He spoke earnestly to Yahweh, God of Israel: "LORD, it is nothing with thee to help, whether with many, or with them that have no power: help us, O LORD our God; for we rest on thee, and in thy name we go against this multitude. O LORD, thou art our God; let not man prevail against thee" (2 Chronicles 14:11). It was a bold prayer by a man whose faith was not born in a panic. He said in affect: "This battle is not ours Lord, we are utterly inadequate – it is your battle Lord. In thy name we are come. Such as we are, we are at thy disposal – our failure will be thy failure. Let not man prevail against thee – not us but thee". Was there in the whole of the Bible a more perfect example of a man casting his burden on the Lord? There was a great victory that day for the Lord and He used Asa – such as he was and such as he had. God often works by what we have. The widow had to give her little oil and meal – the lad had to give his five barley loaves and two fishes. Asa had to fight and it called for faithful courage but he knew his burden was on the Lord. So in this case, God removed the burden but He required Asa's courage to do it. Asa had an active and vital part to play.

**Habakkuk's Burden**

Think of Habakkuk and his prophecy. Remember the first verse: "The burden which Habakkuk the prophet did see". The brother in Christ I spoke about at the beginning – he once said to me: "Dennis, Habakkuk shook his fist at God". Remember the second verse: "O LORD, how long shall I cry, and thou wilt not hear! even cry out unto thee of violence, and thou wilt not save!" Poor Habakkuk – every thing seemed to be wrong. Ungodliness seemed to triumph. The Chaldeans were sweeping over the land and desolation was all around and God who he had trusted would save His people appeared to be utterly indifferent. Habakkuk was perplexed and dismayed – in the midst of darkness and desolation the invisible God seemed helpless. That was Habakkuk's burden and he took it to God. He said: "I will stand upon my watch, and set me upon the tower, and will watch to see what God will say unto me" (2:1). Now consider these words:

"Although the fig tree shall not blossom, neither shall fruit be in the vines; the labour of the olive shall fail, and the fields shall yield no meat; the flock shall be cut off from the fold, and there shall be no herd in the stalls: yet I will rejoice in the LORD, I will joy in the God of my salvation. The LORD God is my strength, and he will make my feet like hinds' feet, and he will make me to walk upon mine high places." (3:17–19)

Notice a remarkable thing. The prophet in the midst of the very same circumstances which hitherto had sapped his courage and intensified his sorrow is saying: "Yet I will rejoice in the LORD, I will joy in the God of my salvation". Dance for joy instead of being downcast and perplexed. Habakkuk is now radiant and exultant. The desolation remains and yet he is jubilant.

Notice again verse 17. Could there be a more graphic description of failure – the fig tree blossomless; the vine fruitless; the olive a failure; the fields barren; the flocks decimated and lost; the stalls empty. In the context of a rural and agricultural people it speaks of absolute disaster. In these very circumstances the prophet is jubilant. He had cast his burden on the Lord and the Lord had sustained him. The Lord had not removed the burden but he had cleared Habakkuk's misty vision and had adjusted his dislocated judgement. In effect God said to him: "Habakkuk, I may be invisible but I am not indifferent. I have not forsaken my people and I have not resigned the government. Everything is under my control and nothing can defeat my purpose. In the midst of all the shattering events which have sapped your confidence, I am there. The great secret Habakkuk is this –the just must live by faith. Trust me and rest". So Habakkuk believed God and rested his soul. He was sustained according to the measure of his faith. The burden remained but Habakkuk understood it and could stay with it in confidence.

**Paul's Thorn in the Flesh**

Think now of the burden of Paul – a thorn in the flesh, a messenger of Satan. Thrice he asked for relief but the Lord sustained him with these words: "My grace is sufficient for thee: for my strength is made perfect in weakness" (2 Corinthians 12:9). The burden remained but when the Lord flashed the light of understanding upon it, Paul would not be without it. Not just "I will suffer it", but he says: "I take pleasure in infirmities ... in persecutions, in distresses for Christ's sake: for when I am weak, then am I strong" (verse 10). When Paul understood it the burden was not one whit less painful, but the sustaining by the Lord was magnificent. So in this case the burden remained, but Paul was equipped to keep it and surmount it.

**The Lord will Sustain**

Observe then the methods which the Lord uses to sustain those who cast their burden upon him. Sometimes He takes the burden away altogether. Sometimes he uses the victim's resources to remove it or overcome it. Sometimes He allows the burden to to remain but equips the sufferer to surmount it. There is an old saying that the Lord tempers the wind to the shorn lamb. It is rarely true. God does not change the wind, but gives the shorn lamb a good thick coat to stand against it. God rarely manoeuvres the circumstances of life, but gives grace sufficient to face them and sometimes to delight in them. So I submit that because this word of God is wholly true, it means that there is no hour so dark, no temptation so subtle, no opposition so strong, no pain so hard, no adversity so bitter – but that if we come in faith to God, He will sustain us. If this is not so then either this Word is false or we have been grossly deceived in our understanding of it. There is a sentence which seems to me to be conclusive – almost the last words of Moses: "The eternal God is thy refuge, and underneath are the everlasting arms" (Deuteronomy 33:27). The word "underneath" in Hebrew is "bottom"; the deepest part. When you have reached rock bottom; when the burden has almost crushed you and you are driven to say: "I was never more down than this" – then listen. Underneath – 'lower' than that – are the everlasting arms. Whatever the abyss – however much it seems to be a dark emptiness – be not afraid. Dare it, have faith, cast it on the Lord and you will find that you are falling through the abyss into the arms of God. The God of the morning is thy dwelling place and the Lord hath said: "I will never leave thee nor forsake thee". Surely this is what Moses is saying – "underneath are the everlasting arms".

Come back to Psalm 55 and the man, probably David, who had suffered treachery from a close friend – perhaps it was Ahithophel, but we must leave that. He had been betrayed by the very one he trusted: "We took sweet counsel together and walked unto the house of God in company" (verse 14). That friendship had proved to be a snare and a burden. Now the point to mark is that what was true of the treacherous friend can never be true of the burden-bearing God. God is the very opposite of the forces which had caused David's sorrow.

So in the midst of the fitful fever of life, in the midst of doubt and denial, faced with the allied forces of ungodliness – it can all be cancelled as we cast our burden on the Lord. We shall find that the promise is true – He will sustain us, until the final rest be won. God grant that we may in our deepest heart feel it to be true. He has said: "Come unto me …". Let us trust in that and take courage.

# 4

## "ALL THINGS WORK TOGETHER FOR GOOD"
### (PSALM 77 & ROMANS 8)

NOTICE that Psalm 77 was composed by a man called Asaph. He lived at the same time as King David and was a member of David's court, and a person of importance and influence. He was a musician and an accomplished songwriter, and was appointed by the king to be chief choirmaster for the services of worship and praise. There were three principal conductors: Asaph, Heman and Ethan. Asaph was the chief. As to his personal details, he was a Levite, son of Berechiah. He composed Psalms 73 to 83. Music must have run in his family and perhaps the high honour of being singers and musicians for God was hereditary, handed down from father to son. But Asaph was more than a great musician, he was a prophet. How else could his songs be included in the great book of inspired psalms? In 2 Chronicles 29:30 Asaph is linked with David and described as a seer of Israel. These are the details of his life as they emerge from the Bible narrative, but there is something more to learn about Asaph, particularly from his songs, as we find in Psalm 77.

### Asaph's View of Life

Most of us have at some time, I suppose, looked through a telescope or binoculars and looking, have found the vision blurred, uncertain, indistinct, dislocated, misty – in other words, out of focus. And then by making adjustment of the lens, suddenly the mists have cleared, the picture is defined, the lines are sharp, the uncertainty has gone, everything is seen in perspective – in other words, in true focus. I think most of us will have had this experience. The point now is that something like this happened to Asaph, but he was not looking through a telescope; he was looking at life. And his experience is recorded in Psalm 77 – the story of Asaph looking at life. How did he see it?

If we look carefully at the first nine verses we shall see. It is a sad, sobering song of perplexity and grief. It is full of complaint, it is heavy with agony, and there is no comfort. His life seems to be a perpetual mystery. Nothing seems right, everything is dislocated. His words come tumbling out; so many personal pronouns and so full of adversity. In the first ten verses you will find 11 references to God and 22 personal references to Asaph. That is not intended to be a criticism but simply to mark the condition of his soul. He is full of trouble and he resolves to cry unto God in his anguish and despair.

Notice his opening words – I quote from the RV because it gives the proper tense:

> "I will cry unto God with my voice ... and he will give ear unto me." (verse 1)

That is what he said to himself in his trouble. But there was no comfort and no healing:

> "In the day of my trouble I sought the Lord: my sore ran in the night, and ceased not: my soul refused to be comforted. I remembered God, and was troubled: I complained, and my spirit was overwhelmed." (verses 2,3)

So remembering God brought him no peace. He complained but was not comforted:

> "Thou holdest mine eyes waking: I am so troubled that I cannot speak." (verse 4)

Even his insomnia he blames on God. Then he tries to get comfort by bringing to mind his past experience and the joy he had then, but it does no good:

> "I have considered the days of old, the years of ancient times. I call to remembrance my song in the night." (verses 5,6)

But the old joy does not return. His perplexity is too real and his adversity is too present to be alleviated by past happiness. At last there stumble from his heart and his lips questions of doubt and utter despair:

> "Will the Lord cast off for ever? And will he be favourable no more? Is his mercy clean gone for ever? Doth his promise fail for evermore? Hath God forgotten to be gracious? Hath he in anger shut up his tender mercies?" (verses 7–9)

Thus the dark desolation of despair filled his soul. That was the vision he saw as he looked at life. Nothing was right, everything was dislocated, the picture was uncertain, the definition was clouded; all was out of focus.

## A New Perspective

This was his view of life in the first nine verses. But here is a strange thing. Mark his view of the same life in the last nine verses. It is the same picture but how differently he sees it. The man who in verse 9 had asked, "Hath God forgotten to be gracious?" is now saying in verses 13–15, "Thy way, O God, is in the sanctuary: who is so great a God as our God? Thou art the God that doest wonders: thou hast declared thy strength among the people. Thou hast with thine arm redeemed thy people … ". The man who previously was full of despair and desolation in the midst of his perplexing life, is now in the midst of the very same life full of hope and encouragement. He is marching with head held high, singing a song of redemption and deliverance. In spite of the very same opposition he is marching on to victory. He is singing, not because the adversity has ceased, but because for some reason it does not matter any more. For some reason he has found the true focus. What is the explanation? Suddenly everything is well. What happened to Asaph to change his vision of life from darkness to light – from one who had nearly lost his hold on God to one who will not let go, come what may?

Now let me be straightforward and say I do not know what happened, though whatever it was I am prepared to believe it came from God. Let me illustrate what I mean. Psalm 73:2 goes like this – the words of Asaph – "But as for me, my feet were almost gone, my steps had well nigh slipped". So what we have said so far is in no way an exaggeration. Look at verse 17 of Psalm 73 and let it follow on from verse 2: "my steps had well nigh slipped … until I went into the sanctuary of God; then I understood …". The result was that Asaph saw something and understood something which hitherto he had missed. It was a realisation of something which in his despair he had not understood. In a moment he made the adjustment and the vision was at last in focus. Now, I believe the "something" is in Psalm 77:10, omitting the words in italics ("but I will remember"). Asaph did not use these words and they do not really help: "And I said, This is my infirmity: the years of the right hand of the most High". Whatever this means, it was this that put the picture into focus. It may be that you need some convincing, so let us go gently and feel our way sympathetically.

Let us think of this to start with. The years which are referred to in verse 10, "the years of the right hand of the most High", are the years of Asaph's life and not the years of God's life. God's existence is outside human time. I suggest that the psalmist is speaking of his own years, measured in his mind and known in his experience, and what he is saying is this: 'This infirmity of mine, these perplexing years of my life, so full of adversity and mystery, have really belonged to God all the time and have always been in the power of His right hand. What I thought to be years of mischance have been years that were, through the strange circumstances of my life, moulded, conditioned, guided and fashioned by the right hand of God. All the time I seemed to be alone and bereft, God knew it and it was part of His pattern for me'. Made within His purpose, encompassed by His law and His righteousness, all those years, though poor Asaph did not know it, God had been working in him, willing and doing of His good pleasure. All through the adversity Asaph was caressed by the love of God. The pressure of the potter on the wheel was sometimes hard, sometimes gentle, but always with a view to making the vessel beautiful and worthy of its destiny. The strange years were held within the right hand of the Most High and what Asaph realised was a forecast of a great New Testament statement:

"All things work together for good to them that love God, to them who are the called according to his purpose." (Romans 8:28)

This was the adjustment that brought the man's life into true focus. And if we would penetrate more the mind of this man, we shall have to think what the right hand of God meant to him as a devout Hebrew. Let me recollect quickly how the idea is used in the Old Testament.

## The Right Hand of God

In Deuteronomy 33:2, Moses, blessing the children of Israel says: "From his right hand went a fiery law for them" – the idea of authority in the right hand of God. In Psalm 48:10 the right hand of God is said to be "full of righteousness" – the idea of truth and goodness. In Psalm 17:7 it is said to be a "right hand" of salvation. In Psalm 20:6 it is the "right hand" of saving strength of the Lord. In Psalm 118:16, "a right hand … doeth valiantly" – that is the idea of action without the possibility of failure. In the Song of Solomon 2:6 the right hand of God is spoken of as a symbol of love and tenderness; and finally in Psalm 16:11 we have those magnificent words which promise so much: "In thy presence is fulness of joy; at thy right hand there are pleasures for evermore". So this is how the Hebrew thought of the right hand of God, and perhaps these ideas were in the mind of Asaph when he spoke of the years of his life being in the right hand of the Most High. It would mean this: a vision of his life encompassed by divine authority, related to God's salvation, sustained by God's strength, guided by God's activity, mastered by God's love and at last fully satisfied with participating in the joy of God's purpose. This was the true focus. No wonder it turned darkness into light and the desolation into a great doxology.

And notice something else, which ought not to surprise us. In the latter verses of his song he expresses his relief and satisfaction in terms of the majesty and power of God, using figures of great waters, thunder and lightning. It is interesting to notice that so often when men of God are in despair and desolate, God revives them by deepening their consciousness of His majesty, and His greatness and His power. It was so with Job. When he was at his deepest desolation, God gave him a vision of His own majesty and glory. As a result of seeing God in that way the soul of Job was healed. So it was with Isaiah: at the time the king died and the prophet faced trial and difficulty, he said, "I saw also the Lord sitting upon a throne, high and lifted up, and his train filled the temple" (Isaiah 6:1). So it was with Ezekiel when he was a poor exile by the river Chebar; there he saw a great vision of glory and was sustained. So it was with Elijah when he wished to die for despair; God gave him a great vision in the mountain. So it was with Jesus; just as he turned to make the bitter journey to the cross-crowned hill, on the mountain where Elijah had stood, Elijah stood again with Moses, and God, through them, deepened His Son's consciousness of the glory to follow. He saw the travail of his soul and was satisfied. Do not be surprised then if Asaph, seeing life in its true focus, tells out the greatness and the healing glory of God. In the deepening consciousness of God's greatness and His purpose, the man loses his consciousness of his own infirmity. Notice the words at the end of Psalm 77:

"Thy way was in the sea, and thy paths in the great waters, and thy footsteps were not known. Thou leddest thy people like a flock, by the hand of Moses and Aaron."

(verses 19,20,RV)

Is not this a reference to the great deliverance God made for His people – saving them from Egypt through the Red Sea? The path of God through the waters was wonderful and awful. His power was manifested then in a way it had never been seen before – hence the words, "thy footsteps were not known". It was something so terrifying that it was never forgotten. "Thou leddest thy people like a flock by the hand of Moses and Aaron". God is revealed as a great shepherd when the people had been ravaged by wolves. So poor Asaph remembered this and his soul was healed. Another little analysis will show this: in the last nine verses Asaph is mentioned three times and God is referred to 24 times. The forces which are mighty and majestic in vision are gentle and healing in their effect upon the soul. The sun is the most powerful force in our experience, yet how gently it brings the primrose to fulfilment and with what tenderness the rose to its glory.

That is the story of Asaph. Notice how it began: "I will cry unto God with my voice". Notice how it ended: "Thou leddest thy people like a flock". The cry for help was answered at last by a realisation of what God is really like. God is a great shepherd: "He leadeth me beside the still waters. He restoreth my soul … I will fear no evil … my cup runneth over" (Psalm 23:2–5). God is a great shepherd, and Asaph found it to be true. It is a story of yesterday, but it is equally relevant for us today. We come with our failures, our weaknesses and our disappointments, but our high priest, the one touched with the feeling of our infirmities, can guide us to the same solution. The right hand of the most High is there. As we contemplate the sacrifice of His son, may we be able to say with Asaph: "Thou art the God that doest wonders: thou hast declared thy strength among the people. Thou hast with thine arm redeemed thy people …" (Psalm 77:14,15). As we consider the ministry of Christ's love, may we see in it the promise of joy for evermore.

# 5

## FEAR GOD
### (PSALM 111)

A S a beginning today, we start with a proposal. It is this: that there are certain passages of scripture which could be regarded as milestones in our understanding of the purpose of God. That is, the ideas which they present have the effect of focussing in an acute way the vital issues of life. They are, in a way, fundamental to our grasping the real understanding of God's way with humanity. I am now going to name four such passages which come in this category.

Our first passage is the Book of Ecclesiastes, because it stresses the emptiness of life apart from God. It tells us that to satisfy the senses fully, at last brings dissatisfaction. That young man who one day came running and kneeling to Jesus, had satisfied all his senses because he was rich, but somehow he was not satisfied, because he saw something in Jesus, which he with all his senses satisfied, did not have. There came singing up through his nature the cry for something else. The force and limitations of sensuality are something to be understood. One man who did understand it well was William Shakespeare. Listen to this about sensuality. And please do not judge me too harshly for quoting him.

> "The expense of spirit in a waste of shame
> Is lust in action; and till action, lust
> Is perjur'd, murderous, bloody, full of blame,
> Savage, extreme, rude, cruel, not to trust,
> Enjoy'd no sooner but despised straight;
> Past reason hunted; and no sooner had,
> Past reason hated, as a swallow'd bait,
> On purpose laid to make the taker mad:
> Mad in pursuit and in possession so;
> Had, having, and in quest to have, extreme;
> A bliss in proof,—and prov'd, a very woe;
> Before, a joy propos'd; behind, a dream.
> All this the world well knows; yet none knows well
> To shun the heaven that leads men to this hell."
> WILLIAM SHAKESPEARE: *Sonnet 129 Th'expense of spirit in a waste of shame*

27

The satisfaction which comes from sensuality is ephemeral – it is no substitute for God. This fundamental truth the Book of Ecclesiastes teaches us.

Our second passage is the Roman letter, especially chapter 2. It marks the great difference between all other religions and the religion of Christ. All other religions proceed in the belief that man is essentially good and all he needs is improvement. Christianity proceeds in the belief that man is lost and that what he needs is redemption and that in the face of that predicament, God has provided a redeemer. Now the Roman letter teaches this incisively and especially chapter 3. You can see it is utterly fundamental to understanding the true purpose of God. There was a man who spent years studying the Bible and he was baffled and then one day he grasped the fundamental teaching of Romans and the scales fell from his eyes and the result shattered the religious world. Martin Luther was the man. So there it is – the Roman letter and especially chapter 3.

Our third passage is the 10th chapter of the Acts of the Apostles and the conversion of Cornelius. I remember when I was coming into the Truth I was deeply impressed by this passage. Here was a man of integrity, a good man, a man who worshipped God, a man who prayed and a man who was kind and generous to the chosen people. Surely a man deserving salvation if any man did. And yet he needed to hear the Truth, to understand it and believe it and to be baptised into the saving name of the redeemer.

As I read the 10th chapter of Acts I knew in my deepest heart I had not done this – the things that needed to be done to secure salvation. How often have we used it to show that human goodness is not good enough. Here in this narrative there is something quite fundamental to a humble reception of the Truth. So we must include the 10th chapter of Acts.

Our final passage is the Apocalypse and especially chapter 14. It is so vital because in that chapter God reveals that the day will come when He will say enough. God says – 'Men have spoiled the creation, ravaged the resources I have given them, ruined the arrangements I have sustained, put the planet in jeopardy and spread evil, violence and corruption throughout the earth. Enough – the end has come, but I will not visit my judgement until I give them warning and one last chance to repent'. That will be a moment of high destiny for all who live on earth – the last chance for humanity. It is told and described in the 14th chapter of Revelation and it is fundamental to realising the great purpose of God.

So there they are – four passages which are milestones in the story of redemption. I have generalised about them but now I want to go back and particularise and would ask you for your careful attention to the words themselves.

## The Book of Ecclesiastes

After a study of the sensual life without God, this is how it finishes:

> "Let us hear the conclusion of the whole matter: Fear God, and keep his commandments: for this is the whole duty of man."                                      (12:13)

So a man who is whole and complete is a man who fears God.

## Romans 3

In this chapter there is a full length portrait of human failure in graphic detail. There in the awful degradation of sin-mastered man, is an explanation of his failure – "there is no fear of God before their eyes". This is the cause of human disaster – the lack of reverential fear in the presence of Divine goodness.

## Acts 10

Remember Peter's astonishment when the Holy Spirit fell on this Roman soldier — that the God of the Hebrews would admit Gentiles to His covenant. He told his feelings in these words of astonishment: "God is no respecter of persons: but in every nation he that feareth him, and worketh righteousness, is accepted with him" (verses 34,35). The criterion is not nation, birth or descent, but this: "He that feareth him".

## Revelation 14

The angel of God will one day go forward with the last chance for humanity – it is called the everlasting gospel. Just recall the words he will speak before the day of enforced humiliation: "Fear God, and give glory to him: for the hour of his judgment is come" (verse 7).

So in every passage there is this one common feature – the fear of God. And whichever way you turn in the Bible, sooner or later you will be confronted with it, so much so that one man has put it like this: "The fear of the LORD is the beginning of wisdom" (Proverbs 9:10); and again: "The fear of the Lord tendeth to life: and he that hath it shall abide satisfied; he shall not be visited with evil" (Proverbs 19:23); and then finally about the Son of God himself it says: "[He] was heard in that he feared" (Hebrews 5:7). In the RV: "... having been heard for his godly fear".

So for all these reasons I submit to you that it is not something to be forgotten as you make progress with the development of love – as is sometimes suggested. Nor is it something you grow out of as you come to understand the will of God better. It is utterly central to living wisely. All of us want to do that – none of us wants to live foolishly. True wisdom should teach us that we ought to understand rightly what the fear of the Lord is and to keep and use it as a vital part of the life of faith.

Can I guess though what you are thinking? You are thinking that the speaker chose those four passages because they suited his argument. He is devious and cunning. But my comrades, that would not be fair. I thought I had your agreement that they were important passages – fundamental in their teaching. The right attitude would be to recognise that in every one there is this common and essential thing – the fear of the Lord. Let us seek to understand it.

**Reverential Fear Provoked by God's Love**

Here is another proposal – it is not that servile fear which a slave feels towards his master, a fear of what the master may do to him by way of punishment. It is the respectful and reverential fear which a good man feels in the presence of the very highest goodness. Looking at it carefully I think we could go further and say that it is more like that filial fear which a son feels towards his father. Not a fear of what the father may do to him by way of chastisement, but a fear of what the son may do to the Father by way of grief. A careful and respectful attitude of homage towards that holy goodness and purity which is centred in God and which through His mercy flows out over all the life of man. Joseph seems to express it well when he is in the house of Potiphar and is being tempted ruthlessly by Potiphar's wife – you remember it is in Genesis chapter 39. Knowing that God had brought him through all his strange experiences and was with him, as he said later on to his brethren: "It was not you that sent me hither but God". Knowing all this he said: "How then can I do this great wickedness, and sin against God?" (verse 9). Somehow he felt it to be such a contradiction, a denial, a shame, that in response to God's care and God's love – he should repay evil. A reverential fear provoked by God's love. This is the abiding secret of living wisely. A principle of action which will set us in a right relationship to all the forces which are about us in the present and in the future.

One of the most profitable passages in the Bible which enforces the idea and gives reason why we ought to fear God

30

in this way it seems to me is in Psalm 111. Notice the last verse – because it is related to all that precedes it. It is the great master principle documented once more: "The fear of the LORD is the beginning of wisdom ..."

**The Beginning of Wisdom**

Pondering the psalm it seems to me that the reasons for this are threefold.

Firstly, God is the Creator:

"Praise ye the LORD. I will praise the LORD with my whole heart, in the assembly of the upright, and in the congregation. The works of the LORD are great, sought out of all them that have pleasure therein. His work is honourable and glorious: and His righteousness endureth for ever. He hath made His wonderful works to be remembered; the LORD is gracious and full of compassion."

(verses 2–4)

The Lord is the gracious Creator, who knows perfectly that which He has created. You are the created, the realised thought of God. In Him you live and move and have your being. He knows the mystic mechanism of your life; by Him you are fearfully and wonderfully made. The majestic dignity of your powers, which enable you to sit here today and understand His holy word – these powers have come from Him. Your life is in His hands. He is the Creator – you are the created. Ought we not to fear Him with holy reverence?

Secondly, He is the Preserver – he careth for you:

"He hath given meat unto them that fear him: he will ever be mindful of his covenant."                    (verse 5)

For you He created the morning and gave you the energy of the morning. For you He created the darkness and giveth His beloved sleep. He makes season follow upon season for your well-being and fills your hearts with gladness every day. Sometimes we are inclined to measure Him by our incompetence and blame Him when we spoil His blessed arrangements. We sometimes criticise His weather, yet He makes His sun to shine on the just and the unjust. It is not just accidental – He *makes* it to shine on the just and the unjust. He makes provision for every need. He gives meat to them that fear him. All the forces of the world are in the grip of His government. Ought we not to fear Him then with thankfulness?

Thirdly, He is the Redeemer of His people: "He sent redemption unto his people: he hath commanded his covenant for ever". Because of sin men have been blasted,

31

scorched, destroyed, and have lost the vision and the consciousness of God. But He has not abandoned them. He has made it possible for the banished ones to return. He has sent the Son to find the wandering boy amid the swine's husks and has lifted the broken one on His own shoulder and brought him through the torrent and the tempest to the place where there is rest and restoration. His love is such which alters not when it alteration finds. In comradeship with sinning men such as we are, He has healed us and remade us – at a cost which cannot be measured in words current in human speech. Yahweh is the Redeemer – He has commanded His covenant for ever. Ought we not to fear Him with hushed spirits and singing hearts?

So then for these three magnificent reasons – the fear of the Lord is the beginning of wisdom.

**Fear Defined**

Think then what that fear really is. Subjectively, it is the recognition of His might and His holiness. It is consenting to the rightness of the claim He makes upon our hearts and minds. It is reverence for Him and a desire to act in conformity with His will. It is a desire for our adjustment to the central infinite truth of the whole Universe – to give glory to that one who is at once Creator, Preserver, Redeemer. Objectively, it is submission and obedience now, in readiness for authority and power and age-abiding life in the world to come.

The book of Proverbs helps us with an exposition: "The fear of the LORD is to hate evil" (8:13). "By the fear of the LORD men depart from evil" (16:6). This shows us that the fear of the Lord is a condition of inward life which produces conduct in outward life. The condition of the inward life is that of hating evil. The condition of the outward life which it produces, is that of departing from evil.

It is little good having the hating without the departing. There was a man who once said: "That which I hate that I do". From this we can draw some solemn conclusions. If a man says "I fear God" and then loves sin – he is deceived. If a man says "I fear God" and then persistently walks in evil ways – he is utterly mistaken about the fear of God. A man who fears God in the true sense is one upon whose spirit there rests the consciousness of God and His holy word. A man, it may be with many faults and who, fails through weakness more than he would like to admit – but who in himself loves the pure and hates the evil and who is therefore striving to shed the one and pursue the other. We stand in the presence of forces which are destructive and forces which are constructive. The wisdom which comes from the fear of the Lord, is the adjustment of our life to those forces. This is the wisdom that leads to the opening of our hearts and minds to the constructive, and the shutting of the door against the forces which hurt and harm and destroy. Insofar as our lives, day by day, are being put into a right relationship to Him whom we fear and love, so the forces which are against us are controlled and at last mastered.

**Final Thoughts**

There are two final things about this master principle:

Firstly, think of the word "beginning" – the fear of Yahweh is the beginning of wisdom. It does not mean it is something you begin with, but which you can dispense with as you become more accomplished. The word here used for beginning does not mean just first in time alone. If you have the RV and look at the reference to Proverbs 1:7 and observe the note there about 'beginning', you will find it means 'chief part', so that it is first in order of time, but first also in order of place, of rank, of value and of importance. The fear of the Lord is the first and chief part of wisdom.

Secondly, we must save ourselves from falling into the fault of thinking that wisdom is an intellectual accomplishment. A man who has wise thoughts but acts in defiance of them is living foolishly. Knowledge may be an intellectual thing, but wisdom is the incarnation of true knowledge in daily life. In the final analysis wisdom is a matter of character. The truth is given to us not to speculate upon but to obey. In a sense a man is half false already who is bent on studying the truth just to talk about it. To fear the Lord is to live the truths we hold, else in the real sense the truth is falsified. This has been vindicated by the experience of men of the past. God spoke to Noah and warned him of things to come. Noah moved with fear, built an ark to the saving of his house. He might have said: 'What you tell me is very interesting Lord – I will organise a seminar about it'. God spoke to Abraham about a land and about a universal blessing through him. It says: "He obeyed and went out, not knowing whither he went". He might have said: 'This is a great thing you have told me, Lord. Thank you for the offer; we will have a family discussion group'. Moses received a solemn call from God to lead his people to freedom. It says: "He forsook Egypt not fearing the wrath of the king". That means he feared God instead and more than other men feared Pharaoh. He might have said: 'This is a wonderful opportunity Lord, I will set up a committee'.

In Hebrews 11 there is a catalogue of men and women who feared God and their reverential fear caused them to act in obedience. They were not perfect but there is one thing about them – they had a reverent fear of God. You see, it is the verbs in Hebrews 11 which are so interesting. Abel *offered*, Enoch *pleased* God, Noah *moved* and *built*, Abraham *obeyed* and *journeyed*, Moses *forsook* and *endured*. Of others it is recorded; they subdued, wrought, quenched, waxed valiant, out of weakness were made strong. They were not spectators – they were doers. Their business was fearing God and working righteousness. Ah – I must be careful, do not misunderstand me. I know it is good to study and read, and listen and learn – it is splendid. But unless the will is energised by the truth we learn we are not living wisely. It is possible to be overfed and yet undernourished. It is possible to learn and utter lofty sentiments of wisdom and yet never experience their meaning. The man who is wise in experience is really living wisely. Remember this word of the King – we hardly ever quote it – John 7:17 – we have difficulty in believing it: "If any man will do his will, he shall know of the doctrine, whether it be of God". Do it and you will learn it best. This is the true wisdom. I leave it with you.

# 6

## ZION IN BABYLON
### (ISAIAH 50)

THINK of the atmosphere of Isaiah chapter 50. That is to say the conditions and the forces which underlie the words. First of all we discover a people who are bereft, motherless and sold into slavery. They are a people who have come to feel that they have no hope of recovery. Verse 2: "Is my hand shortened at all, that it cannot redeem?" asks God, meaning: 'Do you think that I have no power to save you?' This harmonises with some sentences in Isaiah 49: "Thy waste and thy desolate places, and the land of thy destruction ... I have lost my children, and am desolate, a captive, and removing to and fro ..." (verses 19,21).

So pick up the inferences – the words are sent to a people bound, afflicted, desolate and in need of comfort, because they had come to think that God had abandoned them. This is proven by verse 14 of Isaiah 49: "But Zion said, The LORD hath forsaken me, and my Lord hath forgotten me". This was the bitterest feeling of all – to think that God had forsaken the government of His people. So that is the first thing – yearning hopelessly.

Then in the same chapter we read about the suffering servant who was obedient to God, who gave his back to the smiters and hid not his face from shame and spitting; whose ear was opened and whose will was submitted without reservation. With hindsight we know who the suffering servant is. It is the one by whose stripes the people of God are healed, and who bore their griefs, and upon whom their iniquities were laid. So in the same chapter we read about the utter need for redemption and the absolute provision of the redeemer.

With this as the background let us now observe the full vision of the situation. Proof that the words are addressed to a people in captivity is to be found in the words of Isaiah 52:2. "Shake thyself from the dust; arise, and sit down, O Jerusalem: loose thyself from the bands of thy neck, O captive daughter of Zion".

35

It reveals an awful contradiction – Zion in captivity; Zion mastered by Babylon; Zion, the tabernacle of God with men. The divine presence, the ultimate triumph of divine goodness, the city of life and light, overshadowed by the forces of darkness. God's witnesses, called to represent His way and His government, themselves slaves in Babylon – the very force which represents complete antagonism to the government of God.

So the prophet foreshadowed what would happen to the rebellious people of God. They would come to believe God had forsaken the government of His people. That He was unheeding of their need, untroubled by their plight. So in verse 2 of chapter 50 God remonstrates about their pessimism. "When I called, was there none to answer? Is my hand shortened at all, that it cannot redeem?" Now by this they are provoked. They are encouraged to stir themselves out of their despair. So Israel cry to God: "Awake, awake, put on thy strength, O arm of the LORD; awake, as in the ancient days, in the generations of old. Art thou not it that hath cut Rahab (Egypt), and wounded the dragon?" (51:9). They called upon God to rouse Himself and deliver Zion from the bitterness of Babylon.

The reply to their call comes from God in the words of the opening verse of chapter 52: "Awake, awake; put on thy strength, O Zion; put on thy beautiful garments, O Jerusalem, the holy city". If I may put it to you in all reverence, it is as though God is saying: 'Why are you telling me to awake? I am awake, I do not sleep – it is you who are asleep – you must awake and put on your beautiful garments'. And the reason for this is revealed in the vision which comes next: "How beautiful upon the mountains are the feet of him that bringeth good tidings, that publisheth peace; that bringeth good tidings of good, that publisheth salvation; that saith unto Zion, Thy God reigneth" (verse 7). By the declaration "Thy God reigneth", those captive exiles knew that God had not resigned the government of His people. They knew that He had placed salvation in Zion. So they are born again; they are revived; they rise up with joy. With a great song in their hearts and on their lips, the people of Zion make ready to leave Babylon: "Break forth into joy, sing together, ye waste places of Jerusalem; for the LORD hath comforted his people, he hath redeemed Jerusalem" (verse 9). So the inhabitants of Zion cry out and shout because great is the Holy One in the midst of His people.

## Other Applications

This is the historical fulfilment of Isaiah's words – but you know and I know that it is but a reflection of the fulfilment of his words which is yet to be. He speaks of that great day which is soon to be when the great One of Zion makes bare His holy arm in the sight of all nations and all the ends of the earth shall see the salvation of our God.

But now I must bring you to the immediate application. Our messenger has crossed the mountains from Jerusalem to Babylon – how beautiful on the mountains are his feet, and he has come to our captivity and he has brought us this message: "Thy God reigneth". He said: "Look up, and lift up your heads; for your redemption draweth nigh". Notice how the call came to Zion at last: "Depart ye, depart ye, go ye out from thence ...". That call is ageless. It is the call to Zion wherever they may be outside the City of God. It is the call to the Zion of God all down the ages living under the influence of Babylon. It is the call to come back to the established government of God. But go back and notice the exact words, the solemn words which were spoken to them just as they were coming to their redemption: "... touch no unclean thing; go ye out of the midst of her; be ye clean, that bear the vessels of the LORD" (verse 11).

In 2 Chronicles 36:17,18 you can read how the holy vessels of the Lord were taken to Babylon: "And all the vessels of the house of God, great and small, and the treasures of the house of the LORD, and the treasures of the king, and of his princes; all these he [the king of the Chaldees] brought to Babylon". Now those holy vessels are being gathered and are being taken back to Zion in the hands of the returning exiles. "Be ye clean that bear the vessels of the Lord ..."

## "Be Ye Clean"

I am going to ask you to forget the local colouring for a moment and think of ourselves, and about the great principle we now unveil. You are the people of Zion in this generation. You are living every day in peril of the influence of Babylon. You have been waiting, as Zion is always waiting, for your deliverance. You might have thought, as Zion has often thought, that God had resigned His government. But now the conviction has come into your hearts and it is unshakeable "Thy God reigneth". You have seen the messenger upon the mountains – the messenger with beautiful feet – and you have heard his voice and your life has been renewed. And now the call has come to you that your redemption draweth nigh. The bowed head is to be lifted up. In a world where men look horizontally, you are to look vertically. The time has come – you are to awake and put on your beautiful garments and make yourselves ready for the triumphant march. But just as you are about to leave, the solemn word comes to you – to Zion of this generation – "Touch no unclean thing ... be ye clean that bear the vessels of the Lord". Your supreme and ultimate destiny is to bear the vessels of the Lord. Your life will issue at last in being kings and priests in the service of Zion's God. The sanctified and holy things of His kingdom will be your things. The powers and resources of divine life will be your resources. Hear the solemn word then: "Be ye clean that bear the vessels of the Lord". And by way of exhortation this has to be said. That word "clean" is a little word and the tragedy is that it may seem to be so little when it ought to mean so much. If we think of it as being some ceremonial cleansing – some outward ablution only, then we have missed the deepest meaning of the prophet's holy word. It could be put this way – it is not the cleansing of water; it is the cleansing of fire.

There are things which can survive fire and are better and finer – the dross is removed and they are cleaner. There are things which perish in fire – they shrivel and become dust. Malachi tells us that the messenger shall sit as a refiner of silver – it is not to harm but to purify. He, by his process removes the dross – slowly perhaps, now quickly perhaps and he knows when the process is complete. It is when he can see his own image in the bright, clean, molten silver. So the exhortation is that we shall strive to be such men and women of Zion that at last there will be nothing in us to spoil and contaminate the final brightness of the king's silver. The word "clean" here means clean from complicity with Babylon. The holiness of divine government must be borne by holy men and women. So this word of Isaiah calls upon us to shed everything which belongs to our captivity. It calls upon us to reclaim the things of Zion we may have lost.

**Practical Actions**

Getting down to practical things, what does it mean? Well this for instance – we must put away that one thing which we cannot seem to master and which is in danger of mastering us. I shall not need to tell you what it is – you will know it. You can test yourselves if you will face it. Jesus says: "Behold, I come quickly" and the answer of Zion is: "Even so, come, Lord Jesus". Now the thing that makes our lips tremble and falter when we say it – is the thing we must recognise and abandon. The thing that makes us satisfied when somebody convinces us that the Lord cannot come until some distant future date. Whatever ambition or enterprise makes us want the Lord to postpone his coming, to hold back our redemption, is the one thing which produces in our hearts the spirit of disloyalty to the government of God. Leave Babylon behind when you turn your back on Babylon. Do not carry with you to Zion the spirit of the things which are destined to be destroyed. Babylon is tottering – let us leave it altogether. Remember Lot's wife.

I know that these words seem solemn and in some sense frightening – but that is not their purpose. This coming of the redeemer ought not to be a sad thought for you; it ought to be rousing, invigorating, exciting. Remember you are coming to Zion's glad morning. You are not fleeing like wretched criminals – you are going out with joy. "Cry out and shout, thou inhabitant of Zion: for great is the Holy One of Israel in the midst of thee". "The LORD will go before you; and the God of Israel will be your rereward"

**Jesus Knows Your Heart**

And there is another reason why the people of Zion can take courage. The one you are going to meet knows you through and through. He has seen the internal as well as the external. There is more comfort in that than you may realise. Your brethren hear your words but Jesus knows your heart. Your brethren have seen how you blundered and how you failed, but Jesus knows why you did it and perhaps how you did not want to do it and longed not to do it. He knows that your aspirations were a great deal higher than your achievements. He knows about the fire in my blood and yours which drives us against our will. He is an incomparable saviour – touched with the feeling of our infirmity. The last picture of him in the New Testament is this: "His eyes were as a flame of fire". I know sometimes we feel that we dare not look him in the face, but there is one thing which ought to help us struggle on. The conviction that under the scrutiny of those eyes of fire we may hear the voice of love: "Fear not". This is the teaching of the New Testament: "I will never leave thee, nor forsake thee", and in the Old Testament this in Isaiah: "Behold, God is my salvation; I will trust, and not be afraid … Therefore with joy shall ye draw water out of the wells of salvation" (Isaiah 12:2,3).

So you may come to Zion with a song in your heart, with a lilt in your step, and with hope and blessed assurance in your soul. May you come to that one from whose face shines out the love of God and whose beautiful feet are clothed with advent glory.

So in this solemn moment of remembrance when we are alone with our redeemer – when we break bread in memory of his bruising for love's sake and for our redemption, let us pray to God that in His strength we may come with shining faces to Zion's glad morning – and especially at this moment as we bow our heads and hush our spirits – in our deepest heart may we feel it to be true.

# 7

## GOD'S WITNESSES
### (DANIEL 12)

*THIS exhortation was given to the Oxford ecclesia in 1957 to encourage support for a specific preaching effort. Although the passage of time has made the details irrelevant, they have been retained out of historical interest. Of course, the principles on which the appeal was made are timeless and they are expressed in a way that deeply probes the conscience.*

TODAY this is a special exhortation. I know that sounds shockingly immodest and so I must explain that it is not special in its words or sentences or the manner of its presentation – in all those things I am afraid it is going to be very ordinary. But it is special in this sense – it has an especial relevance to this ecclesia. It seeks to take in a situation which exists in our own meeting and so it is for you especially. What I mean will become obvious as we go along.

Let me first of all bring you to a principle which we know so well but which we sometimes forget. It is this: that all the works of God, whether they be works in the natural sphere of things or works in the spiritual, all the works of God are done on the basis of certain fundamental laws which never change and which never fail.

Let me illustrate: "God is not mocked: for whatsoever a man soweth, that shall he also reap" (Galatians 6:7). We know it is true. If we want to reap wheat we must sow wheat. No man ever sowed corn-cockle and reaped wheat. There is a law which says that what you reap is what you have sown multiplied many times. The germ of harvest is in the seed which is sown. The one is the Divinely natural outcome of the other. Be it for good or ill.

### Shining as the Stars

Now this principle is revealed for us again under another figure in Daniel 12: "And many of them that sleep in the dust of the earth shall awake, some to everlasting life, and some to shame and everlasting contempt. And they that be wise shall shine as the brightness of the firmament; and they that turn many to righteousness as the stars for ever and ever" (verses 2,3). "Shining as the brightness of the firmament – shining as the stars for ever and ever". It is a figure to describe the regenerated, resurrected, incorruptible condition of the saints in the Kingdom of God to come. And notice who will come to that condition: "They *that be wise* shall shine as the brightness of the firmament".

And notice "wise" means something more than just wisdom. It is not just a condition but an action. The meaning is: 'They that make others to be wise' – which is an equation with the other phrase: "they that turn many to righteousness". In confirmation of this look in your margins to see the meaning of the word "wise" – in my Bible it says "teachers" – I expect it does in yours. Here then is the meaning. Those who are to shine as stars in God's firmament are in the age to come those who now are His teachers, converting others from sin unto righteousness.

But we have not come yet to the real issue. Remember we said that this phrase was an example, under another figure, of the unchanging principle that the effect is related directly to the cause. You reap what you have sown – the harvest is the sowing multiplied many times. How is it true in this case? What is the direct connection in the figure in Daniel 12 between teaching righteousness now and shining as stars in the age to come?

Recall how the Bible speaks of stars. In Genesis 1 they are said to be for "signs" – they signify something. Jesus' miracles are said to be signs too – they manifested something. In Psalm 50 we read: "The heavens shall declare his righteousness for God is judge himself" (verse 6). In Psalm 19:

> "The heavens declare the glory of God; and the firmament showeth forth his handywork. Day unto day uttereth speech, and night unto night showeth knowledge. There is no speech nor language, where their voice is not heard. Their line is gone out through all the earth, and their words to the end of the world." (verses 1–4)

It is evident therefore according to the scriptures that the heavens – their brightness of the day and their glory of the night – are witnesses to God. They declare His glory, they testify unto Him, they show forth His handiwork. They witness.

## Personal Witnessing

But one more step to bring us to the real issue. Come with me to Romans 10:

> "How then shall they call on him in whom they have not believed? and how shall the believe in him of whom they have not heard? and how shall they hear without a preacher? and how shall they preach except they be sent? as it is written, How beautiful are the feet of them that preach the gospel of peace, and bring glad tidings of good things!" (verses 14,15)

Here then is the very centre of the figure. The brightness of the firmament and the shining of the stars in its very deepest and noblest intention is that witness borne to God by preaching His word of salvation.

And so going back to the figure in Daniel 12 and how it reveals the Divinely natural law of cause and effect, it can be stated like this. If you want to witness to God in the age to come – with heavenly brightness, as the shining of the stars in glory – you must witness to Him now by teaching and turning others to righteousness. Those who are God's witnesses now will be God's witnesses for ever. What you sow you reap. Be it for good or ill.

When the New Testament speaks of witnesses it uses the word in a very deep and significant sense. It does not mean men who merely talk – though it certainly means speaking. The Apostles were brought before the High Priest and the rulers for daring to preach in the name of Jesus of Nazareth, saying that he was alive and had been seen. Think of the scene. Here is the High Priest in the robes and the phylacteries of his office and on the other side Peter in his simple homespun cloth. Yet he has a rough and rugged splendour about him, and if I am not mistaken the light is gleaming in his eyes. He says: "We must obey God rather than men – we are witnesses of these things ..." (see Acts 4:19,20). And when he said that he did not mean that he had come merely to argue or to discuss – what he meant was this: 'We men as you see us to be, we are the witnesses that these things are true. We ourselves are the proof. We prove our preaching by the transformation our lives'.

A man in a court of law has only to speak and he is by that very thing a witness; but a witness for God is more than that. A witness for God is a man who has heard the Truth, who is convinced that it is true and then yields his life to the claims of the Truth of which he is convinced. So finally a witness is

43

a specimen, an evidence, a sample, a credential, a proof that what he believes is true. And as we look back through the pages of the holy scriptures we can see that this meaning is true. We can read of men who formerly were consumed by lust and passion for destruction, changed to men consumed by zeal for the salvation of men and for the glory of God. We can see that it is the prime duty of the church to confront the world with living witnesses. If the church does not witness, she is dead. A mere recitation of a statement of faith is not witness.

**Preaching is for All**

"We are witnesses of these things". Are *we*? We cannot escape the responsibility. Any man or woman who names the name of Christ becomes his witness. Every disciple is an ambassador. "The Spirit and the bride say, Come. And let him that heareth say, Come". Whoever knows and believes the Gospel is obliged to make it known. Sometimes it is said that cannot be. The preaching of the Truth is for a few to do, but not for all. I do not believe that. In the New Testament church the very humblest and simplest of men who answered the claims of the gospel and became transformed thereby, became also a force in its proclamation. And I believe that each one here, if the truth is believed by him and he is changed by it, becomes by that very thing appointed a witness in apostolic succession. In cooperation with God, he becomes part of that movement for teaching and turning many to righteousness.

Please God deliver us from the heresy of imagining that the only way of witnessing is on the public platform. But let us also never forget that it is by the preaching of God's word that men are brought out of darkness into His marvellous light. Where the preaching of that word is halted, or thwarted or smothered by our failure, indifference or neglect – so our witnessing for Christ has become a blasphemy. If any man says, "I am Christ's witness", and then will not aid the preaching of Christ's word, he is either a liar or a fool. His salvation is in jeopardy.

**Light for the Future**

Recall the law of salvation once again as it is revealed in Daniel 12: "They that be wise shall shine as the brightness of the firmament; and they that turn many to righteousness as the stars for ever and ever" (verse 3). One star differeth from another in glory, but the light of glory which we may enjoy in the world to come will be the light we have generated now multiplied many times. And if the light we have generated now is really only darkness – so that darkness will be multiplied many times with weeping and gnashing of teeth. We sometimes say that this Ecclesia is a lightstand in this city. I pray God that is how it appears in the high court of Heaven. We have special efforts and not many are made wise and not many are turned to righteousness – but insofar as we have been blessed with an act of salvation here and there, let us be thankful and let us never be discouraged. Remember the commission to preach the Gospel is not a human project – it is a Divine commandment. It is the work of Jesus Christ but he has committed it into the hands of men. But it is his work. "I am with you alway even unto the end of the age". "We are witnesses of these things". Let us hold fast to that high heritage come what may.

**A Special Effort**

Brethren and sisters, our next act of public witness will be a special meeting in the Oxford Town Hall, on Sunday evening November 24th [1957] at 8.0pm – the showing of a colour film to proclaim the good news of coming salvation. I speak to you now with the full authority of the Arranging Brethren.

We believe that this may be one of the most promising opportunities that this Ecclesia has had to attract a good audience. It has been arranged with some shrewdness to follow on immediately a number of meetings which have been held recently at the Town Hall on Sunday evenings – whereby people have got used to going to the Town Hall at that time for religious purposes. Furthermore, a colour film is calculated to attract where perhaps an ordinary address would not. The great problem is to make it known. We believe that a really powerful advertising effort is necessary – large newspaper advertisements and large and numerous posters. The will is there but we need the money. Advertising is costly. Next Sunday, therefore, November 10th, there will be a special collection to enable the effort to be advertised properly. Whoever gives to that collection will be making their witness to Christ – whoever refuses to give when they could, I will not seek to judge nor criticise, but they must in their own hearts justify their refusal to witness. I am appealing to you brethren and sisters to give generously – no, more – to give recklessly. Do it with something of daring – do it with something of heroism. If any man says giving money is easy – let it not be easy – make it a sacrificial giving. Give us, say, £50 and do it with cheerful hearts and shining faces. We are witnesses of these things. If you are not going to be here next Sunday, see that your contribution reaches the Lord's treasury.

Brethren, just lately in our reading of the Acts, we have been in the company of men and women who imperilled their lives for the sake of being true witnesses. They made others wise and turned many to righteousness. They did it lovingly but not without effort and endurance. Their shining glory will be revealed in the day which is coming.

But today, brethren, we are in the presence of that one who came into the world to bear witness to the Truth. Because of his fidelity to that cause he came to stand alone at the last at the place of execution. In a little while, two brethren will rise up to thank God for the faithful witness of His Son and for the Son's love towards us expressed in that faithfulness. You have to look Jesus in the face today and say whether you will follow him in sacrificial service. If you have seen something of his love I do not think you will be able to refuse. He calls us to witness. He does not ask us if it is convenient – he never has. God grant that we may obey because our response could be the measure of our gratitude to him for the things to which these emblems bear witness. In a few simple words he gave us the measure of our service as disciples – "as I have loved you".

Brethren, today we have come to the green hill as men who once needed salvation and who, by some indescribable grace of God, have found it. We come as a little company of the children of God, to thank Him for His unspeakable gift. And the deepest, noblest and shining act of gratitude to Him is this – that we shall let the truth of this sacrifice be incarnate in our lives, because "We are witnesses of these things".

Let us therefore by our faithfulness when the gospel is being proclaimed, by our prayers for its blessing, by our self-denying gifts, large and small, by our seeking contact with any who might be willing to hear, by the incarnation of its teaching in our lives – let us go back to our life tomorrow as shining lights in the midst of a dark world, with the angel's promise to Daniel deep in our hearts.

# 8

## THE STORY OF HOSEA
### (HOSEA 1–3)

THE ninth chapter of the Roman letter is an especially significant chapter because in it Paul deals with what theologians have come to call *theodicy* – that is the attempt to vindicate the goodness of God in the face of the existence of evil. All theodicies try to explain evil by seeing it as making for a greater good than is attainable without it. As far as this exhortation is concerned I am not concerned with the problems addressed by theodicy – save to remark that in the course of dealing with them Paul reaffirms a great truth that salvation is not dependent upon human ingenuity or human endeavour or human caprice, but that firstly and finally it is wholly dependent upon God's mercy. Once again it unveils the supreme truth that in the presence of human helplessness and utter failure, God is the initiator and the perfecter of salvation. To quote Paul's own words: "So then it is not of him that willeth, nor of him that runneth, but of God that showeth mercy" (Romans 9:16). And Paul is anxious to show to these Romans that the mercy of God is not something which is confined and cramped – rather it is broad and expansive and full. Insofar as it was exclusive to the Jews at first, it was but a pattern of what God would do for the Gentiles at last. The people of Israel were representative. God was showing in one nation what He would do for all nations in due time. And Paul then proceeds to show that it was the Hebrew prophets who foretold the blessing of the Gentiles. The men of God raised up in the midst of Israel proclaim the blinding of Israel and sight to the Gentiles. "Even us whom he hath called, not of the Jews only, but also of the Gentiles ..."

"As he saith also in Osee, I will call them my people, which were not my people; and her beloved, which was not beloved. And it shall come to pass, that in the place where it was said unto them, Ye are not my people: there shall they be called the children of the living God."

(Romans 9:25,26)

"As he saith also in Osee". Those are the words I ask you to lay hold on today. At Paul's direction let us see what Hosea

47

says about the mercy of God and try to discover the feelings and forces which underlie the prophet's words: "I will call them my people, which were not my people".

Some of the books of the Minor prophets are stories in themselves. They are narratives like, say, Jonah or Habakkuk – narratives having a prophetic and teaching purpose. Other books are not stories or narratives at all but plainly straightforward prophecy and teaching, like Amos or Micah. Hosea comes in between these two categories – that is to say it is not a story in itself and yet underlying it there is a story which comes to light incidentally, and we discover that the story is linked unmistakably with the teaching and ministry of Hosea the prophet.

**A Tragic Story**

The first verse of the book tells us the period of his ministry and that he was a prophet sent to the northern kingdom of Israel. This was the darkest period in the history of the people of Israel. It was descending into that deep dark condition of degenerate self-indulgence which was to end in captivity. We learn of that condition: "The land hath committed great whoredom, departing from the LORD" (1:2). As you read the prophecy it is evident that Hosea's domestic circumstances are a microcosm of the nation's life. In other words, God's feelings about Israel were repeated in Hosea's feelings about his own life and circumstances. Remember briefly and bluntly what Hosea's life was like.

He married a woman named Gomer. Subsequently three children were born – Jezreel, Lo-ruhamah, and Lo-ammi. Gomer played false and was unfaithful to Hosea. As a result she was cast out as the judgement demanded. In her infidelity she was rejected. In the course of time she descended deeper in degradation – to the very darkest condition of all. She became a mere slave, bought and owned just as a piece of property by someone else. In that bitter condition of degradation Hosea sought for her and found her and forgave her. He bought her at the price of a slave for himself and restored her to his side as his wife and bride again, in love.

The first part of the story is tragic and more common than it should be – the second part, the restoration, is very uncommon but when it happens it is wonderful and it did happen to Hosea. This is the narrative that lies behind his prophecy.

## A Moral Problem

May I pause just for a moment to try to deal with something which may be a problem to some. Reading verse 2 of chapter 1 it looks as though God commanded Hosea to marry a woman of sin and a prostitute. This has been a difficulty for some, and I would like to help in some way to relieve it. In the Revised Versions, both English and American, the 2nd verse reads thus: "When the LORD spake at the first by Hosea ..."; and in the margin for the word "by" there is an alternative "with", so it reads: "When the LORD spake at first with Hosea", and suggests that God was at first speaking to Hosea as a man and this was before he spoke by him as a prophet. And the words "at the first" are important. Remember at the end of his ministry Hosea put down on parchment the record and words of his prophecy and looking back on his life he is saying in effect – 'Right at the first when God spoke to me, He told me to marry Gomer'. Now the statement quite clearly calls her a woman of whoredoms, but I do not think we are necessarily meant to understand that she was such at the beginning. But Hosea looking back on it, and seeing what she became, so describes her. Perhaps she was not openly a whorish woman at first and perhaps at first there was joy and happiness in the life of Hosea before the tragedy of his wife's infidelity.

When you read the rest of the prophecy you get the impression from the words which are spoken to and about the unfaithful wife that she is a wife which at one time was true but now has become false. Hosea's life was to be a picture of the life of Israel espoused to God. Israel at first was true but at last became false.

## Pain Caused by Sin

The domestic scene at first is one of peace and happiness but the naming of the children as they came along is prophetic and indicative of Israel's destiny. Jezreel – 'judgement to come'; Lo-ruhamah – 'without mercy'; Lo-Ammi –'not my people – people rejected'. God knew the kind of wife Gomer would prove to be when He commanded Hosea to marry her, but I do not think Hosea did then. The result of the tragedy in Hosea's life was that he was admitted to an understanding of what infidelity means to a condition of love, and therefore to an understanding of what the sin of Israel meant to God who loved His erring people in spite of their unfaithfulness. Hosea has been called the prophet of the broken heart. The pain and agony of his experience is apparent in his prophecy and it became to him an interpretation of the feelings of God

49

in the presence of Israel's sin. The infidelity of Gomer was for him an interpretation of the infidelity of Israel. So he was prepared for his great work. He preached the word of God out of the experience God had arranged. The process of inspiration is more than strange, brethren. Observe its strangeness in the case of Hosea. Thus he was prepared for the high calling of being a prophet. Doubtless he could have been a prophet without it and yet in the purpose and wisdom of God it was necessary that his prophet should preach the word of the living God out of his own experience. By that experience he came to understand more surely and more deeply the tragedy of Israel's sin against her Divine Husband. The book of Hosea reveals most strongly what sin is really like in the sight of God. Sin wounds the love of God. In his psalm of penitence when he had sinned against Bathsheba and against Uriah, David said to God: "Against thee only have I sinned". It shows that in the final sense we sin against God. We may sin *with* others as David did with Bathsheba, but it was of a nature which in the real sense was against God – and this he confessed.

If I may use the expression without being misunderstood – the pain of the sin was in the heart of God. Once a man wrote a book called *The Impassive God* and it sought to show that God was untouched by and indifferent to the doings of men. This is not the God revealed in the Bible. For once I read this about God and His people: "In all their afflictions he was afflicted". And if you can find your way this day into Hosea's soul and catch something of his feelings when Gomer played him false and left him, then you will better understand how the sin of the bride which was true but became false, wounds the love of God. And learning that, we can best learn also the strength of that love which seeks and saves that which was lost. God's love is wounded by sin but His love is such that presently He is going to find a way for the sinner to be rescued and to come home.

**A Note of Tenderness**

The second chapter of Hosea begins with the prophet delivering a message from God to adulterous Israel. Hosea is not speaking of Gomer and yet the bitterness of his own experience adds feeling to the words. And then suddenly in the midst of the sorrow there is a note of strange tenderness:

"I will allure her, and bring her into the wilderness, and speak comfortably unto her [to her heart]. And I will give her vineyards from thence, and the valley of Achor for a door of hope: and she shall sing there, as in the days of her youth, and as in the day when she came up out of the land of Egypt ... Thou shall call me Ishi [that is my husband – the voice of a wife]; and thou shalt call me no more Baali [that is my master – the voice of the slave] ... and I will sow her unto me in the earth; and I will have mercy upon her that hath not obtained mercy; and I will say to them which were not my people, Thou art my people; and they shall say, Thou art my God." (verses 14–16,23)

"As he saith also in Osee, I will call them my people, which were not my people; and her beloved, which was not beloved. And it shall come to pass, that in the place where it was said unto them, Ye are not my people: there shall they be called the children of the living God."

(Romans 9:25,26)

Observe then how Paul takes the word spoken of Israel so long ago and uses it in its final and supreme interpretation to describe any man who will come to God through Jesus Christ – even us whom He hath called.

**A Door of Hope**

Let me bring you back to a strange sentence in Hosea 2. Remember verse 15: "I will give her ... the valley of Achor for a door of hope". Hosea had seen the rejection of Gomer for her infidelity and the corresponding judgement of God upon Israel for the same wickedness. And in the midst of the double sorrow he hears this strange note: "The valley of Achor for a door of hope". The name Achor means "troubling". We remember Achan for he was prophetically named. His name means "trouble", and he troubled Israel by his sin. The trouble which God refers to in this strange sentence is the troubling of sin. By the very nature of sin and the Universe, the law of sin is inevitable – its penalty cannot be avoided. It is a blessing that it cannot, for if sin had no penalty in its wake, men would go on unheeding to utter destruction – content with it and unmoved from it.

The troubling of sin is a real thing. Because of it ere long Gomer is going to say: "I will return to my husband". That poor wandering boy in the parable in the midst of the mighty famine and the troubling said: "I will arise and go to my father". It was the door of hope for him. Desolation is the opportunity to think again and remember and retrace the steps and seek the way of rescue. "I will return to my husband". "I will arise and go to my Father". It is the loving discipline of God which makes men turn back when to go on is to be lost. "The Valley of Achor for a door of hope".

51

## Bought with a Price

So now again God broke in on the life of Hosea and gave him another command. "Go yet, love a woman beloved of her friend, yet an adulteress. So I bought her to me for fifteen pieces of silver and for an homer of barley, and an half homer of barley". May I remind you of her condition when he found her? How much did he pay? 15 pieces of silver. 30 pieces of silver is the price of a slave. The poor woman had sunk so low he bought her for half price – and then a homer and half of barley. This was exactly the rations given to a slave for a day. Half price and a day's ration.

That is the best way of apprehending her condition. I will leave you to measure it. And the outcome? Brood and meditate upon the whole prophecy – therein is the answer. Hosea goes on to experiences of joy and love and life on the highest plane. It can best be explained by a sentence from the New Testament: "Rejoice with me, for I have found the sheep that was lost".

It is difficult to explain such joy to somebody who is in the world and has no knowledge of God and has never been conscious of being lost or losing anything – but Hosea would know its meaning deeply and magnificently. The valley of Achor is the door of hope. He passed through it into the sunshine of divine life. It was a prophecy of God's purpose with His people – even with us whom He hath called, not only of the Jews but also of the Gentiles.

In this last minute may we leave the historic and come to the present. As we face these emblems, that word "troubling" needs interpretation. We shall need to move from Hosea to John. Hear these words: "Now is my soul troubled; and what shall I say? Father, save me from this hour ... Father, glorify thy name" (John 12:27,28). "Now is my soul troubled". The troubling of the Lord to the uttermost bounds opened the door of hope – and let us make no mistake, the troubling which created the door of hope was not the troubling of Israel nor of Hosea – it was the troubling of God in Christ Jesus. God was in Christ reconciling the world unto himself. So he bore the sin of the world and banished it and opened the door so that we might make our way to the heart and the kingdom of God. So those who had not obtained mercy shall obtain mercy – those who were not His people shall be called the children of the living God.

Observe then what the word of exhortation is. If God so loved, we ought to love one another. "Love so amazing, so divine, demands my soul, my life, my all". If a man say, "I love my brother", but it is only a doctrine and never made truly incarnate, that man has failed. Hosea came to know the heart of God closely and deeply and came at last to full fellowship with the Lord – how? Because he obeyed God when God said: 'Hosea, go after Gomer and love her as I have loved this people. Make true in your life the things you have seen in me'.

So in that obedience, Hosea came to know, nay feel, the meaning of the love of God. God speaks to us today out of the life of Hosea. He says to us: "Go and love – somebody who is in need, in sorrow, in danger. The derelict in the faith, the weak, the despised. Somebody you would not naturally want to love – somebody you do not like very much, the undeserving, somebody who is only worth half price and a day's rations. Care for them, seek them out, serve them, bring them back, gather them in. Teach them that through the Valley of Achor there is a door of hope. And in the doing of it you will rise into the circle of those who know God best and to the secret of true fellowship with him.

In this memorial of the Lord's troubling – God grant that each one may feel it to be true.

# 9

## "I CAME NOT TO SEND PEACE, BUT A SWORD"
### (MICAH 7 & MATTHEW 10)

AS a beginning to this little exhortation, think of what we have read in Micah chapter 7. Recollect the conditions which provoked the prophet's censure. There was bribery and corruption in high places. The rulers and the judges were at the command of the highest bidder. The upright had been swept from power and the evil were doing their deeds unhindered – as the prophet puts it: "with both hands".

One of the worst features was a loss of confidence at all levels of society. Nobody dare trust anybody. Your best friend may be an informer. Remember verse 5: "Trust ye not a friend, put ye not confidence in a guide". In modern parlance: 'Do not trust a neighbour nor put any reliance on your friends'. But even worse: 'Be careful how you confide in your wife'. As the prophet puts it: "her that lieth in thy bosom". Then the prophet sums it up succinctly in verse 6: "For the son dishonoureth the father, the daughter riseth up against her mother, the daughter in law against her mother in law; a man's enemies are the men of his own house". Now of course you can hear the bells ringing – you have heard this many times before. As you know well it is in the gospels – in Matthew chapter 10 and Luke chapter 12. Let us take Matthew chapter 10 verses 34–36.

"Think not that I am come to send peace on earth: I came not to send peace, but a sword. For I am come to set a man at variance against his father, and the daughter against her mother, and the daughter in law against her mother in law. And a man's foes shall be they of his own household".

This, as you will perceive is a direct, quotation from Micah chapter 7 and it is an interesting example of the way in which the New uses the Old Testament. The important thing to notice is the sentence which the King used to introduce the quotation: "Think not that I am come to send peace on earth: I came not to send peace, but a sword". Here is a startling thing. The one who is called by Isaiah the "Prince of Peace", is standing in the midst of God's people and saying: "I came not to send peace, but a sword".

Just come to Isaiah with me and remember that sublime Messianic prophecy in verse 6 of chapter 9. "Wonderful, Counsellor, The mighty God, The everlasting Father, The Prince of Peace". Or more accurately – 'Wonderful Counsellor, God Hero, Father of Eternity, Prince of Peace'. There is a sense in which these four couplets are a revelation of the purpose of God in human history.

Think of it:

• Wonderful Counsellor – the one of perfect understanding, out of whom comes the perfect law for the final government of humanity

• God Hero – *El Gibbor*, the God of Battles, the Warrior God – who will fight for the salvation of His people in their extremity

• Father of Eternity – that is the begetter of the ages – literally the creator of the vanishing point, the source of immortality

• Prince of Peace – the one who harmonises opposing forces – who brings agreement and concord

Now as we listen to the voice of the man of Nazareth, there seems to be a conflict: "I came not to send peace but a sword". May I detain you for a moment on the word "send". In the margin of the RV the word is translated 'cast' – the actual Greek word is *ballo*. It is submerged in our word 'diabolical' – that which casts against. Used in the sentence from Jesus, it has the flavour of casting as in the sowing of seed, falling in all kinds of places. So the Lord Jesus may mean: "I have not come to cast peace promiscuously or carelessly – willynilly. My peace, when it comes, has purpose and plan, and the purpose necessitates a sword. I have come to bring a sword, ere there can be peace". We know that this principle is true in the great realisation of bringing peace to the world. We know from our understanding of the prophetic word that peace will come by way of judgement. The Messiah will come in the name of God to declare war on all the forces which prevent peace. It means that at last the rule of the irremediably wicked will be ended. Those who make war on the Lamb will be destroyed in the cause of peace.

**Family Divisions**

But in Micah and in Matthew this principle of the sword bringing peace is applied to the individual. The sword divides the family – two against three, a son from his father, a daughter from her mother. This is no mere figure. We must know that the nature of the Truth is such that sometimes this happens. Commitment to the King sometimes has to mean detachment from the next of kin. The King did say: "He that loveth father and mother more than me is not worthy of me". Sometimes the sword cuts and divides and we have to face it honestly. Now here is an interesting thing – the man who wrote the passage we read today for our third portion – knew this very well. He discovered the sword in his own family. He was the brother of Jesus by family ties, but not his brother by faith. In fact James was an unbeliever, and to that extent divided from him and against him. So, in the family of Nazareth there was this very division referred to in Micah and re-discovered in Matthew. There was disagreement and disunity as a result of Jesus' ministry. I came not to cast peace but a sword. On one occasion his family came to him seeking to urge him to give up his ministry – it is in Matthew chapter 12. I think we can  be sure that James came with his mother and the others. So James would have heard Jesus say this: "Whosoever shall do the will of my Father which is in heaven, the same is my brother, and sister, and mother" (Matthew 12:50). How far that impressed James we cannot tell, but with hindsight we now know that after the Lord's resurrection James becomes a faithful believer and eventually writes a great letter to those who are scattered abroad by the dispersion. Remember he is writing to those committed to the will of God the Father, who by that very fact become brethren of the Lord Jesus Christ, and of each other, in peace and unity.

## My Brethren

Now in the light of these circumstances concerning  James, have you noticed how often in his letter he uses the expression, "My brethren"? Be patient while I just remind you. "My brethren, count it all joy when ye fall into divers temptations" (1:2); "Do not err, my beloved brethren. Every good gift and every perfect gift is from above" (1:16,17); "My brethren, have not the faith of our Lord Jesus Christ … with respect of persons" (2:1); "Hearken, my beloved brethren, Hath not God chosen the poor of this world rich in faith?" (2:5); "What doth it profit, my brethren, though a man say he hath faith and have not works?" (2:14); My brethren, be not many masters, knowing that we shall receive a greater condemnation" (3:1); "Out of the same mouth proceedeth blessing and cursing. My brethren, these things ought not so to be" (3:10); "Can the fig tree, my brethren, bear olive

56

berries?" (3:12); "Take, my brethren, the prophets, who have spoken in the name of the Lord" (5:10); "But above all things, my brethren, swear not" (5:12); "Brethren, if any of you do err from the truth, and one convert him" (5:19); "Wherefore my beloved brethren, let every man be swift to hear, slow to speak, slow to wrath" (1:19).

You see what I mean – it tolls like a great bell – my brethren ... my brethren ... my brethren. And my suggestion is that James is like this because he has been greatly affected by the fact that at one time he was a brother of the Prince only by name and that there was a time when his family was spoiled because they were not brethren in the truest, realest sense. Remember the gospel says that even his brethren did not believe on him. I feel that James in the words "My brethren" is speaking in harmony with his anxiety that in the family of the Prince of peace there should be no forces which divide and harm, which spill and sunder. James does not beat about the bush. He asks in chapter 4 verse 1: "From whence come wars and fightings among you?" James, brother of the Prince, is anxious to warn his brethren about the forces which can harm the family. If you think I have over stated, then let us read again the passage we have read already from chapter 3 verses 13–18:

"Who is a wise man and endued with knowledge among you? let him show out of a good conversation his works with meekness of wisdom. But if ye have bitter envyings and strife in your hearts, glory not, and lie not against the truth. This wisdom descendeth not from above, but is earthly, sensual, devilish. For where envyings and strife is, there is confusion and every evil work. But the wisdom that is from above is first pure, then peaceable, gentle, and easy to be intreated, full of mercy and good fruits, without partiality, and without hypocrisy. And the fruit of righteousness is sown in peace of them that make peace".

Why do you think James is careful to say about heavenly wisdom, that it is first pure, and then peaceable? I have a suggestion. It could be that James once heard his brother say: "I came not to send peace, but a sword". You see in a way here is a revelation – the word "pure" relates to the sword. It means this Prince of Peace is at war with the things in my life and yours which are impure. He is in conflict with the forces in our discipleship which could shut out God. The Prince of Peace is a warrior with a flaming sword and flashing eyes – the God of Battles, ready to fight the things which harm those upon whom His love is set. He will make no peace with the opposing powers which assault those who are called, blood-sprinkled and chosen. He is merciful and full of compassion, but first the wisdom is pure and His word cuts through our impurity and sophistry like a knife.

## Purity before Peace

In Psalm 32, David tells of his great relief when pardon came to him at last. He reveals one of the conditions for full pardon – it is this: "… in whose spirit is no guile". What is guile? My comrades, I know about it so well. It is pretending that bad things are not so very bad. I am half ashamed to tell it. It is hiding our claimant desires in some artful kind of justification. It is giving doubtful things high sounding names in order to make them plausible. This was how David was and God gave him no rest. The controversy which David wanted to forget was kept alive in his soul by God. At last the sword of God was contained in four words which fell from the lips of Nathan: "Thou art the man".

David himself had pronounced the sentence – it was God who identified the sinner. So there was no lullaby for David until he shed his guile. It had to be first pure, before he could find peace. This I believe is what James means. Peace with God comes through honesty with ourselves. End the pretence, stop the window dressing, put away the sham, be done with the guile. James is saying, all this talk, talk, talk of religion – in God's name give us the reality. Be ye doers of the word, not hearers only.

A disciple is half false who only talks and argues but never acts. Notice what James is saying about the wisdom which is first pure, then peaceable. He says it is gentle, it is easy to be intreated, it is full of mercy and good fruits. He says it is without partiality and without hypocrisy. Think of being gentle – gentleness is power held in check. Think of the sea, able to destroy the strongest vessel, able to break up the sturdiest defences, to destroy the boldest endeavour, but it laps over the feet of a little child in perfect safety. This is gentleness. When I could be hard and unyielding, instead I must try to be forbearing, understanding and kind. It calls on me to behave to others as I would like them to behave to me; that is by being full of mercy, says James, and full of good fruits.

Good fruit is fruit without rottenness, without taint, without sourness. James exhorts us to be full of mercy. He means be merciful because one day you will need mercy. His brother said once: "Blessed are the merciful: for they shall obtain mercy". James exhorts us to be without partiality.

Partiality means being true in one way and untrue in another. The word integrity is the opposite of partiality. Integrity means being true in every way, through the wholeness of character. We speak of something being an integral part of something else. We mean it is entire, not partial. If we are to avoid being partial, it means we must urge on our brother's behalf every defence and every clemency we would want to claim for ourselves. When James says "without hypocrisy", I think he means avoid professing one thing and then doing another. Hypocrisy means proclaiming high principles and then living on low ones. I know these things are incisive and are not nice, and if you feel angry with me then I shall have to bear it, but my defence is that I am seeking to put to you what James is concerned about. The wisdom from above is first pure then peaceable and he is saying that there are some things which spoil it and impede it. What I have done is to draw your attention to James' words.

I know that James is a popular writer because he is so practical – he gets down to the nitty gritty – but I must say that having prepared this exhortation, I am not so sure that I like James that much. I feel he has caught me out – as it were in the very act, with the blood on my hands. But I think I have learned more about what the King meant by: "I have not come to send peace, but a sword", and I know I must give James a fair chance. I must not ignore it; I must give it a fair run, in my mind and in my conscience. The point is this. Is there a better place to do it than now, at the bread breaking? Confronted with the one who is pre-eminently the wisdom from above – who once said: "Whosoever shall do the will of my Father ... is my brother, and sister". Micah knew it, Jesus knew it, James knew it. They wanted us to know it.

So in this solemn moment of the memorial let us renew our resolution to know it more and more, now and in the coming days, sowing and making peace. As you handle the emblems, ask this question: 'What is the sword-bearing Prince of Peace saying to me – not to any other, but to me?' This, my brethren, is the word of exhortation.

# 10

## "BE STRONG ... AND WORK"
### (HAGGAI 1,2)

I WILL come to the point straight away and say that this exhortation is based upon the prophecy of Haggai – and the central idea is focussed in the first four verses of chapter 2.

"In the seventh month, in the one and twentieth day of the month, came the word of the LORD by the prophet Haggai, saying, speak now to Zerubbabel the son of Shealtiel, governor of Judah, and to Joshua the son of Josedech, the high priest, and to the residue of the people, saying, Who is left among you that saw this house in her first glory? and how do ye see it now? is it not in your eyes in comparison of it as nothing? Yet now be strong, O Zerubbabel, saith the LORD; and be strong, O Joshua, son of Josedech, the high priest; and be strong, all ye people of the land, saith the LORD, and work: for I am with you, saith the LORD of hosts."

The words I want to emphasise are: "Be strong ... and work". This is the central theme of our exhortation. I am going to ask you to look at it ere long in the context of Haggai. It is a wonderful thing how the words of the old Hebrew prophets have such a striking relevance to our own times. The messages written so long ago seem to have an uncanny application to our situation. This I think is true of the message of Haggai and it is concentrated in these words: "Be strong ... and work".

**Vigour and Vision**

First of all though, I am going to ask you to think in a somewhat fundamental way about the idea of strength. Very often when we think of those who are strong on the human level, we think of the young. Youth is the time of strength. When the prophet Isaiah wanted to express the very deepest sense of failure in God's people he said in chapter 40: "Even the youths shall faint and be weary, and the young men shall utterly fall" (verse 30). Or John the Apostle wrote: "I have written unto you, young men, because ye are strong ..." (1 John 2:14). Youth then is the time of strength.

But there is another element about youth which will help us. Joel says: "Your old men shall dream dreams, your young men shall see visions" (2:28). When you are young the emphasis is always on possibility, and when you are old it is more likely to be on limitation. I mention this to draw attention to the fact that with strength there is associated the idea of vision and aspiration. In the Bible the two ideas are joined – vision and vigour. It teaches us that on the spiritual plane the first element in spiritual strength is strong conviction. An uncertain mind issues in a half-hearted life. A double-minded man is unstable in all his ways. Doubt may sometimes be honest but it often saps the strength.

But strong convictions are not enough – they must generate strong feelings. It is passion which drives men to attempt the difficult and overcome the insuperable. Do not be ashamed of passion and emotion. Jesus wept over the death of his friend and over the desolation of his city.

But strong feelings are not enough unless those feelings energise the will. Strength is useless unless it results in volition. Strength only becomes real when it is exercised strongly. Strength perpetually in reserve but never in use becomes weakness. Remember the man with the withered arm whom Jesus cured. I wonder what he did afterwards. Perhaps he showed his friends the strong muscles rippling under the skin – proud of the new strength in what was before a helpless emaciated limb. But imagine they said: 'Now you will be able to do some hard work ...', and that he said: 'I am going to wrap it up and keep it in a sling. I must protect it at all costs and not expose it to injury by using it for work'. Suppose he did so and ere long the limb became atrophied and useless. The last end of the man would be the same as the first. The new strength would become weakness. Strength is real only when it acts strongly.

**The Power of Restraint**

But there is one last element in spiritual strength which must be remembered. The power of restraint. The power of strong command. Sometimes actions we intend must be held in check – sometimes our will must be submitted to another and higher authority. Sometimes we must learn to wait. Sometimes we must change our course. Real strength is force under control. Force out of control is weakness. It teaches us that sometimes we must measure strength by the power of the feelings which we subdue, not by the power of the feelings which subdue us. Real strength is in the man with strong passions who remains chaste, who having the manly power of

61

indignation, is not provoked; who having a keen sense of injustice is able lovingly to forgive. There is a kind of courage which rightly named is foolhardiness. There is a kind of strength which rightly named is bravado. Having irresistible impulses is not the same as having spiritual strength and sometimes, the strength of the passion not expended, makes us stronger still. Sometimes real greatness and real gentleness consists of power held in check. Think of Jesus and the long calm waiting at Nazareth. All the things he was to redress and rebuke were there – the hollowness of religion, the misinterpretation of the scriptures, the priestcraft, the cowardice, the hypocrisy, the culpable blindness. The Son of God waited, matured his energy, prepared his soul and then when his hour was come went out to speak and do and suffer. This is strength – keeping power until it is wanted. All this is said brethren, in order to try to expose what we ought to mean by spiritual strength.

**"Be Strong … and Work"**

With these thoughts in mind then we can return to Haggai and meditate upon his message: "Be strong … and work". You will recall well enough the situation in which these words were spoken by God. The house of God lay waste for 15 years. Its rebuilding had been started but it had been left and now it was in a condition of utter desolation, overgrown and moss covered – neglected. The need then was to build the house of God, and issuing out of that need there was the responsibility that the people should be strong and work, and the encouragement was in the word of the Lord: "I am with you, saith the LORD of hosts". In the command to be strong and work there is the suggestion that hitherto, and even still, weakness had prevented them from building the house of God. Something had sapped their strength, and so fostered the neglect. Before we come to look at the things which made for weakness I need hardly remind you of the relevance of this matter to our own day. The need is always there to build the house of God. In those days it was a material house and it was the sacramental symbol of the people's relationship to God. Today it is a spiritual house, but the principle remains the same. The house of God is the pillar and the foundation of truth, the place of praise, of testimony and of light – a city set on a hill – the place where men may find God and worship him. The need now as then is that we shall be strong and work for the building of that house lest it become a reproach.

Mark the forces of weakness which had halted the building of the house: "The time is not come, the time that the LORD's house should be built" (1:2). This is the voice which says in the presence of superabounding need: "The time is difficult, the situation is not favourable, we had better postpone the idea". This is the voice of men cowed by obstacles, whose enthusiasm is lulled into carelessness by pessimism. I have no doubt they said these words when somebody wanted to have an Isolation League, or the Auxiliary Lecturing Society or the Care Homes or the Bible Mission. Difficulty is not a valid reason for capitulation. Notice the magnificent turn of expression used by Paul in 1 Corinthians 16: "I will tarry at Ephesus until Pentecost. For a great door and effectual is opened unto me, and there are many adversaries" (verses 8,9). The majestic opposition constituted for Paul the best reason to remain.

The next element of weakness is revealed in this question: "Is it time for you, O ye, to dwell in your cieled houses, while this house lieth waste?" (Haggai 1:4). Luxury and comfort had made them anaemic and indifferent. Enervated by the affluence of their times they had no will nor strength for God's rebuilding. Brethren I am not going to moralise about the influence of our times because I enjoy it as much as you do. Things which our fathers spoke of as luxuries we speak of as necessities. We have changed as men are always changed by their environment. They tell me that the truth was stronger when there was less luxury. The heroism of our fathers was born out of a simple life and hard times. Be that as it may – I cannot tell. But I would say this – never was there a time when the pressures of living bore so hardly on the young. The constant call to get on, to achieve success, to secure the best positions, to make a place in life which is worthwhile. I am told that there are not many young men becoming speakers and there may be a crisis ere long. Whether that is likely to be so I know not, but I know that the philosophy of this age is the philosophy of prosperity and in order to get it the young have to dedicate themselves to more education, more study, more ambition. And then comes marriage and they have to dedicate themselves to being parents and acquiring possessions. So perhaps the opportunities for building the Lord's house are limited and the chances of work are hindered by the daily responsibilities of living in the affluent society.

The third element of weakness is discovered in another question: "Who is left among you that saw this house in her first glory? and how do ye see it now? is it not in your eyes in comparison of it as nothing?" There are those who are always looking back and making comparisons and sighing for departed glories – for the voices of those who are now asleep, for the days when men read their Bibles and cared for their religion. So they look with doubt and misgiving on any new methods – they cannot bring themselves to accept any change – they lament the enthusiasm which looks for new ways and new ideas. The bottles become hard and unyielding and sometimes the new wine is lost. The strength and enthusiasm of youth needs sympathy and wisdom – where it is lacking the strength is sapped and the enthusiasm frustrated.

If you ask 'Why do you draw attention to these factors?', I reply that the prophet urges us to discover our strength by first of all examining our weaknesses. He says: "Consider your ways". The Lord's word to us is: "Be strong and work". I affirm that we cannot travel a hundred yards from this house without discovering some need; some opportunity to build the house of God; some word of kindness; some sentence of encouragement; some ministry of immediate help; some proclaiming of the Lord's purpose.

The truth is that the people in your street, apart from some ministry external to themselves, are likely to perish. You are that ministry. So the Lord's strong man by his example will halt the spread of corruption and throw back the frontiers of darkness within the orbit of the little world in which he moves. In the work of building the house of God, nothing is mean – the whole glorifies every part. Nothing is unimportant when it is done for God. But we must be strong and work. The first way to strength then is to discover your weakness.

The second is this – a discovery of the need. Twice the prophet says: "This house lieth waste". What was needed was a strong conviction that the Lord's house must be built. The next element of strength is confidence in the promise and power of God. "I will fill this house with glory ... the glory of this latter house shall be greater than the former ... in this place I will give peace" (2:9). When they were convinced of that they rose up and builded. The strong convictions entering into their hearts, they felt the pain of the ruin in their souls, so their convictions and their feelings energised their will, and they became strong and worked for the Lord.

64

## I Am With You

And the final point of strength is encouragement: "I am with you, saith the LORD". Therefore the weakness can be turned into strength because they were conscious of the Lord's nearness. How often in our lives is the nearness of God undiscovered because of the poverty of our faith.

Hear the word of Paul to Timothy, the young: "My son, be strong in the grace that is in Christ Jesus". Those words were sent to a young man who was called to endure hardness as a good soldier of Jesus Christ. Paul uses three great words which indicate the way of strength for Timothy. *Flee* youthful lusts; *Follow* after righteousness, peace, love. *Fight* the good fight of faith.

Flee – Follow – Fight. This is the pattern for the channelling of youthful vigour. The young must flee from those things which are manifestly evil – they must consciously follow those things which are good – and perpetually fight for those things which belong to the King. Every man who has yielded himself to the king is called upon to fight the battles of the king. It calls for courage and vigour but remember the King is the file leader. The man who takes short cuts devoid of principle has forgotten who he serves. Remember a traitor is not one who fights against the King from outside but one who tolerates in his life the very things against which his King is fighting.

Hear the story of the young man who came to his father who was an old warrior and said: "Father, my sword is just a little too short for me". And the old man said: "Then add a step to it". This is the vigour of youth – enhanced by the wisdom of the aged. Be strong and of good courage.

Remember how on one occasion God said: "Let all the faint hearted return home" and 23,000 left forthwith. They were good men no doubt and may God bless them all, but the force was made stronger by their going. Young brethren and sisters – this is your calling: "Be strong ... and work: for I am with you, saith the LORD of hosts". But remember the word of John Zebedee because it reveals the source of your strength: "I have written unto you, young men, because ye are strong, and the word of God abideth in you" (1 John 2:14).

Shall we not put ourselves at his disposal so that having our vigour disciplined by the power of that wisdom which cometh from above, we may together in balanced harmony, young and old, share the high and holy enterprise of building the house of God.

# 11

## THE WAY TO THE ALTAR
### (MATTHEW 5)

I WOULD like to tell you how this exhortation came to be conceived. I knew it had to be based on Matthew chapter 5. How could I pass it by? The manifesto of the King – the sermon on the mount, the revelation of the perfect ethic. The things which are at the centre of our faith – the divine blueprint for discipleship. So how could I pass it by?

So I read through it carefully – and of course it is full of ideas for exhortation – a dozen themes present themselves in the first 16 verses. But I applied another measurement. Was there something here in the great sermon on the mount which at the same time as being hortatory has an especial relevance to the memorial service? Something peculiarly right for our presence here today? And as I read through it seemed to me that there was. It is in verses 23 and 24:

"Therefore if thou bring thy gift to the altar, and there rememberest that thy brother hath ought against thee; leave there thy gift before the altar, and go thy way; first be reconciled to thy brother, and then come and offer thy gift."

Can we first of all settle in our minds that the altar referred to by Jesus can reasonably be equated with this table of remembrance?

Quickly think what the altar meant to the Hebrew mind. Going back to the Old Testament it is the place appointed by God where He and men can meet. It was the place where, in God's presence, adjustments are made. Where having made the adjustment men go forward, renewed and re-determined. The altar is the place of worship. In the presence of the altar men prostrate themselves and speak with reverence. Here at the altar they recognise the utter sovereignty of God, they confess the supremacy of His will. In the Hebrew mind, coming to the altar was drawing closer to God in fellowship. The altar was the place of mediation and sacrifice – the place where pardon was extended to those who came with contrition and confession. It was the right place for every occasion of life. In times of joy and in times of sorrow men came to the altar. In times of success and in times of failure they built an altar. In times of brokenness and in times of exultation they came to the altar. The altar was for the mercy seat and the best place of all to find succour and blessing. The very proof is in the word of God himself. Exodus 20:24: "An altar of earth thou shalt make unto me, and shalt sacrifice thereon thy burnt offerings, and thy peace offerings, thy sheep and thine oxen: in all places where I record my name I will come unto thee, and I will bless thee". So it was a holy but common conception in the Hebrew mind that men should come to the altar of God bringing a gift and so drawing near to God should find blessing and fellowship. "I will come unto thee" – fellowship: "and I will bless thee" – the favour of God.

Now here is an interesting thing. We are not left to our intuition about making the transition from the Hebrew altar to our own. The Hebrew man says: "We have an altar, whereof they have no right to eat which serve the tabernacle" (13:10). That this altar is the cross, there can be no doubt: "For the bodies of those beasts, whose blood is brought into the sanctuary by the high priest for sin, are burned without the camp. Wherefore Jesus also, that he might sanctify the people with his own blood, suffered without the gate. Let us go forth therefore unto him without the camp, bearing his reproach" (verses 11–13).

We have an altar – the cross of Christ. It is the place of sacrifice, the place of pardon, the place of readjustment. It is the place where men meet with God and bow their heads in reverence; the place where men draw close to God in fellowship and receive blessing. The place to which they bring their gifts and make their dedication. This is no stretch of the imagination. As truly as the Hebrew had an altar, so do we. It is holy, sanctified and exclusive. We come in times of joy and in times of sorrow, in times of success and in times of failure. In times of brokeness and in times of exultation. It is for all conditions of life. This table is the mercy seat.

When men are surveying and they find the place on their plans where all lines meet and from which all lines proceed, then they go out and fix the place on the land and they drive in a stake and they call it the place of triangulation. Thereafter it is the place from which all measurements are taken and all calculations are made and all judgements proceed.

Once men drove in a stake and on it they crucified the Son of God. Thereafter it became the place of divine triangulation, the place from which all measurements are taken and all judgements are made – the place by which your life and mine will finally be calculated. The mercy seat – the altar of God.

## We have an Altar

Now we have to be fair. When Jesus spoke of offering gifts before the altar, he was referring to the existing order of things. He was referring to the altar in Israel to which men came to offer sacrifice through the high priest. But the Lord was no mere ritualist – he was not a formalist. When he said "the altar", he was referring to all that the altar stood for, measured by the very highest values of the spirit. That is, men drawing near to God by way of sacrifice to gain pardon and blessing. When he uttered this word on the hillside he knew that the day would come when under the constraint of the Spirit, a Hebrew man would say: "We have an altar".

He knew that in himself all the foreshadowing values of the altar were to be fulfilled. So let us have no doubt in our minds. These words in Matthew chapter 5 are truly the word of the Lord for us. What he said about coming to the altar was said in a passage of scripture which in every way we know to be the supreme measurement of life for those who profess to be his disciples. This is his manifesto, and our master plan for life. So let us look at the word carefully – for it has to do with our presence here today especially on the first Sunday of a new year. I beg you receive it reverently, for this thing is holy and God will not have His holy things to be profaned.

"Therefore if thou bring thy gift to the altar, and there rememberest that thy brother hath ought against thee; leave there thy gift before the altar, and go thy way; first be reconciled to thy brother, and then come and offer thy gift.

As you know I often say that in the Bible every word is important and this passage proves it yet again. Notice the word "therefore". "Therefore if thou bring thy gift ...". "Therefore" means 'because of what I have just said'. Notice what he had just said:

"Ye have heard that it was said by them of old time, Thou shalt not kill; and whosoever shall kill shall be in danger of the judgment: but I say unto you, That whosoever is angry with his brother without a cause shall be in danger of the judgment: and whosoever shall say to his brother, Raca, shall be in danger of the council: but

68

whosoever shall say, Thou fool, shall be in danger of hell fire." (verses 21,22)

In these words the King emphasises the sacredness of human life – murder under any guise is forbidden. Then he warns his disciples against anger – especially the anger which quietly rejoices in the suffering of another against whom the anger is felt. *Raca* in the Hebrew mind was the supreme form of contempt and those who used it were in danger of the council – that is citation before the whole Sanhedrin. If a man should say "Thou fool", the language of malice, of insult with the clear intention to harm and wound – then the only fit punishment is to be cast into Gehenna – the place of refuse and burning outside the city.

Under the old law a man was condemned if he was caught red-handed. Under the new law a man is condemned because of his attitude of soul, which unless it is checked and changed may end in wounding and murder. So the word "therefore" is related to this. Because these mental attitudes of contempt, anger and despising are forbidden, therefore if these moods exist in a man, he is at once to act so as to remove them. "Leave there thy gift ..."

**First be Reconciled**

Here is a strange thing. Notice how drawing near to the altar activates the conscience: "... and there rememberest". Somehow it compels a man to remember his failure. The first value of the love of Christ at the altar is that of conviction. In his presence we know that we are undone – we have failed.

The altar will not harbour the man who wants to nurse his sin. It is not the place where we may hide in our pollution – it compels us to come out into the light and to confess our weakness. If we are honest there is no escape from the reality of our wilfulness. Here there is no cloaking of the wrong done. Window dressing is outlawed. I know how easy it is. We give our motives the very highest intentions. We invest our attitudes with the purest purposes. We justify our ways with the contention that the Truth is being defended or advanced. I know how it is – I do it myself.

But in the presence of the altar we are exposed. We say so often that this is the time to examine ourselves. At this place, we can know our own hearts and cry out with the psalmist: "Search me, O God, and know my heart: try me, and know my thoughts: and see if there be any wicked way in me" (Psalm 139:23,24). Understand the altar is the way to purity and peace. So "first be reconciled ... and offer thy gift".

Here is a strange paradox. A man, realising and remembering there is some impediment in the way of coming to the altar – some dislocation that needs to be adjusted – moves away from the altar geographically and leaves his gift. And if he goes in the right spirit and intention to be reconciled to his brother, then every step away from the altar geographically is a step nearer its spiritual reality. As he travels away from it he draws nearer to God.

And here is the opposite which is frighteningly true. If he stays nursing his bitterness, satisfied in his prejudice, ready to cover and hide his sin, then as he draws near he gets further from God. Understand properly the purpose of the journey. Is it for his own peace of mind? Inevitably it will be, but that is not its noblest intention. It is for love's sake. It is to save his brother from those attitudes of contempt, malice, offence, anger, despising, opposition, which could lead to sin. Every journey from the altar which eventually leads back to the altar is a journey to serve someone else for love's sake. None of us lives to himself. Love cannot be independent. Fellowship is not capricious.

The obedience to this command is co-operation with God for the restoration of your brother first of all, and then for yourself. We are to deal with that which is remembered between ourselves and our brother or sister. We are to make confession. If need be, we are to make restitution. We are to find our way into his heart. Will it work? Of course it will work. How often do you hear of a refusal to be reconciled? It is a remarkably rare thing. You may read about it in novels but rarely in real life. True souls need to be at peace. They are glad for the healing forces of the altar.

I am compelled to say to this congregation today that I am grieved if I have to believe that in this house there is any one who has some unreconciled thing against me. If there is, then they must come to me and tell me frankly and let it be ended and restoration be made. That is not spoken for effect. It is quite possible for those who serve the ecclesia to do harm as well as good. It is possible to walk over other people's dreams and other people's feelings without intention, and so fellowship is fevered and bitterness is provoked.

The complications and intricacies of ecclesial life sometimes lead us to do wrong things when we think we are doing right. You may think that this exhortation is unnecessary – it is out of place here. But my reply is, I draw attention to it because Jesus drew attention to it in our hearing today. It does have a very real application to this memorial service and every other occasion when we come to break bread.

This is always a holy occasion. It would be a sad thing if we came week after week to the altar and never had a twinge of conscience and never blushed with shame. So let us take the word of the Lord as he has spoken it to us. Let us look carefully and honestly at our hearts and consent to what has to be done if need be. I am not suggesting that we leave the altar now. But what we can do now is to resolve that before we come again, the reconciliation will be made; peace will be established; the breach will be healed. Finally, notice the blessed welcome: "Then come and offer thy gift". It means that we come no longer as a formalist but in truth and in reality. In the moment that the conscience is awakened, the way is clear to the altar. If our coming is sincere and free from rancour then the altar may rebuke us but we shall find pardon and peace and power for all the coming days. Is there a better way to start a new year? Clear from the impediments, free from the forces which could taint our fellowship; pure in our friendships and true in our service. So on this day, within this hour, amid this congregation, through this memorial service, let us thank God for the altar – let us rejoice in its meaning and its mystery and depend always upon its mercy.

# 12

## "BY THEIR FRUITS YE SHALL KNOW THEM"
### (MATTHEW 7)

TODAY brethren, we have heard some solemn words from the lips of Jesus Christ. Words, perhaps which we wish he had not found it necessary to utter – words perhaps which to some extent we wish we could tear from the New Testament but we dare not. "Every tree that bringeth not forth good fruit is hewn down, and cast into the fire" (Matthew 7:19).

We know that the arithmetic of God is not the arithmetic of the market place – very often that which is golden to men is but tinsel to God, whilst that which men despise, is counted great in heaven. Nevertheless Jesus reveals to us this principle; that it is both Divinely natural and humanly natural to judge a tree by the fruit it bears.

In the judgement of most men a barren tree is not worth keeping. Jesus says that that judgement has its roots in the Divine law – it is also the judgement of God. It is a universal and eternal law. The words which Jesus used had been used before by a great prophet. We can read in Matthew 3 of how John Baptist came preaching in the wilderness of Judea and crying: "Repent ye: for the kingdom of heaven is at hand". He said it was a day of Divine judgement: "And now also the axe is laid unto the root of the trees: therefore every tree which bringeth not forth good fruit is hewn down, and cast into the fire" (verse 10). He spoke those words to some who were seeking to justify themselves, not by the fruit which they bore, but by the name which they used. Said John Baptist to the Pharisees: "Think not to say within yourselves, We have Abraham to our Father" (verse 9). It was not by using Abraham's name that they would escape, but by bringing forth fruit meet for repentance.

In private gardens the fruit trees are very often marked with small metal labels tied to one of the branches. On one it says *Newton Wonder* – another *Ellison Orange* – another *Doyen du Comice*. They tell the gardener the kind of fruit that tree ought to bear – they do not guarantee any fruit. The label is not an insurance against barrenness. The name is not without significance, but the fruit is the real test. In the garden of God there are some trees marked *Christadelphian.* The name is not without significance, but it is not a guarantee of fruit. It tells the gardener that this tree is within the orbit of every possible influence designed to produce the most desirable fruit. It tells the gardener that this tree has access to the very highest powers, the very richest source of strength toward fruit bearing. That tree in a sense is in the midst of the paradise of God. It is in the most exalted position, with the very finest opportunity to be fruitful. Its roots are set in the most fertile part of the Divine garden. But that tree therefore bears a heavy responsibility. For to be barren when the possibility of so much fruitfulness exists – after so much care on the part of the gardener – is a great tragedy. It is that which at the last causes the axe to be laid to the roots.

**The Gardener**

Suppose Jesus is the gardener. We need not suppose it, brethren, for it is true. I will take you to the proof of it.

"Jesus spake also this parable; A certain man had a fig tree planted in his vineyard: and he came and sought fruit thereon, and found none. Then said he unto the dresser of his vineyard, Behold, these three years I come seeking fruit on this fig tree, and find none: cut it down; why cumbereth it the ground? And he answering said unto him, Lord, let it alone this year also, till I shall dig about it, and dung it: and if it bear fruit thenceforth, well: and if not, then after that thou shalt cut it down."          (Luke 13:6)

Of course the parable is oriental in its flavour but it would be doing it no violence to change the word 'vineyard' to 'garden' and 'dresser' to 'gardener'. The owner of the garden is God – the gardener is Jesus Christ.

Have you ever noticed how so often in the teaching of Jesus he made the men to whom he spoke the judges of their own actions – to pass a verdict upon themselves? Recall on another occasion after giving the parable of the wicked husbandmen he asked: "What will he [the owner of the vineyard] do to those husbandmen?" and his audience replied: "He will miserably destroy those wicked men, and will let out his vineyard unto other husbandmen, which shall render him the fruits in their seasons" (Matthew 21:40,41). They were really passing judgement on themselves, though perhaps they knew it not. This little parable is something like that. When you read it did you not within yourself feel that the judgement of the owner of the garden was right? If

73

you were in that position would you not feel that an irretrievably barren tree is best removed? This is teaching us again that it is both humanly and Divinely natural to judge a tree by its fruit.

**Expectation of Fruit**

If you had a garden and purchased at cost to yourself a tree and planted it and nurtured it and tended it – is it not right to say that the tree is yours and you have a right to expect fruit? Is there any man or woman in this congregation who would quarrel with that? Do you not feel it to be true and reasonable? Then take the truth which you admit and the reasonableness which you feel and apply it to the realm of God.

There are some men and women who have been purchased by God at a very great price. In a peculiar sense they are His property. Furthermore they live in His world and all the forces of their life are forces which have come from Him. They use resources which God has provided. In Him they live and move and have their being. He is caring for them and seeking to protect them and strengthen them and renew them. Taking up the figure again – therefore has not God the moral right to expect fruit? If in the human sphere of things we have admitted the truth of this principle, is it not now ten thousand times more true in the realm of God?

Do not be surprised therefore that in the parable, the owner speaks as though he had the right to expect fruit. "Behold, these three years I come seeking fruit on this fig tree ...". What is the fruit he expects to find?

Brethren, the simplicity of the parable is magnificent. If I went to your Sunday School this afternoon and asked one of the children what he would expect from an apple tree, you know what he would say – or what he would expect from a fig tree, you know the answer he would give.

When God comes to a man He is seeking manliness – manhood. Somebody may say: "But that is only a word – what is manhood?" Brethren, in our thesis we have come to the green hill. Behold the man. He is called the last Adam and you know what Adam means. He is the man Christ Jesus. He is the realised idea of the perfection of humanity. In the beginning God said: "Let us make men in our image, after our likeness ... and let them ... have dominion over all the earth". This is that resolution of God realised and perfected. The meaning of humanity has once been perfectly revealed in the man of Nazareth. Jesus is what God means by manhood. All the things which you can think of as being part of the Christian life are all comprehended in that word. When the Apostle says: "Quit you like men", this is what he means. Jesus is the Archetypal man – the true revelation of what God intended our own nature to be. Manhood is greater than angels. The letter to the Hebrews says so.

## Producing Fruit

If therefore you come to ask yourself whether you are producing fruit for the goodman of the house – make your test by comparison with the life of Jesus. It is so easy to test our lives by comparison with others. That way we can become satisfied with our lives on the basis that there are many worse than ourselves. It is still so easy to stand in the sanctuary and say: "God, I thank thee, that I am not as other men …". May God forgive us.

We may be able to say of ourselves: I do not swear, I do not drink, I do not smoke, I have never fallen into blatant vulgar sin, I have been brought up in a good Christian home. Thank God you can – I am glad, I respect you for it – I never despise a man who can say that. But consider if that is all we can say and if Jesus is the standard, I wonder if when God comes seeking fruit in us He will find only leaves? No drunkenness, no adultery, no profanity, no blatant worldliness – but no fruit. What I mean is this – fruit is a positive thing. It is not only an abstemious refusal of certain vices, nor a punctilious performance of certain virtues. Fruit does not come by magic overnight – it grows. Baptism is not a conjuring trick which produces perfection in a flash. The word fruit presupposes life, and life is growth.

The Apostle says the fruit of the spirit is love, joy, peace, longsuffering, kindness, goodness, faithfulness, meekness, temperance. Fruit is something which happens in the realm of life. In a sense it is mystical in its substance. We can know it by observation but we cannot analyse it and explain it. Fruit is God's work – it is true in the natural life – it is true in the spiritual life. Men can paint it on canvas and make it in wax for a glass case but they cannot make it grow. Notice the Apostle says the fruit of the spirit, but he never says the fruit of the flesh. He says the *works* of the flesh. Consider the difference – think about the words. Fruit suggests a garden where things are alive and pre-eminently God is at work. Works suggests a – yes a factory. At Cowley we have the Morris Car Works. God does not work there. It is where men are working with dead things. The metal and the timber are all dead. I will grant you they will do wonderful things with them but they are all in the process of disintegration. That is the difference between fruit and works. One is the work of God the other the work of men. It means that the very finest thing which is man-made and man-centred is really a thing of decay. Your life and mine could be like that – works but no fruit.

I said that fruit implies life – it also implies cultivation. You know well enough that the tree which runs wild without cultivation and the pruning knife will gradually cease to bear good fruit. It is well to remember this always. It may be that some soul has come here this morning into the assembly of the saints with a heavy heart – perplexed by life, pressed by difficulty, puzzled by God's treatment, inclined to say "Why this hardship, this buffeting, this beating …?"

My brethren, hear the word of the Lord. "No chastening for the present seemeth to be joyous, but grievous: nevertheless afterward it yieldeth the peaceable fruit of righteousness". By that process God is perfecting the fruit – may He help you in the time of cultivation to see the afterward, and understand.

We started with a solemn thought: "Every tree which bringeth not forth good fruit is hewn down, and cast into the fire". It is the word of the Lord and is unmistakably true – but there is reason for solemn confidence. Go back to the little parable in Luke 13. Notice the word of the gardener – he is in fact an intercessor. "Lord, let it alone this year also, till I shall dig about it, and dung it: and if it bear fruit, well: and if not, thou shalt cut it down" (verses 8,9). Notice that the anxiety of the gardener is not that a barren tree shall be allowed to cumber the ground, but that the tree shall bear fruit. Notice there is no quarrel whatever between the gardener and the owner of the garden. There are no disagreements between God and Jesus Christ about man.

Recall that in Matthew 7 today we have read that it will be Jesus himself who will say at the last to the barren: "Depart from me, ye that work iniquity" (verse 23). Jesus has not come into the world to persuade God to accept men who are determined to be an eternal failure. The work of Jesus is not to influence God to let off the man who is irremediably barren. The work of Christ is to produce in that barren man the fruit that God is seeking. He came – to use the words of the figure – to dig about the tree, to dung it. He came to infuse into it new life, to introduce to it resources which make for fruit-bearing. Never believe that into the kingdom of God Christ is leading a great procession of failures. I do not believe it and it is not the language of the Bible. Hear words from Jude's elevating ascription of praise: "Now unto him that is able to keep you from falling, and to present you faultless before the presence of his glory ..." (verse 24). Or Paul's prayer that: "Your whole spirit and soul and body be preserved blameless unto the coming of our Lord Jesus Christ" (1 Thessalonians 5:23). There is room for solemn confidence. Notice the patience of the goodman of the house: "Behold, these three years I come" – nay four. Notice the patience of the gardener: "Let it alone this year also, till I shall dig about it ..."

Let us take heart. Though by ourselves we be barren fruitless men, yet in the yielding of our will and our life to him, forces can be at our disposal to make us neither barren nor unfruitful in the knowledge of our Lord Jesus Christ. So the words of the old prophet can be true in our lives – the fruit shall shake like Lebanon and the desert shall blossom as the rose.

# 13

## "BE OF GOOD CHEER"
### (MATTHEW 9)

AS bush-beating rarely does any good, I will come to the point straight away and tell you what this little exhortation is about. It begins in Matthew 9:2. This is the case of the man sick with the palsy – and not only that but he is troubled in heart on account of his sin. His friends with commendable resolution carry him into the presence of Jesus and the Lord says to him: "Son, be of good cheer; thy sins be forgiven thee".

Now it is those words I want you to fix on because I think you will recollect that the King used them on other occasions – and your memory is correct. Indeed in this very same chapter (verse 20) the next occasion occurs. This time a woman is in trouble of quite a different kind. Twelve years of suffering from a particularly distressing disease which brought her not only personal suffering, but also divorce from her husband and ostracism from her friends. A woman with an issue of blood. When she touched the hem of the King's garment the Lord turned to her and said: "Daughter, be of good comfort; thy faith hath made thee whole". Yes, I know that the Authorised Version says "be of good *comfort*" but I can assure you that it is exactly the same phrase as in the case of the man sick of the palsy – the very same words – "be of good cheer". So let us pass on.

The next occasion is Mark 6:45 onwards. You will recall it well – those men in peril on the sea. The wind was rough and contrary and their seamanship was being tested to the hilt, but that was not the real trouble. It was not the wind that filled them with so much fear, but something else. It was that mysterious thing that moved across the face of the sea – a phantom, a ghost, a spectre of the night. Then suddenly, out of the apparition, a voice speaks – a familiar voice: "Be of good cheer: it is I; be not afraid". And then he was in their midst and there was a great calm.

Then there is John 16:33 and the record of Jesus with his disciples in the upper room and he is telling them that he is shortly to leave them. They are bewildered and are deeply worried about their weakness in the face of antagonistic forces ranged against them and without his presence. They are troubled by fear of the future. The Lord said to them: "In the world ye shall have tribulation: but be of good cheer; I have overcome the world".

And then the last occasion is in Acts 23:11. The Apostle Paul is in prison, hindered in his high and holy enterprise of preaching the gospel and in peril for his personal safety. The Lord appeared to him and said: "Be of good cheer, Paul: for as thou hast testified of me in Jerusalem, so must thou bear witness also at Rome".

So there we are – five different occasions – in each one people in trouble of different kinds, but the self-same words to each: "Be of good cheer". In each case the King challenged the fear and the trouble which surrounded these people with the same comforting words. I think we can be sure of one thing: he was not telling them to cheer up. Let nobody suppose that there is anything wrong with cheerfulness – let nobody think that I am against it. I think cheerfulness is splendid; but the man of Nazareth never told people to cheer up when they were in trouble. To do so would have been to deal with the mere externals and the surface of things and he never worked like that. What *we* mean by cheerfulness is a circumstantial thing, an external thing. The proper New Testament word for cheerfulness is a word translated "joy" and is a very different thing. Joy is inward; it does not depend upon outward circumstances and can exist at times when cheerfulness would be impossible. Let me quickly give you the proof.

In Acts 27 there is a ship in peril on the sea – exactly the same situation as in Mark 6. Paul is on his way to Italy in a ship of Alexandria, and they, in the midst of a wind called *'Euraquello'*, are in great trouble. Paul says, by way of encouragement: "I exhort you be of good cheer" and again: "Wherefore sirs, be of good cheer". The word used for cheer here is *euthumeo* which means 'cheerfulness'; that is 'to be well minded', to be the opposite of glum, to cheer up. But the word that Jesus used in the above five references was not this one. It was the word *tharseo* and is used only on these five occasions by Jesus and on one other. It means 'courage'. So let there be no mistake, when he said "Be of good cheer", he was calling them to show courage. It seems that this was something quite personal to the man of Nazareth; no one else ever used the word or made the call: "Be of good courage". Let us retrace our steps and think again of the occasions.

To the man whose body was paralysed and whose conscience was troubled – to the woman abandoned and destitute, trembling and fearful – to the men on the sea filled with fear of mystery and the unknown – to those disciples threatened with opposition and deeply conscious of their weakness without their Lord – to that man in prison, hindered in his great purpose, mobbed, barely rescued and in peril for tomorrow, cast down and disappointed – to all those the very same word: "Be of good courage ..."

## Protected by Jesus

Can I put into words what I think you are thinking. That being told to have courage does not make us really courageous. To be told to put a brave face on it may help for a little while, but in the end it does no good because the old agony and the old fear returns. With reverence we are compelled to say that if this call to courage is to be real and practical, then we must be given a good reason for having courage. Now here is the thing – we are given that good reason. The central argument of this little exhortation is not just the words: "Be of good cheer", but more the thing which makes them true and valid. Did you notice in all these five cases where Jesus called these people to courage he had only one argument why they should respond – that was himself. To every force which came against those in trouble he placed himself. Let us notice one other thing. He did not seek to minimise the reality or the power of the forces which were against them. He did not say that pain does not matter and that sin is nothing to worry about and that evil can be brushed aside and that loneliness can be ignored. He did not laugh at those men on the sea because they were afraid of what they thought was a ghost. Jesus never minimised the fact and force of those things which are against his kingdom and which confront his disciples. What he did do was to place himself between the one who was in trouble and the force of the trouble. He placed himself between the assaulted disciple and the assaulting foe. Let us notice how this is true in the cases we are considering.

To the man crippled by paralysis and hardened with sin, Jesus said: "Thy sins be forgiven thee ... Arise, take up thy bed, and go unto thine house". Jesus placed himself between the sin and the sinner, cancelled the guilt and removed the disability.

To the woman he said: "Thy faith hath made thee whole". She was healed before he said it. His power came between her and the foe which assaulted her. I think we can be sure that when she heard his voice, courage filled her heart.

Those men in peril, faced with dark mystery on the sea, heard the familiar voice which said: "Be of good cheer: it is I; be not afraid". A dimmed vision of their Lord had turned him into a phantom and they feared, but when he was known to them, the fear ceased and there was a great calm.

The men in the upper room, fearful of the forces against them, to them he said: "Be of good cheer; I have overcome the world". It meant that over the very forces which they feared, he had been victorious. He meant: 'In fellowship with me your battles are won'.

And then in the stillness of the night, in prison, he appeared to that man who was threatened by evil men, deeply frustrated and hindered from achieving his goal at Rome, and said: "Be of good cheer, ... so must thou witness also at Rome". The word of the Lord became the stay of Paul. So his fears were calmed, his hopes renewed and his joy was sustained. That night he slept the sleep of the just. At the risk of wearying you – I repeat once more – the fact of Christ was the source of their courage – "It is I be not afraid".

## Courage in Christ

Now brethren and sisters, the local conditions we have pondered have now all faded. The king does not any more walk the streets and hills of Galilee nor stride across Gennesaret. No hem is touched nor prison invaded. The palsied are still set in their paralysis. The voice that spoke the word of courage is now silent. And yet although the local conditions have gone, do we not know in our deepest heart that the principle remains unchanged? That is, if we are to have courage it will be because of the fact of Christ.

There is nought else for those who are called and blood-sprinkled and chosen. All the wonderful things to which we have become related, and for which we long, are centred and focussed in him. All the promises of God in him are 'yea' and 'amen' to the glory of God the Father. The one lonely concentric man, the man of God, and yet of our humanity, has passed to the central place of power and authority. No power on earth can defeat his enthronement.

All the forces which seem to trample over God's world and seem bent on halting His great purpose, have been mastered in this one lonely man, the man of the seamless robe. He is Lord by the victory of life over death; Lord by the appointment of God; Lord by the administration of the Holy

Spirit. He is perfect in his humanity; mystic in his divinity. His master passion is the kingdom of God. Paul says if this is not true we are of all men most pitiable. The fairest dream that ever made human hearts throb with new hope has come to nought. We can hide our shame and creep back to our doom. If he never rose and presented himself in that upper room when the doors were bolted; if he never stood on the shore and prepared breakfast for cold, tired fishermen; if angels never said to those few disciples: "This same Jesus, which is taken up from you into heaven shall come again"; if there is no advocate after all and we are deceived, what would our lives be worth?

But the opposite is wonderfully true. He is alive and is the central fact of our hope. Our faith is not vain. Our sins are forgiven. We are not pitiable. We have come to know a joy which has eluded other people. Think of all those wonderful prophecies which we have lingered over so long and which we have loved so much, and which have become the polestar of all our hopes. He is the central figure in them all. The Immanuel, the Branch, Shiloh, Dayspring, Daystar, Daysman. Think of that great word of Isaiah in chapter 32:

"A man shall be as an hiding place from the wind, and a covert from the tempest; as rivers of water in a dry place, as the shadow of a great rock in a weary land." (verse 2)

Here is the picture of a man coming between the tempest and those who are exposed to it. Here is a man succouring the weary and refreshing those that are bruised and broken; resting their tired hearts and easing their burden. No wonder he said: "Be of good cheer". Who else could ever say it? Without him all life is emaciated; without him it is hard and cold and dry; without him it is empty and we are forlorn and wasted. So I put to you the affirmation – again. Because of the fact that he is, and all his being means to us, we are called to courage. In him all the promises are assured and all the doubts are dispelled. Because he is central in our lives there is no cause for fear, or panic, or trembling or despair. The courage he calls us to is appropriated by our faith in him. He is as much our courage as our faith will make him. It means we may come with our wounds, and with our bruises and with our failures and with our weakness and find grace to help in time of need. The voice is silent and yet it speaks to us from the parchment of this holy word as surely as ever it did. We may take our stand upon it and renew our courage.

Think of Hebrews 13:5: "He hath said, I will never leave thee, nor forsake thee". Therefore we may say with good courage: "The Lord is my helper, and I will not fear what man shall do unto me". Peter says "He careth for you". Either that is true or Peter has deceived us. We have come today because in our deepest heart we believe it is true, wonderfully true, and the caring providence of God for His people is focussed most sharply in this celebration. For love's sake, Armageddon of the Ages was begun on the green hill, and the victory which was won will issue at last in his great triumph over the forces of ungodliness in the day of his coming and his kingdom. So this is the summation. When he says to us: "Be of good cheer" – if your faith in him is sound and true and strong and unassailable, he stands between you and all the forces which apart from him could bring ruin and failure. Therefore in the truest sense you can have courage.

So in this moment of bread breaking, as we with solemn hearts and hushed spirits handle these emblems, when every third party is excluded and we are alone with the redeemer, let us renew our faith. Let us seek more truly our heavenly Father's blessing; consent more willingly to his examination; and submit more gladly to his commandments, so that we may be fortified for the days which lie ahead and our hearts may be garrisoned against the forces of ungodliness, so that in the very best sense we may be encouraged. May there be a spring in our step, and a song in our heart. Let us remember him therefore; the Christ of the virgin birth; of the virtuous life; of the victorious death and of the victorious resurrection. This is the source of our courage. Let us eat and drink and be of good cheer.

# 14

## FAITH WITH DILIGENCE
### (MATTHEW 16 & 2 PETER 1)

"From that time forth began Jesus to shew unto his disciples, how that he must go unto Jerusalem, and suffer many things of the elders and chief priests and scribes, and be killed, and be raised again the third day."

(Matthew 16:21)

FOR the Apostle Peter at this time the whole tragedy of the King's purpose is gathered together in the little word, 'this'.

"Then Peter took him, and began to rebuke him, saying, Be it far from thee, Lord: this shall not be unto thee."

(verse 22)

He saw wicked and brutal men harming and hurting the Master whom he loved. He saw the King bruised and broken. But we know that although Peter spoke out of love, his outburst was utterly mistaken. He was a man of faith – it was he who just before had made the great confession: "Thou art the Christ, the Son of the living God" (verse 16). His faith was genuine and yet when the incarnation of that faith demanded diligence – that is the prosecution of the faith to the uttermost in the face of forces which are antagonistic – he was urging the opposite. The one who made the great confession was urging the King to turn back from his high destiny. We can understand the vehemence of the King's reply. He of all men had manifested diligence. He had followed God's purpose with undeviating fidelity, never once being subverted from the high enterprise of godliness, though he had been sorely tried. Peter, with the best intentions was advising the Lord to turn traitor.

### Lessons Learned

So when Peter exhorts us to add to our faith with diligence (2 Peter 1:5), I think we can legitimately turn back to the great occasion when the lesson was learned so penetratingly. I am not saying that Peter, when he wrote the words in his second letter, was thinking back consciously to this occasion, but I submit that the association is permissible and I hope may be profitable for the following reason. If we can discover what it was that made a man of faith like Peter refuse the call to diligence – for what seemed to him the best reasons – it may help us to look penetratingly at our own lives and in the interrogation of our deepest heart, know the truth about ourselves.

In this situation we must understand that these two personalities as they stand facing each other – the King and Simon Peter – are at that particular time representatives of two opposing ideals. One displays humanity at its natural best and yet really at its deepest failure, and the other, humanity as God intended it to be. And the real issue at this memorial feast is that ere this day is over we shall in some measure be identifying ourselves with one ideal or the other. One demonstrates the things which be of God and the other, the things which be of men.

## Human Thinking

What was it then that made a man of faith turn back from diligence (as understood in its deepest meaning)? Peter's response firstly expressed a misconception of man's primary duty. Peter said in effect: 'Lord spare thyself'. He meant: 'Lord, your first duty is to yourself'. And how often have we heard it since, from our own lips and from the lips of others. 'Charity begins at home'; 'A man must look after himself'; 'Every man for himself and the devil take the hindmost'. Make no mistake, it is all a lie, humanly conceived and humanly proclaimed. A man's first duty is to God. The King said: "I must be about my Father's business". 'Spare thyself' was the philosophy which ran exactly opposite. No wonder it did the work of the adversary.

Secondly, Peter revealed a misconception of the value of sacrifice. Peter was saying in effect: 'Lord you have just approved my faith; you have commended my confession; I believe in you and you have spoken of building a great church; but what you propose to do now will bring all this to disaster. Sacrifice means ruin and failure to all your plans. Sacrifice is a mistake. To follow it is failure'.

I will pass over for a moment the result if Peter had had his way. We know now that by what Peter called 'defeat', the Armageddon of the Ages was fought and won. If you think I ought not to have used that expression, then consider this language:

"The kings of the earth stood up, and the rulers were gathered together against the Lord, and against his Christ."

(Acts 4:26)

85

As the poet has put it:

"He death by dying slew;

the grave in hell laid low".

Peter's words revealed a further misconception concerning the value of men to God. I speculate for a moment to say it seems to me as I read the narrative that somehow in the mind of Peter there was the idea that his Lord was by some method going to Jerusalem to save the very people who sought his life; that the purpose of his sacrifice was remedial; that a measure of love for the undeserving was his motive. So Peter's words were saying in effect: 'Lord you are mistaken – these people are not worth dying for. See how much you have endured because of them. Deliver yourself from any more pain and suffering – they are not worth it'.

We know now from the Lord's reply that his estimate is that, however dark the sin, the sinner is worth recovering. The obligation that drives him is godly love directed towards men in the midst of their ruin. It reveals God's diligence to seek and to save that which was lost. Perhaps we can understand better why the Lord used words like 'Satan', 'stumbling block' and 'offence'. He did it out of the compassion of his heart for all men, including Simon. This then, it seems to me, is an analysis of the reasons why Peter, a man of faith, did not at that time add to his faith with diligence. Recall again what the reasons are and then by contrast comprehend the forces which drive us and should compel us to diligence.

**True Realisations**

The first essential is a realisation of the fact that man's primary duty is to God. Every ambition humanly conceived must be subservient to the great ambition; every purpose must be remitted to the King's command.

Secondly, there must be a realisation of the value of sacrifice. "Whosoever will lose his life for my sake shall find it" (Matthew 16:25). We are always telling ourselves and each other that we must enter into sacrificial service for the King – but why? Because the truth is, that service which is sacrificial is done for love's sake. Blind submission to mechanical force may be all right sometimes but the submission which derives from love is glad, true and diligent. Sacrifice is the life force of diligence.

Thirdly, there must be a comprehension that, for some reason which defeats our full understanding, God cares for men immeasurably. His love for broken humanity is the master passion which underlies His purpose.

## The Need for Diligence

When Peter says "give diligence to make your calling and election sure" (2 Peter 1:10), he does not mean that we only do so to get something for ourselves. Our hope is not a selfish hope. It is not just that by diligence we shall gain a great harvest for ourselves. Our real hope ought to be for the glory of God and the realisation of the divine purpose in the world. For God's desire is to heal the wound of humanity – the satisfaction of the immeasurable love of God towards those who are undeserving. The harvest we look for is God's victory and God's triumph. Such diligence as we put into the business of advancing the cause now, will fit us to advance it in the age to come. In that sense we make our calling and election sure. Men who have bent to the wrong throne now, cannot serve the right one in the kingdom of God. So then God's love for broken humanity so powerfully manifested in the Cross, ought to provoke us and impel us to diligence for the sake of those who are in need of succour and salvation. Paul expressed it well. When he thought of man without God he felt himself to be in debt. So then he said:

"I am debtor both to the Greeks, and to the Barbarians … I am ready to preach the gospel to you that are at Rome also … I am not ashamed of the gospel of Christ: for it is the power of God unto salvation …"

(Romans 1:14–16)

Put those three sentences together and you have a definition of diligence. "I am a debtor … I am ready … I am not ashamed". I know that the things which halt us in our search for diligence are not the low, vulgar, sensual things of the world. Rather they are often the things which respectability and prudence can approve. They sound most reasonable and most sensible; most rational and most sane. But we ought to learn today from Peter that there is a kind of sanity which rightly named is madness. The truth is that whether we like it or not, in our daily lives we are answering one of two master principles. One is saying 'Spare thyself'. The words are in the centre of our mind whenever duty calls, when some sacrifice has to be made, some effort set forth, some temptation resisted – when God says "Who will go for us?", and the voice within says, 'Here am I – send him'. The temptation is to say, 'Let somebody else bear the burden; let them take the responsibility and do the work'. And too often perhaps in the house of God, seats are empty when they should be filled; too often the wall is not built around the city of God;  too often the King's business is neglected; too often the ecclesia is weakened and the Lord's needy ones are not succoured; too often the gospel is not advanced – because somehow we have spared ourselves. I know you will not love me for saying it – it is as uncomfortable for me as for you – but this is the issue we must face if we really want to add to our faith with diligence.

## Faith in Action

The other master principle compels us to realise that diligence should be at the very centre of our faith. It may mean preaching when there seems to be no result – and yet continuing to preach. It may involve teaching in Sunday School when our heart is breaking to see our Sunday work undone on Monday. It means living by truth and love and grace when in the world we are surrounded by hardness and hate and indifference. Perhaps it involves being steadfast when life means putting into hard ground what seems to be lifeless seed and never seeing the golden glow of harvest. For some it is keeping going in a day when there seems to be no light and the birds have ceased to sing. That is diligence. I have tried to show that the real issue of diligence is going on purposefully when conditions and common sense would say 'Give up, spare thyself'.

Hear this final word – it is a word from the great Galatian letter:

"Let us not be weary in well doing: for in due season we shall reap, if we faint not."  (Galatians 6:9)

Not being weary in well doing is the very essence of diligence; fainting is the opposite. If we are to escape the peril of failing diligence, we need as never before to have a clear conception of our calling, to practice our fellowship with God and with His other children and never to deflect our strength into unfruitful channels.

I leave you with one last thought – imagine the outcome if Peter could have had his way. The promise of redemption through Christ's blood would have been made hollow; the tomb seals would never have been broken; the Emmaus journey would have had no burning heart; Thomas never have been convinced; five hundred brethren would have been without manifestation. For some apostles there would have been no spirit-blessed Pentecost; for another no blinding light on the Damascus road; for yet another, no Apocalypse. And for ourselves there would have been a creeping back to our shame and disappointment: sins unpardoned, death triumphant, despair unabated. But thankfully this is only imagination. Our Lord was utterly faithful to his Father's business as we are reminded in bread and wine, and consequently all things are ours.

# 15

## "WATCH AND PRAY"
### (MATTHEW 25,26)

THE object when we gather round these emblems is not so much to discover new things in the Truth, as to deepen our understanding of those things that are well known.

I mention this because today in our third portion we have a chapter with which we are very familiar and which must have formed the basis of many an exhortation. For this reason an exhorting brother may be somewhat reluctant to speak upon a chapter which has been so often explained and considered. And yet the further we go in our course, the more we find ourselves thrown back for strength upon the things which are elementary and yet so essential.

We must remember that things that are deepest are usually at the centre and things which may be doubtful are at the edge. And so today I would like to speak to you about the exhortation that comes to us from the parable of the talents in this 25th chapter of Matthew.

When we read the New Testament we cannot escape the conclusion that Jesus counts it an especial virtue in his disciples, that they are eager and alert for the day of his return. There is some profound advice for those who await his return, particularly those that await it in the last hours. It is—Watch!

Jesus was hurt at the indifference of his apostles to the great crisis of his life—"And he cometh unto the disciples, and findeth them asleep, and he saith unto Peter: "What, could ye not watch with me one hour?" It would not be amiss to reflect how he may feel at the great crisis of his second advent—with regard to those who ought to be watching and praying and thereby being delivered from temptation. For that reason, therefore, I feel the parable of the talents may be able to guide us and help us in these things. And in order to understand it in the way I have in mind, I feel we must not take it out of the context of the life of Jesus. And so it is necessary to observe a certain submerged situation in the life of Jesus, evident almost from the beginning, and becoming more apparent as it progresses. It is the inevitable consequence of the manner of man that Jesus was. It seems to be summed up clearly and profoundly by the Apostle John in the first chapter of his Gospel: "He came unto his own, and his own received him not" (verse 11).

We must remember that Jesus came to Israel—he bore the sins of the world, but he came to Israel and they rejected him. He came to a people full of the expectancy of a Messiah, but this expectancy became his greatest hindrance. Their Messiah was not Jesus of Nazareth. They did not think of him, as he thought of himself. The light was shining in the darkness, "and the darkness comprehended it not" (verse 5).

He came into contact with the religious leaders of his day and they challenged him. He had tried to keep on speaking-terms with them for two years but he had his work to do and in the doing of it he shocked them. He healed a man at first hand in the Synagogue. He healed a man on the sabbath day and exposed the evil of their hearts.

And so he tore their system into tatters and they hated him for it. On that day the die was cast; the daggers were drawn. When his disciples tell him that he has offended the leaders he says: "Every plant, which my heavenly Father hath not planted, shall be rooted up" (Matthew 15:13). This plant is not of his planting — it will have to go.

His enemies, knowing that he must be dealt with carefully, for he had a way of making them look foolish, use subtlety in trying to ensnare him. They requested that he would "Shew them a sign from heaven", and he gives his reply: "A wicked and adulterous generation seeketh after a sign; and there shall be no sign given unto it, but the sign of the prophet Jonas" (Matthew 16:4), and he left them and departed. They had heard that as Jonah was three days and nights in the fish's belly, so the Son of man was to be three days and nights in the heart of the earth. But I want to suggest to you that this reply was far more than a prophecy of his death and resurrection, but a deep and subtle accusation of the leaders of his day.

For the men of Nineveh repented at the preaching of Jonah but Israel stoned and rejected the prophets that were sent to her. The sign of Jeremiah or Isaiah would not have stung them so much, but the story of Jonah—how they hated that story. The men of Nineveh were riding in judgement upon them—for they repented at the preaching of Jonah and a greater than Jonah was among them. "He came unto his

91

*disgrace*

own, and his own received him not". And so he left them in their silent anger and departed.

**Among Friends**

And so in his rejection we find him at Cesarea Philippi and he turns to those who were his friends and those who first called him Messiah and asks them whom men say that he is now. They tell him that Israel still respects him as one of the prophets but nothing more.

The Truth of God comes from the heart of Simon – "Thou art the Christ, the Son of the living God". This Simon, who two years before had greeted him as the Christ, confounded by his people's rejection of his Master, browbeaten by the priests, perplexed by what the Christ was proving to be—this Simon declares the sublime truth: "Thou art the Christ".

Let us look at this little company of outcasts from Israel, within a stone's throw possibly of the Imperial Majesty of Rome, on the wayside of a mighty empire. Jesus stands there in all his loneliness and apparent weakness and says: "I will build my church". How hopeless the task of Jesus might have seemed on that day in Cesarea. Against force he puts love; against lust he puts service; against self he puts the cross. The gates of hell will close upon all the empires of the world, but his church will not perish.

He then formally takes up his Messiahship. It is a rejected Messiahship but he affirms himself and proceeds on his way. Let us not leave him on this day without reflecting upon his words of sorrow, upon all that might have been and now can never be: "O Jerusalem, Jerusalem … how often would I … and ye would not".

"From that time forth began Jesus to show unto his disciples, how that he must go unto Jerusalem, and suffer many things of the elders and the chief priests and the scribes, and be killed, and be raised again the third day."
(Matthew 16:21)

And out of the incidents that follow comes the most amazing demand of the Master. He knows the perplexity, the consternation, the disappointment that he has thrown upon these men. He knows that although they hoped to see him rule the world, instead they will see him nailed to the tree. Men do not think much of you when you are crucified on a cross. They are ashamed of it as a rule. And yet Jesus expected his men to stand it, to stick to him, to love him and accept him—crucified. He expected it and he won. He wins even Simon, for the day will come when Simon will shout to

92

Israel: "God hath made that same Jesus, whom ye crucified, both Lord and Christ" (Acts 2:36).

Can we begin to see the meaning of those words that he spake?—"If any man will come after me, let him deny himself, and take up his cross, and follow me" (Matthew 16:24). He was going to mocking, to rejection, to the hate of men. If any man is to be with him, he also will have to carry his obloquy and bear his shame. And I say unto you today— he speaks with authority: "Whosoever will save his life shall lose it: and whosoever shall lose his life for my sake shall find it" (Matthew 16:25). From those who stand by him in his darkest hour he calls for utter devotion of life to the cause of his church and kingdom.

## The Call to Serve

You may have perceived that we find ourselves in almost an identical position. Here are we, few in number, gathered round a crucified Messiah, who has been rejected by the majority—and he still expects us to stick to him, to stand firm, to accept him and to love him. It is here that the exhortation comes to us from the parable of the talents and its message is this—that everyone has certain opportunities to serve, and those opportunities must be used. The greater the opportunity, the greater the responsibility.

The Lord defines for us the meaning of talents: "To every man according to his several ability" (Matthew 25:15). In Luke 19 we have a similar parable, where the man with one pound hid it in a napkin. It is interesting to note that a napkin is intended for two purposes. The first is for a sweat rag, in which case the wicked servant should have used it to mop his brow, after working hard. Or it is used as a towel like this: "He [Jesus] riseth from supper and laid aside his garments and took a towel, and girded himself ... and began to wash the disciples' feet". That, brethren and sisters, is humble service. The purposes of a napkin are work and service, not to conceal talents.

It is not uncommon to hear that there are very great difficulties in living the Truth today. That may be true, but the point I am trying to set before you today is that Christ expects us to carry on. Consider the difficulties, the utter disappointment, the dismay and helplessness thrown upon those disciples on the wayside at Cesarea Philippi. Jesus expected them to follow after him. We cannot all give the same in service and work—the qualification is "each according to his several ability", but it has occurred to me

93

that perhaps we find the service of Christ and his church irksome because we try to do too many other things as well.

As far as serving the church is concerned,we cannot all do what seems to be the most impressive work. But let us avoid the "I can't help at all" outlook. The one talent man was not condemned because he failed to make five talents. His condemnation was that he made nothing. If he had made one talent he would have equalled his five talent brother servant. "God is not mocked: whatsoever a man soweth, that shall he also reap".

It is the story of service, to the ecclesia, to our brothers and sisters in Christ, to all men and to God. And we cannot escape the responsibility—everybody has some opportunity and Christ expects those opportunities to be used. We cannot become detached from the ecclesia; we cannot stand aside and offer our criticism as though we had no responsibility. We are the church of God—it is not made of stones and cement and timber—it is made only of living stones—of men and women.

Let me tell you a story to illustrate what I mean. I submit that, perhaps as never before in the history of the church, there is a need for humble and selfless service. Perhaps more than ever the Christ is pleading with us to fulfil our great calling. He asks for the man who is wholehearted, who is willing to abandon himself to the cause. The man who is steadfast, who will stick with him to the end—this he expects—for who is not with him is against him and who will not take up the same obloquy and follow is not worthy of him.

The exhortation then that comes to us today is—"What, could ye not watch with me one hour? Watch and pray". It is a day that ye think not—Watch and pray. And as we shall go in a few moments in spirit to that place where the Christ is hanging between heaven and earth, let us ask ourselves; Are we standing at a distance? are we fearful of persecution? are we so dismayed with the difficulties that beset us? Now is the time once again to declare ourselves true followers of the Nazarene, yoked with him in enduring service to his Father and our Father, in meekness, in purity, in holiness, because that question which was asked all those centuries ago is shortly to be answered, and each one of us will form part of the answer. "When the Son of man cometh, shall he find faith on the earth?"

# 16

## IMPRESSIONS OF THE LORD OFFERED UP
### (MARK 14,15)

TODAY we have a double blessing. Not only the emblems to assist our remembrance of the redeemer's death, but a chapter read which gives us in a graphic way the details of those things associated with the very thing we have come to celebrate. I said "in a graphic way" but the truth is that we have read it so many times that to some extent the drama has lost its awful impact. We cannot help it. The very familiarity diminishes the dramatic effect.

I once heard about a girl of 20 years who read the gospel for the very first time. When she came to the part describing the passion and death of Christ she broke down and wept. That could rarely happen to us now. The strong impressions that once might have stirred us are weakened. The pathos is diluted by the foreknowledge of what is revealed.

I was thinking of this as I read through Mark 14 and 15 trying to prepare for today. It occurred to me – shall I try to put down my impressions, my reactions, as I read again the account of the saviour's sacrificial death? This is what I have done and this is what the exhortation is about. Blunted though my feelings are by the familiarity, and notwithstanding my weakened sensitivity, these are the ideas that came to mind as I looked at these events once again.

The first impression I want to emphasise is about the trial of Jesus. Caiaphas must have been worried when the witnesses put up such a bad case. A man who said that he would destroy the temple of God and rebuild it in three days, might be regarded as boastful, possibly even showing signs of devil possession, might even be guilty of religious treason; but Caiaphas knew that Pilate would not be very impressed by this kind of evidence. Caiaphas was in a rage. Then regaining his composure he saw a way out of his dilemma. Matthew records it specifically – Caiaphas put Jesus on oath. It was illegal and a violation of the very law he was supposed to be upholding but he is a man who believes that the end justifies the means. "I adjure thee by the living God, that thou tell us whether thou be the Christ, the Son of God"

(Matthew 26:63). The reply was categoric. Jesus said: "Thou hast said ... Hereafter shall ye see the Son of man sitting on the right hand of power, and coming in the clouds of heaven" (verse 64). Caiaphas rent his clothes. This was illegal – the Law forbids the high priest to rend his clothes (see Leviticus 21:10), but what matter if this sign of shock and sadness will secure the condemnation of this obstinate prisoner. Of course there was no real sadness, only deep satisfaction. "He hath spoken blasphemy; what further need have we of witnesses?" He is worthy of death, they said. The trial was over.

All this we read yesterday in Mark 14. Of course we know they were not really bothered about blasphemy. The real ground of their opposition to Jesus was hatred of the light. But this was not the reason they put forward. Eventually when it comes to the Roman trial before Pilate it will be public zeal, patriotism and loyalty to Caesar. What could be purer than to protect the name of God from blasphemy, and to defend the nation and government against treason? But we know it was all shallow and superficial. The real accusation was that this man was a danger to their position, their influence and their power. For our soul's sake the thing to notice is how easily men justify their deeds with the highest motives. People tend to sugar over their dark guilt with a crust of superficial whiteness which seeks to make them innocent, pure, injured by an unsympathetic word. When they have something to be ashamed of they complain about others or the injustice of the case against them or the alleged slander of the witnesses. It may be that Caiaphas really did think he was doing God service by condemning the king. He was blinded by his own prejudice. What a solemn thing it is and how carefully we ought to mark it. The lesson is the need to look at our own prejudices and self-justifications, lest we be blinded and desensitised.

May I detain you here for one moment about one detail in the evidence such as it was. The witnesses they brought were so futile, and so flimsy was their testimony, that even the high priest was disgusted. Then at last came two witnesses who alleged they had heard him say something which could convict him. They reported that he had said: "I will destroy this temple that is made with hands, and within three days I will build another" (Mark 14:58). He had never said any such thing. What he said was: "Destroy this temple" – not "I will destroy it" (see John 2:19). His supposition was that *they* would destroy it. They were the destroyers, he was the

96

builder. By their distortion they turned his supposition into affirmation.

Then the other thing – notice his silence. He answered nothing until the high priest put him on oath. Then he confirmed plainly that he was the Messiah. When he added that they would see him coming in the clouds of heaven, they knew he was quoting from the prophecy of Daniel. Remember Daniel 7:13: "And I saw in the night visions, and, behold, one like unto the Son of man came with the clouds of heaven". And then Jesus said: "Nevertheless" – he means in spite of your unbelief you will see it and you will have to bend to it at last. The king laid claim to triumph in the hour of what they thought was his defeat.

**Where were the Witnesses for the Defence?**

The other thing about the trial which impresses me is that there were no witnesses for the defence. It was provided for in the Roman law. There had to be a properly formulated accusation supported by witnesses, and there should be a proper defence supported by witnesses, then the verdict was given. But in this case there was not one witness in support of the accused; not one soul to speak for him. There were plenty who had good reason to speak well of him. Many who could testify that he had done good. What about Jairus the ruler of the synagogue? He was a man of some influence and his young daughter was a living witness to the goodness of this man. What about the widow of Nain? Her son was alive because of this man's compassion – surely she could have testified. What about Lazarus and Martha and Mary? Bethany is only a stone's throw from Jerusalem. They were his special friends. What about the woman who had the issue of blood? Well, you could go on – the man with the lunatic son – the man who leaped out of the pool at Bethesda – the bridegroom whose marriage feast was saved at Cana. Where were they all? Not one soul was allowed to speak for this lonely man.

**Peter's Denial**

Another thing which leaves me with a strong impression is the account of Peter's falling into failure. I remember Psalm 1 about the method of falling into failure. Remember how it goes: "Blessed is the man that walketh not in the counsel of the ungodly, nor standeth in the way of sinners, nor sitteth in the seat of the scornful". There is the process – walking standing, sitting. This is what happened to Peter. Walking, he followed him afar off. Standing, he went into the court of the high priest and stood. Sitting, he sat by the fire. I dare not feel superior when I read it. I know in my deepest heart that I too have walked, have stood and have sat where a disciple ought not to be. There is no warmth sat by the fire lit by the hands of the scornful. Then consider what the maid said: "Thou *also* wast with Jesus of Nazareth". Why the "also"? Is it not because John was there somewhere and probably Judas was there too – watching fearfully to see the outcome of his folly. Then this – could there be any thing more dramatic? As Peter uttered his final oath – the cock crew. What a simple thing. Jesus had foretold it and it came to pass – the cock crew. There seems to be nothing in it at all, but here is the thing to notice. God will use the simplest things to bring back those who are in danger of falling away. He will use the crowing of a single cockerel to arrest the failure of a man in jeopardy. He will bring into play the song of a bird if that can halt and restore a soul in the agony of remorse.

The gospel writer is so careful not to intrude upon Peter's grief. He says simply that when the cock crew he thought thereon and wept. What a strange and complex grouping of forces are here in this chapter. Hate set on murdering the king, and love, through weakness, denying him. Discipleship affirmed at first, and now at a distance through fear.

**The Anointing**

Then retrace your steps to that account of the supper at Bethany – we read it in chapter 14 yesterday in verse 3. The woman with the alabaster box of ointment – and the one who condemned her. We know from Matthew that it was Judas. Here we have the personification of two forces; one the force of tender beauty and the other the force of flaming covetousness. The woman is generous with the precious ointment to such an extent that Judas protests. To her it is right; it is fragrant and full. To Judas it is a waste. He does not understand that love must be prodigal. Love is not prudent when it sees the need to be generous. Jesus understood it. He said: "she did it for my burial". If we have read it rightly, there was no tremor in his voice – he was calm and serene.

Then he said something which he had never said about any other creature. "Verily I say unto you: Wheresoever this gospel shall be preached throughout the whole world, this also that she hath done shall be spoken of for a memorial of her" (Mark 14:9). Notice the extent of his intention – wheresoever in the whole world. Not a stone monument which in the course of time will crumble away. Not a marble statue or a golden pillar. Not a temple or a great cathedral. But a memorial nevertheless and indestructible. Here we are almost 2,000 years afterwards, remembering her today. A memorial of devoted love. Love never faileth, said Paul. It shall be her memorial – said Jesus. One frail woman, regarded perhaps by the apostles as emotional; despised by Judas as a wastrel; and then suddenly the room is filled with fragrance where she is and the fragrance penetrates to all the world. Somehow because of this woman, life is sweeter everywhere. The rancid stream of human failure is for a moment forgotten. Judas' baseness is lost and covered.

If we want to follow in any succession it ought to be in the succession of this woman with the alabaster cruse of ointment. Follow the ministry of love which overlaps the bound of prudence – just occasionally for love's sake. Follow by being daring with your sympathy – be prodigal in the cause of God.

## The First Last Supper

The final impression for today is that passage in chapter 14 verse 17 where our Lord institutes the first last supper, as his memorial. It was passover time – the feast of deliverance from bondage, the memorial of the Exodus. Imagine it. Israel was keeping the feast of the passover for the last time in the old economy, because all that was foreshadowed came to be fulfilled. Jesus took the forces of the old economy and he suddenly made all things new. In a sense, it was the first action of the new age. That night the future began. He touched the bread and suddenly it became the emblem of life and joy for ten thousand Lord's Day celebrations. He gathered the cup and suddenly the red wine became the symbol dedicated to provoke a multitude of disciples to seek for pardons and renewal down the ages. Think of this. A Roman soldier dedicates himself to the Emperor's cause without reservation. It is called his *sacramentum* – the act of allegiance. This is our sacramentum. Here we pledge our lives to his cause.

What a holy and solemn thing this memorial service is. Think how you regard it. Once long ago, two men offered strange fire at their altar and were consumed. The Hebrew man says: "We have an altar" and it is not one whit less holy. Three great forces are here established – *commemoration – communion – covenant.*

The old passover was a feast of the Exodus – it looked forward through the sprinkled blood in hope. This new feast is also a feast of the Exodus – but it is the exodus which

99

Christ has accomplished at Jerusalem. It does not look forward in hope as they of old. It celebrates the certainty of achieved victory through the cross of Christ.

We are not hoping that he may be able to save us – we are celebrating that he has achieved the salvation. Remember those who sit at the table to eat and drink are one with him in all the enterprises of his glorious purpose – now and hereafter. This is the covenant. He has done his part. This is the time to declare that we will do ours. God grant that in this solemn moment of bread breaking we may declare it gladly and joyfully and resolutely and keep it faithfully until he come.

# 17

## THE SOLDIER AND THE PROSTITUTE
### (LUKE 7)

LUKE 7 is a most interesting chapter – there are things in it which are fascinating and startling. For instance we are confronted with the fact that Jesus has contact with and a relationship toward two people, who as a community we rarely meet and even more rarely have any relationship with at all – a soldier and a prostitute. Neither of these professions come within the orbit of our life in the Truth. I mention it only to stress that there are things in Luke chapter 7 which are most startling. So my plan in this little exhortation is to look enquiringly at these two incidents, since from our point of view they are so unusual.

Think of the Roman centurion – what do we imagine? A strong man of dedication and discipline, a man of authority, feared and respected because of his calling. A man of iron. Now listen to this: "And a certain centurion's servant, who was dear unto him, was sick, and ready to die". This man of iron was moved with anxiety over his servant. This is a startling thing – a Roman officer who loved his servant. Then this – the faith of this Roman soldier made Jesus marvel. It was the best he had met up to that time. Only twice did Jesus marvel – once at the unbelief of his own people and once at the faith of this Gentile soldier.

Come back to the centurion. A man of the master race is saying to a man of the despised race: "I am not worthy that thou shouldest enter under my roof: wherefore neither thought I myself worthy to come unto thee: but say in a word, and my servant shall be healed". Quite evidently the soldier believed that Jesus could heal at a distance. Perhaps he had seen the healing of the nobleman's son at Capernaum – Jesus healed then by remote miraculous therapy. It has been suggested that perhaps the soldier and the nobleman were friends. Anyway the report of this remarkable cure at a distance could well have encouraged the soldier's hopes. The secret of the centurion's faith and the thing which caused Christ to marvel was not only that he recognised the power of Jesus to heal at a distance, but it is focussed in one word spoken by the centurion and recorded in verse 8: "For I *also*

101

am a man set under authority, having under me soldiers". The critical word is 'also'. It implies the meaning: 'I perceive I am like you Jesus – I submit to authority so that I can wield authority'. The soldier saw superlatively in Jesus what he had realised dimly in himself – that submission must come before responsibility.

The centurion submitted to the Emperor on the throne so that he could represent the Emperor's will to those under his command. He submitted to the throne so that he could exert the influence of the throne. "I am under authority" – submission. "I have soldiers under me" – responsibility. What did the centurion submit to the throne? The answer is everything. Possessions, time, talent, strength, will. It was for the purpose of his own perfecting, for the accomplishment of the work to which he was called. This he saw in Jesus and confessed: "I understand Jesus that you are under the authority of your God, so that you can wield His authority in this world. I perceive that you have submitted so that you can command. I say, come, go, do this – and it happens. I believe you do too Jesus – therefore say but the word and my servant will be healed".

Now what is the word of exhortation? This first of all – every soul submits to some throne. Every personality is mastered by some authority. The influence that masters you is the influence you exert in the little world in which you move – be it good or bad, lifting up or flinging down. It all depends upon the throne to which you bend the knee.

The Lord Jesus Christ could have said with perfect accuracy and the most complete meaning: "I am a man under authority, having under me soldiers". His soldiers are true, faithful and strong, only insofar as they have submitted to his authority. The thing they have to guard against is the possibility that their submission is partial, spasmodic and fragmentary. There are other thrones claiming allegiance. The throne of the flesh; the throne of the world; the throne of the devil. Human nature being what it is there is always the temptation to say: 'In this particular thing I cannot submit. I must have my own way. I must retain my own control. I must insist upon my own will'. It may be a small thing or a large thing, but whatever it is the reservation results in you exerting the power of the wrong throne. That which you are under, you transplant into that which you are over. So the word of exhortation urges you to ask this solemn question. In the deep recesses of your life, which throne are you submitting to the most? What are the true sanctions of your daily life? To what authority do you remit the decisions you take? Can I assure you I know how searching these questions can be when faced honestly. I know about the claimant cry of the flesh. I know about the daily demands of self; I know about that old liar, the devil and Satan who is urging us inside ourselves so often to compromise. He is the prince of subtlety. It is not the things we say; it is not the poses we make in the sight of our comrades – what matters is the throne to which we bow the knee in the secret part of our life. It is not *singing*: "Take my life and let it be ...", it is *seeking* to make it true in practice.

The evangel to which we have confessed proclaims that if we hand over our submission to the king, we can exert the right influence now and reign with him for ever in his blessed kingdom. This is the issue which the soldier's case enforces upon us. Finally one thought – my mind goes back many years to the conscientious objector's tribunal. To a young man standing there the judge says: "Are you not embarrassed by the fact that the one man in the whole of the gospel most commended by Jesus for his faith was a soldier?" Was it an unfair question? It probably was because the young man was ill-equipped to answer difficult questions. I leave it with you.

## The Prostitute

We have thought of the soldier; let us come to the prostitute. It starts at verse 36: "And one of the Pharisees desired him [Jesus] that he would eat with him". From what we read later on we know his name was Simon. It is a strange story. Simon invited Jesus and then treated him with consummate discourtesy. No water; no kiss; no anointing – all the things common and essential in Eastern hospitality.

Why, think you, did Simon invite Jesus? Could it be curiosity? But curiosity is usually polite. Surely rudeness would hamper the possibility of satisfying the curiosity. Did Simon want to catch Jesus out, so to speak, so as to disgrace him? It is possible. I suppose any conclusion we may come to will be mostly speculation. The woman is the other mystery. It says a woman of the city, a sinner. It is one way of saying she was a woman of the streets, a harlot. Have you ever wondered how a harlot came to get into the house of Simon the Pharisee, at a private dinner? Let us face it – Simon would not have touched her with a disinfected barge pole! The scenario is so startling – these two characters are so different. They come from opposite ends of the social spectrum. To put it in modern parlance, he from Acacia

Avenue in the suburbs – she from the red light district of the inner city.

Why was she allowed to get in and occupy such a prominent place in the proceedings? I notice that some commentators, in order to get over this difficulty, say that when there was a dinner party, people used to wander in and out of the house to see how the meal was progressing. There is no evidence for this whatsoever. It sounds very much like a contrivance. There is something here we do not know. Evidently Simon knew the woman and her profession. How did he know that? She seems to behave in the house as though she is very much at home. I get the feeling that she is acting as though she had a right to be there, doing for Jesus what Simon had neglected.

What do you make of this – that sentence in verse 37: "[she] brought an alabaster box of ointment"? The word translated "brought" occurs ten times in the New Testament and on every occasion it is translated "received" because that is precisely what it means. Now if the woman received the ointment when she knew Jesus was in the house, from whom did she receive it? Could it be that she received it from someone in the house – possibly the servants? If that is true then it means she was in some way part of the household – possibly a black sheep relative of Simon.

Brother Harry Whittaker mentions this possibility in his *Studies in the Gospels*. It could explain the invitation and the strange discourtesy of Simon. Perhaps it was the woman who really initiated the invitation and Simon to save face accepted it but was anxious not to sully his reputation among his fellow Pharisees by offering the usual courtesies to this suspect guest.

### Simon's Reaction
We must leave this speculation to look at something more certain – the reaction of Simon to the compassion of the woman. "This man, if he were a prophet, would have known who and what manner of woman this is" (verse 39). The little parable of the two debtors brings the issue out into the open. Notice Jesus so led the conversation as to make Simon assist in the interpretation of the parable. "I suppose that he to whom he forgave most", said Simon. Simon might have agreed that he was a sinner but not at all as bad a sinner as the woman. Remember, another of his party had said in a prayer: "God, I thank thee, that I am not as other men". Simon was a Pharisee and when they began in the time of the Maccabees they were a great force for good in the nation,

holding the people together in the face of infiltrating paganism. But as time went by they went wrong. They added tradition upon tradition; they lifted the incidental on to the plane of the essential; and their conception of righteousness became essentially external and wrongly exclusive and in the end evasive of the real truth about God. This was Simon's trouble.

He was blind to the Truth about this woman. He could see only what she had been and never what she was now. But this was the argument of Jesus in the parable – she acts as she does because the massive debt of sin has been cleared and cancelled. She is a splendid example but not a unique case. The reason for our gratitude, for our loyalty, for our willing service, is precisely that through the bruising of this man unto death, *our* sins have been pardoned and cancelled altogether. The teaching of Luke chapter 7 is that it ought to affect us radically, as it did this woman. All through the New Testament the writers are saying the same thing – the atonement ought to have a practical effect upon our lives – not only in the great things but in the commonplace things as well. Remember: "The grace of God that bringeth salvation hath appeared to all men, teaching us that, denying ungodliness and worldly lusts, we should live soberly, righteously, and godly in this present world" (Titus 2:11,12). Out of Simon's dinner there is a word of exhortation in harmony with that word to Titus. It is this – Simon neglected Jesus. He brought him no water; he gave him no kiss; he provided no anointing for his head. Jesus said no word at the time, but later Jesus revealed that he noticed the neglect. We ought to remember that. He notices neglect and he values care and compassion.

## Our Reaction

A question, therefore, comes leaping at us from the page of Luke 7. What kind of a reaction are we giving him? We have made the invitation – but are we careless about his service? Are we neglectful about our appointments at his celebration – our meal with him? Are things undone because we are too busy elsewhere? What are we saying within ourselves about him? All I want to stress is that he notices it. Remember how he valued the prodigal care of the pardoned woman. Her memorial is no great statue, no massive cathedral, no scroll of honour, but simply this; that for a little while the rancid stream of life was made sweeter by the love that broke a box of precious ointment on the man with beautiful feet. As you break the bread and sip the wine in his memory, recollect

105

that he noticed it and valued it and said: "Thy faith hath saved thee; go in peace". God grant that in this celebration we may hear that voice.

At the last, let us come back to the soldier. The complete dedication of his life to the Empire, as we have said, was called his *sacramentum*. We have a sacramentum and when this day we take the bread and sip the wine we ought, every man and every woman, to reaffirm it in the presence of the Lord's memorial. Think what it ought to mean. When his voice speaks we hear; when he looks we see; when he beckons we go; when he commands we act in order to advance his cause. He is waiting for that kind of obedience.

There is no vision; there is no passion; there is no mission; there is no victory – apart from the master-person on the throne. So in this solemn moment of bread breaking let us bow the knee to his throne, kiss his sceptre and place ourselves unreservedly under his authority and at his disposal. Let our voices be ready to speak; our feet ready to run; our hands ready to work. That is our sacramentum.

God grant we may feel it to be true in our deepest heart.

# 18

## THE HEALING OF JAIRUS' DAUGHTER
### (LUKE 8)

I WOULD like to speak to you today brethren about the healing of Jairus' daughter. I shall try to draw a lesson from that story which may be of help to you but it is a lesson difficult to draw and more difficult to learn. The full lesson cannot be gained unless the miracle of the healing of the daughter of Jairus is considered in conjunction with the miracle which preceded it – the healing of the woman with an issue of blood – it is when these two miracles are taken together that the true lesson is seen.

Let us first of all recall the facts as the gospel writer reveals them. The daughter of Jairus is very ill and she is dying. Jairus comes to Jesus and asks him to come at once to help, and Jesus responds immediately and makes his way to the house. A large crowd is with him. On the way another person – a woman ill with an issue of blood – also seeking a cure, touches from behind Jesus the hem of his garment and is cured at once. Jesus knows it. He stops and comforts the woman, but while this is happening a message comes from the house of Jairus that it is too late now – the girl is dead. Jesus undismayed, encourages Jairus and proceeds to the house where there is also a great crowd. Jesus goes in with the girl's parents and his three disciples only and though the girl is dead raises her up from the sleep of death, and tells them to let her eat, for doubtless she was weak from her illness. Those are the bare facts. Let us look at it again and try to find the heart of the story.

Jairus was an important man. He was the ruler of the local synagogue, the first citizen of the town – equal to our Mayor – a man of importance. Anything which happened to Jairus therefore would receive full publicity. He was well-known and probably well liked. The illness of his daughter would almost certainly be common knowledge and a subject for continual and sympathetic discussion among the citizens. The sight of Jairus coming to Rabbi Jesus and falling down at his feet beseeching him to come to his house to his sick child would evoke a great deal of curiosity and interest. The whole situation was out in the full glare of publicity – Jesus was caught up in it and without willing it, had a stage all set for a great miracle to be done in public with all the attendant excitement and interest.

The case was urgent – a matter of life and death – delay might be fatal. A few minutes might make all the difference between living and dying. Jairus was a great man and it was a great occasion. Jesus responded with his usual sympathy, and a great crowd moved with him to the house of Jairus.

In that crowd was an unknown woman with an unspectacular affliction but a wearisome one – perhaps nobody there knew of her illness and nobody cared. The situation was certainly not as urgent as the one at the house of Jairus. You know what she did – she said: "If I may but touch his garment I shall be whole", and she pushed her way through the crowd and touched the border of his coat and instantaneously was cured of her trouble.

And though Jesus was on his way to a most important case – an urgent matter of life and death – he stopped and unhurriedly took time to enquire who touched him. He took time to teach the lesson that although dozens of people were thronging and touching him, someone had touched him differently from them all, with the touch of faith. And when the faithful one was discovered, he comforted her before continuing on his way. Whilst on his way to perform a very great act of love he took time to succour and hear a call from the ordinary commonplace crowd of onlookers.

Had we been there to see it we might have thought that Jesus was careless about the urgency of his first call; thoughtless for the feelings of the man whose daughter was at the point of death; that he had things out of perspective to take time to bother about an unknown, commonplace, less important need, when a greater more urgent need was waiting and where needless delay might be fatal. We know now of course that the delay was only apparent. Jesus was able to perform the miracle of resurrection just as ably as the miracle of restoration. We know now also that the miracles of Jesus were subject to the laws of the spiritual world – it was not possible to convey a great blessing to an unbelieving heart. So we read at one place he could not do many miracles there because of their unbelief. And his perpetual question was:"Believe ye that I am able to do this?"

Now here is a point to notice. Jairus saw this miracle to the poor woman. He saw her modest touch towards the hem of his garment and saw the abashed look with which she shrank from public gaze and exposure. He heard the words of the Rabbi Jesus: "Somebody hath touched me". He heard the great principle laid down that the only touch which reaches God is a touch of faith. And so my brethren, remembering this, is it not almost certain that the soul of Jairus was made more capable of receiving a blessing than before? Is it not true that he must have walked home with a more hopeful step and that he must have heard the words: "Thy daughter is dead" with less dismay? Do you not think that the words: "Fear not, only believe" must have come to him with a deeper meaning and altogether received with a more implicit trust, than if Jesus had not paused to heal that woman on the way, but had instead hurried on?

## The Call of the Commonplace

As we look at it now does it not seem that out of that apparent delay – that interruption with a great work, that turning aside to something by comparison so unimportant and commonplace, a great deal of good came? It might be that the faith needed for the performing of the great miracle of resurrection arose as a result of seeing the poor woman cleansed on the wayside. It may be that the glory of the last miracle had its roots in the commonplace of the first. That which was done so quietly and unobtrusively by the poor woman was the very thing which caused the faltering heart of Jairus to rise up once again. Of the two miracles perhaps the cure of the poor woman was the greater.

Now brethren, observe what the lesson is. It is not that we ought to take on a lot more work than we can perform, nor that we must answer every call that comes to us, come what may – though if any one feels that is their duty I should be the last to try to change their mind. The lesson I draw is this, though whether it is intended I cannot tell – that we ought not to be so consumed with the things which to us appear the most important, as to be unable to recognise the call of the commonplace when it comes. Naturally our lives are most occupied with the things which we judge to be the most important to us. Good things, true things, legitimate things. Yet it could be that we are so engrossed in the things which are important to us, that when the commonplace requires our attention or sympathy, we cannot feel the need to turn aside from the path we have planned. Sometimes we are so occupied with what we believe to be a set of duties that we have no sensitivity for anything else. We feel ourselves monopolised by our particular fancy and so feel discharged from any other obligation.

Sometimes men are said to be interested in a cause because it has some peculiar charm for them. I do not deny that this is good. But here is the difference between human goodness and Christian love: one is partial, the other is universal.

Have you never met the brother or sister who is so taken up with the things which appear to be the most urgent – in the view of the world's show – open to the notice of all and having all the signs of the important – that you would tremble to ask them to render some mundane service and answer some commonplace call? Yet so often the commonplace things have in them the opportunity to be great in the true sense.

The other day I heard of two men who thought their duty lay in doing a simple service for another who was in need and in order to do it, they had to use whitewash and wallpaper paste. Whitewash and paste might seem a long way from the greatness of our high calling, yet who can tell how that commonplace action was judged in the high court of heaven? It may be that there the commonplace takes on a new glory. Sometimes God calls us to service in the commonplace, and it is a tragedy if we cannot perceive it.

**Rejection in Samaria**

There is an example of this in tomorrow's readings in Luke 9:

"And it came to pass, when the time was come that he should be received up, he stedfastly set his face to go to Jerusalem, and sent messengers before his face: and they went, and entered into a village of the Samaritans, to make ready for him. And they did not receive him, because his face was as though he would go to Jerusalem. And when his disciples James and John saw this, they said, Lord, wilt thou that we command fire to come down from heaven, and consume them, even as Elias did? But he turned and rebuked them, and said, Ye know not what manner of spirit ye are of. For the Son of man is not come to destroy men's lives, but to save them. And they went to another village."                    (Luke 9:51–56)

"And they went to another village". The villagers refused him hospitality and when he arrived at the gate he was forbidden to enter. There was no fuss, no fury, no fire – he turned away silently and the destiny of the village was sealed. God came in the commonplace and they could not perceive it. The Lord sent his messengers to prepare his way but they did not come with pomp and splendour. There was no demonstration of

110

power, no important announcement. I can imagine those Samaritan villagers smiled when Jesus turned from their gate and thought themselves happily rid of an awkward visitor. They slept that night and many a night after undisturbed – though they had turned away their Saviour. He had come to them in the commonplace and they could not perceive it. It is a silent tragedy.

## Significance in the Trivial

Sometimes great and momentous issues turn on such seemingly trivial events. Sometimes in our lives the things which we have not bothered about turn out in the end to be the only worthwhile things – while the things upon which we have bestowed all our thought and care and labour have come at last to nought.

An example of this is to be seen in the case of Jude the Apostle:

> "Beloved, while I was giving all diligence to write unto you of our common salvation, I was constrained to write unto you exhorting you to contend earnestly for the faith which was once for all delivered to the saint".
>
> (Jude verse 3, RV)

It seems that Jude had been entrusted with the task of writing a great treatise to the Gentiles – as his brother James had written to the Jews. It was to be a big thing – perhaps a standard work for all the churches to set forth and expound the Gospel of the common salvation. It seems Jude had devoted himself to it with enthusiasm – it filled all his time – took all his thought. Notice he says: "I was giving all diligence". That means he was very busy with it indeed. And then an interruption came and he had to set aside his work on the great treatise to deal with something which called for his immediate attention. He turned aside to meet the emergency. An exhortation was written to which no special labour was devoted and no great literary importance was attached. Perhaps it was a word sent to settle immediate questions which were to be dealt with at length in the treatise. But brethren, the treatise never came and all that remains of Jude's diligence, his toil and his preparation is a half sheet of note paper written when he was interrupted on his great work. The commonplace has survived – the great came to nought. But it is the half sheet that counts. That was the really important thing. Perhaps if Jude had neglected the lesser claim in order to get on with the greater, we should have neither treatise nor exhortation. But brethren, do not think his preparation was wasted. Jude could probably never

111

have written such a letter to us had he not laboured diligently on his treatise. Good work is never lost. What we learn in preparing for the important, we can use in doing the commonplace.

Brethren, is not our life so often full of unfinished tasks? We begin to write a treatise and finish up with a half sheet of notepaper. Life is full of broken plans. It is full of important things which we are never able to realise. Let me not dissuade you from good true ambitions in the Lord. Great ideals can ennoble small duties. Devotion to true principles can impart dignity to ordinary tasks. But brethren, do not lose your eye and ear for the commonplace. Sometimes men sigh for wings to be away from that which is everyday – but wings do not always bring rest. We long and strive for something different. We are fascinated by the clamour of the important – but think of the one who turned aside when he was on a life and death mission because he felt the touch of the commonplace. Never come to the position where you have to despise small opportunities. God calls sometimes in the least likely places.

We are exhorted by the Apostle to "redeem the time because the days are evil". Men waste time, kill time, while it away – but never redeem it. The Apostle takes an ordinary thing like time, adds to it a religious word "redeem" and gives the use of it, however commonplace, a new significance. Never become so insensitive that you cannot feel when the hem of your garment is touched.

Now you may ask: "What has all this to do with these emblems?" Brethren, I have urged you to dwell upon he who heard every cry of pain, who responded to every kind of need – the need of the woman, the cry of the father, the wail of the oppressed, the helplessness of the child. He heard them all, and none in vain. He is like the great ocean which receives into itself every stream and every river and responds yet is never too full.

He who felt the touch of the commonplace on the way to raise the dead, has been touched with the feeling of our infirmities, and these emblems are the tokens of his response. If you can feel this to be true, I do not think you will participate in vain today.

# 19

## "REJOICE, BECAUSE YOUR NAMES ARE WRITTEN IN HEAVEN"
### (LUKE 10)

THERE are, in Luke chapter 10, several significant ideas which could well provide a basis for exhortation, but there is one which seems to me to be particularly interesting and fruitful. It has to do with Jesus sending out his disciples to preach and heal in his name by using his remarkable powers. They return full of excitement and satisfaction, and were specially delighted that they had power over the demons.

Now it is the observation of Jesus that we must notice. He said: "Notwithstanding in this rejoice not, that the spirits are subject unto you; but rather rejoice, because your names are written in heaven" (verse 20). That is the crucial phrase: "Rejoice that your names are written in heaven".

People in and out of Christ rejoice for all kinds of different things such as when they fall in love; or get married; or graduate at college; or have children; or get promoted in their job, or their bank balance increases significantly; or their business prospers; or they come to retirement. Doubtless they are all legitimate reasons for rejoicing, but Jesus is saying that for the disciple the first and best reason for rejoicing is that the disciple's name is written in heaven. This idea then we must follow in order to find the word of exhortation.

When Jesus used the figure of names being written in heaven he was taking up an idea which is scattered right through the word of God. It first emerges in Exodus with Moses descending from the mountain to realise that the people have turned to idolatry. He intercedes for them with the Lord God and says:

"Yet now, if thou wilt forgive their sin – ; and if not, blot me, I pray thee, out of thy book which thou hast written."
(Exodus 32:32)

We find it in the Psalms:

"Thou tellest my wanderings: put thou my tears into thy bottle: are they not in thy book?" (Psalm 56:8)

Or David speaks of his enemies and says:

113

"Let them be blotted out of the book of the living, and not be written with the righteous." (Psalm 69:28)

Or in the prophet:

"And it shall come to pass, that he that is left in Zion, and he that remaineth in Jerusalem, shall be called holy, even everyone that is written among the living in Jerusalem." (Isaiah 4:3)

Ezekiel, speaking against false prophets gives God's pronouncements and says:

"They shall not be in the assembly of my people, neither shall they be written in the writing of the house of Israel." (Ezekiel 13:9)

Or in Malachi, a familiar verse:

"Then they that feared the LORD spake often one to another: and the LORD hearkened, and heard it, and a book of remembrance was written before him for them that feared the LORD, and that thought upon his name." (Malachi 3:16)

Or in Daniel where the angel speaks of Michael standing up for God's people and says:

"And at that time thy people shall be delivered, every one that shall be found written in the book." (Daniel 12:1)

When we turn to the New Testament the same thing appears. In Philippians, Paul speaks of my

"fellowlabourers whose names are in the book of life." (Philippians 4:3)

To the Hebrews:

"Ye are come ... to the general assembly and church of the firstborn, which are written in heaven." (Hebrews 12:22,23)

In the Apocalypse:

"He that overcometh, the same shall be clothed in white raiment; and I will not blot out his name out of the book of life." (Revelation 3:3)

Concerning the worship of the Beast:

"All that dwell on earth shall worship him, whose names are not written in the book of life of the Lamb slain from the foundation of the world." (Revelation 13:8)

Or:

"They that dwell on earth shall wonder, whose names were not written in the book of life from the foundation of the world." (Revelation 17:8)

114

About the second death:

> "And whosoever was not found written in the book of life was cast into the lake of fire."  (Revelation 20:15)

And then about the Holy City:

> "And there shall in no wise enter into it any thing that defileth, neither whatsoever worketh abomination, or maketh a lie: but only they which are written in the Lamb's book of life."  (Revelation 21:27)

Pardon me for deluging you with all those quotations but I am quite anxious to show how the Bible is impregnated with this idea. It throws light on why Jesus used it to demonstrate that, when all is said and done and in the final analysis, this is the vital thing – that your names are written in heaven. It transcends every other consideration, it exceeds every other ambition, it surpasses every other aspiration. It is crucial in this world and in the world to come. As we think on it, let us ask why the figure is used so liberally? Probably the symbol is related to the practice of Biblical times, especially in the Old Testament period, when the king would record in a book the deeds of his subjects; deeds which were notable or especially worthy, brave or courageous, so that they could be rewarded accordingly and in due course. There is an example of it in Esther chapter 6 verses 1–3:

> "On that night could not the king sleep, and he commanded to bring the book of records of the chronicles; and they were read before the king. And it was found written, that Mordecai had told of Bigthana and Teresh, two of the king's chamberlains, the keepers of the door, who sought to lay hand on the king Ahasuerus. And the king said, What honour and dignity hath been done to Mordecai for this? Then said the king's servants that ministered unto him, There is nothing done for him."

So God has used the practice, common in Biblical times, as a symbol of His Divine memory; the unerring and indelible record of those who are in relationship with Him and therefore have a responsibility of service.

We shall understand of course that it is a symbol and we are not to suppose that God needs to keep a literal record to ensure that He makes no mistakes. It looks as though the name of the newborn – the follower of God, called and blood-sprinkled – is written in the book of life as soon as the rebirth takes place; as soon as the submission is made, as soon as the covenant relationship is formed. The book of life is not yet a book of the saved, but is a record of those who have been offered salvation. It is a register of the faith-impulsed, truth-governed souls who are willing to begin the pilgrimage of life. Their names are written in heaven because they seek a heavenly country on earth. Those who enter the heavenly country, the kingdom of God, the life eternal, are those who at the last and final assessment are worthy to have their name retained in the book of the living.

**Removal of Names**

I am reluctant to face it but I have to – it is possible to have a name blotted out from the book of life. We saw it just now. A name once written can be removed. If you do not agree then you do not have an argument with me; you have an argument with the Holy Spirit. We cannot avoid it: "So then every one of us shall give account of himself to God" (Romans 14:12).

Now I am sure I know what you are thinking because I am thinking the same myself. It sounds so cold, so clinical and so calculating. It fills us with anxiety. Now partly it is the very figure which makes it so. The fact is that if our names are retained in heaven it will be by the mercy of God and not because we are entitled to claim it. But we must not ever forget that our name will be retained or blotted out because of what we are at last. Measured by the one true man – the archetypal man. He is the touchstone of life and destiny. He is the point of triangulation from which all the measurements will be taken and every judgement made. If that sounds very solemn it is because it is very solemn. Think of this – you can have a sight now of part of the book of life – it is in Hebrews chapter 11: "These all died in faith, not having received the promises ... for he hath prepared for them a city" (verses 13,16).

Some of the names written there might surprise us, but God sees more than we do. There ought to be comfort in that for all of us. It means that alongside those names in Hebrews 11, yours is written, except that it is not yet as permanent as theirs. Can I tell you something? – indeed I am half ashamed to say it. There are times when I look at the 11th chapter of Hebrews and try to imagine my own name there and when I see it, there are times when I think it must belong to some other man who has the same name as mine. Some days when I rise with hope and consecration in my heart, ere noon has come I am assaulted by the forces of sin. So you will understand why I say that at last we shall need very much the abiding mercy of God. Remember Jesus did say *rejoice* that your names are written in heaven – so he is urging us not to be downcast or despairing. I know the Bible says: "It is a fearful thing to fall into the hands of the living God" (Hebrews 10:31), but the solemn truth is that it is safer and more blessed to fall into His hands than any other.

It is better to give account to His Son than any other and to draw on his mercy. He knows all about us – this man of Nazareth, who has been touched with the feeling of our infirmity. He knows about the poison in my blood and yours which drives us against our will. He knows that our aspirations are always better than our achievements. But most of all he loves us with an imperishable love. He wants us to succeed. It is his Father's good pleasure to give you the kingdom. That is why you ought to rejoice.

## Hopefulness of the Truth

I must tell you something which is on my heart – I hope you will forgive me for making a personal reference. I have been in the Truth now nearly fifty years and I must tell you that it has left upon my mind one over-riding impression and it is this. Bearing in mind the frailty of human nature, how hopeful the Truth is. In spite of the human predicament, this is a marvellous thing – the hopefulness of the Truth. Let me just illustrate what I mean. I bring you now to what I believe to be the most hopeful declaration in the whole of the Bible. It is in Colossians chapter 1:

> "And you, that were sometime alienated and enemies in your mind by wicked works, yet now hath he reconciled in the body of his flesh through death, to present you holy and unblameable and unreproveable in his sight: if ye continue in the faith grounded and settled, and be not moved away from the hope of the gospel, which ye have heard, and which was preached to every creature which is under heaven; whereof I Paul am made a minister."
>
> (Colossians 1:21–23)

He is able to present you holy and unblameable and unreproveable. Is there anything more hopeful than that?

So it is what this man is able to do for you that will ensure your name is retained in heaven for ever. Not by some great work which you will accomplish or through some outstanding application of strength. This is the point of the incident in Luke 10. The disciples were elated because of the great works they had been able to do and because of their newly found power over the demons. Jesus said: "Rejoice not, that the spirits are subject unto you; but rather rejoice, because your names are written in heaven (verse 20).

117

Let us mark the perspective. Truth is greater than strength. The reality is greater than the sign. The internal is greater than the external. Being is better than doing. Character is nobler than miracles. Paul once said: "And though ... I could remove mountains and have not charity [love], I am nothing" (1 Corinthians 13:2). The greatest deed is discredited if the character is false. It is better to obey than to do many mighty works.

The day is on the way when there are some who will be surprised in a conversation with the King. They are going to say: "Have we not ... done in thy name many wonderful works?" and by some mysterious measurement of greatness he is going to disown them: "I never knew you". In this age of sensationalism we do well to remember it. In the revival of psuedo-pentecostalism we do well to remember the real issues. In the day to come when names are erased or confirmed, the verification of a faithful life, lived quietly and lovingly cannot fail. We may die but the truth of character survives. It is better than a trumpet or a clanging symbol or a big whistle. This will ensure that names will not have been written in vain. It is the optimism of our faith which should help us look forward hopefully and with rejoicing. Remember this: he careth for you. Either that is wonderfully true or else we have been grossly deceived. We believe in our deepest heart that is is true.

So I beseech you my comrades, when this service is over go on your way rejoicing – impulsed by joy. Jesus said it – *rejoice*. This joy is not some great burst of ecstacy which happens once and then it is gone. Rejoicing is a common delight which sings as truly in December as in June – a singer which never tires. It transmutes every dark cloud; it illuminates every sorrow; soothes every wound; gives new hope to every endeavour. Men may laugh at this but we know it is true. We are not pitiable. You have discovered a joy which has eluded most other people. There is a lilt in your step and a song in your heart. Remember this – the things that you do and the things you are at his bidding – your obedience in the common places of daily life – will give you access at last into Emmanuel's land of light and love, unto the heavenly Jerusalem, where your name has been written forever if you will have it so. But most of all as you break the bread and sip the wine, remember this – he is an incomparable saviour. Take courage – he is able to present you holy and unblameable and unreproveable, if you continue in the faith, grounded and settled. God grant in the solemn moment of memorial you may feel it to be true in your deepest heart.

# 20

## JESUS AND SINNERS
### (LUKE 15)

HAVE you noticed in the gospel narratives how from time to time the enemies of Jesus say things about him which are derogatory and intended to condemn him? Yet because of the wonderful personality of the man of Nazareth, the very things which were spoken to oppose him and degrade him, turn out to be to his glory. Things spoken to denigrate him, at last express some of the noblest things of his gospel. Without willing it and without knowing, his enemies testify to his glory. Indeed you might call it the gospel according to the enemies of Christ. Let me illustrate what I mean.

Once they said about him, in a tone of disdain: "Is not this the carpenter?" What they meant was "He is nobody – we know who he is, he is no better than we are. Why should he set himself up as a teacher in Nazareth, when really he is only a carpenter?" But the truth is that the fact he was a carpenter has equipped him to sympathise with all such toilers, so that by the lowliness of the long years in the carpenter's shop he has dignified the reality of honest labour and wooed to himself the reverence of men who recognise the truth of his humility. So the question is asked today in quite another tone – Is not this the carpenter? the man touched with the feeling of human infirmity and close to the reality of human experience? a working man who knows the meaning of toil?

Or again – the High Priest said once: "It is expedient for us, that one man should die for the people, and that the whole nation perish not" (John 11:50). He said it to justify his corrupted sense of justice and to ensure the condemnation of the one who ought to have been set free. But without knowing it he spoke a prophecy about the Messiah which came to be central in the purpose of God. By this man's death the children of God scattered and bereft were gathered and saved.

Or again – in the dark hour of his bitter agony, cruelly they flung this taunt in his face: "He saved others; himself he cannot save". Was not this the deepest truth about his death? If he had saved himself he would have saved no other – and because he refused to spare himself he is able to save all them who come to God through him.

This is what I mean then, and I draw attention to it because today in Luke 15 we have heard something said about him by his enemies which was full of bitter criticism and hostile antagonism, and yet it enshrines something wonderful and simple and sacramental, and the very thing we have come to celebrate. They said: "This man receiveth sinners and eateth with them" (verse 2). They said it to condemn, but when we hear it we are compelled to say – thank God he does. Thank God he does receive sinners, and thank God we are privileged to remember it, and please may we eat with him in blessed fellowship in the day which is to come.

Think for a moment upon what they meant when they said: "This man receiveth sinners, and eateth with them". There is no doubt it was a criticism. Upon what was it based? This – as it appears to me. They had heard the man of Nazareth say some incisive and solemn things about sin. They had doubtless blanched with fear when he spoke of divine judgement upon hypocrisy. He had scorched them with his penetrating assessment of human wickedness. The strange thing is that these scorching things which on other lips would have repelled, on the lips of the Nazarene had the effect of drawing men to him. Here is the paradox – when Christ said the severest things, the greatest sinners drew near to him. The scorching fire seemed to have a fascination for those who, measured by human measurement, were without hope. "Then drew near unto him all the publicans and sinners for to hear him" (verse 1). Now the Pharisees could not help but notice this. They were astounded that when these people drew near to him he received them. He not only received them, but received them in a spirit of friendliness – even of comradeship. Although he said the severest things about sin he did not stand aloof from sinners. He even went as far as to actually sit down with them at table and eat bread together with them. The severity of his gospel and his teaching did not harmonise with his friendship for the sinner.

So, the Pharisees were perplexed and conscious of the contradiction. "The Pharisees and scribes murmured saying, This man receiveth sinners, and eateth with them". But there was something else behind their murmuring. Based on their understanding of sin and sinners, they meant: 'He

120

cannot receive these sinners and fraternise with them and not be polluted himself. He cannot take this fire into his bosom and not be burned'. Measured by their own assessment of the situation, no doubt they were right. Had he been such as they were, no doubt it would have been true. If you choose bad companions no doubt you are exposed to the influence of the bad. They would feel that he would blight his career as a Rabbi by his association with the undone. Make friendship with sinful men and you will be spoiled. The worst of the Pharisees were sceptical and scornful, the best were disappointed.

Looking back on it now we know in our deepest heart that they were wrong. They did not know this man. They did not understand him. They did not realise that he was able to receive men unto himself and remain unpolluted – to take men with the virus in them and the contamination upon them and not be harmed. But more – the polluted, the contaminated and the undone as they drew near to him in friendship were themselves purified, cleansed and healed. They did not harm him but instead he, by the communication of the gospel, remade them.

The secret of this strange paradox is fixed in the words "this man" – "*this man* receiveth sinners, and eateth with them". This man – the man of integrity with no double dealing, as clear as crystal water is clear. This man – a man of probation, who lived his life in the midst of its realities, its joys and its sorrows as other men. This man – a man of workmanship who knew how to face a day's toil in order to win a day's bread. This man – a man of temptation, who felt it more keenly than any man because he was more sensitive than any man. This man – a man of trust, who lived upon earth and depended upon heaven, who transformed all earthly relationships by his utter trust in God. This man – a man of sorrows. Not so much the sorrows of his own life but the agony of bearing other men's failure and other men's rebellion. The sorrow of sympathy that moved him to compassion. This man – a man of victory. The one lonely concentric man of the centuries who met sin face to face and front to front and mastered it; who moved in quiet kingly dignity to the place of battle and won the Armageddon of the ages.

Because he is the man of integrity, of toil, of temptation, of trust, of sorrows and of victory, he is finally and superlatively the man of atonement. The man of the mercy seat – who stands between earth and heaven at the place where the failure of men and the grace of God may meet and merge – the perfect instrument of Divine love. The Lamb of God.

Here is the mystery. Although he is seated now at the right hand of God in heaven and soon to be set upon the throne of universal empire in Jerusalem – although he is so far above us in stature – although we are dazzled by the full blaze of his glory – although he is transcendent and immanent – although to him every knee shall bow and every tongue shall confess, yet here is the mystery – this man receiveth sinners.

The day is coming when men will have to kiss his sceptre and submit to his unchallengeable rule – yet now he is near to us, as near as our own soul is near. In the moment of our failure and in spite of our guile and our sophistry, he is taking us as we are. In the knowledge of our recurring sin, with the confession on our lips, with the resolution in our hearts, with the amendment of life determined, he will pronounce upon the contrite soul the verdict of the guiltless. In that blessed verdict the scarlet corruption is ended and the pollution is cleansed.

This man receiveth sinners – not to patronise them but to give them pardon and renewal. The work is not yet done. Such men as we are, seeing the clear shining of two ways, are too often tempted to take the way which is wrong. For such the work is not yet done. The succour will be needed again, the tides of life will need control again, the tempests will need to be stilled again. This man receiveth sinners – continuously.

Let us come back to where we began. You will remember we were pondering the Pharisees' criticism of the King's conduct – why he was the companion of the outcast; why he laboured with the guilty; why he spoke tenderly to the undone; why he was there amidst the wreck of human life. Had they remembered their own scriptures they would have recalled that Isaiah had written of their Messiah: "A bruised reed he shall not break, and the smoking flax he shall not quench (42:3). Other men will say about the bruised reed: "It is broken; it is no good". He will say: "It is broken; it can be mended". Other men will say about the smoking flax: "It is smoking; put it out". He will say: "It is smoking; it can be fanned into flame".

Think of that parable the King spoke about the Two Sons (Luke 15:11–32). He did it to personify for the benefit of the Pharisees that spirit which complained that he had received sinners. The elder brother was the incarnation of their criticism. They said concerning the man of Nazareth: 'These

122

sinners are outcasts; why does he not exercise more discernment; why does he not leave it at that?'

## The Parable of the Two sons

In effect Jesus replied: 'You say I am like that; very well I will show you what you are like'. And he told them the story of the two sons and in the elder son he personified the very attitude which the Pharisees had taken up. So we see the elder brother resentful at his father's sympathy and understanding of the younger son. He is sullen and sulky – he complains, he is angry and resentful. Notice the elder brother calls the younger "*Thy* son" (verse 30) – he will not admit that the younger was also *his* brother. Notice how the father in reply goes out of his way to call the younger son *thy* brother. "It was meet that we should make merry, and be glad: for this thy brother was dead, and is alive again; was lost, and is found" (verse 32). Yes, Jesus in the parable was marking carefully exactly what the attitude of the Pharisee really meant.

But here is something to ponder finally. This parable told of the Father and the two sons – and in the parable the elder son was true to the facts on earth – true to how the Pharisees behaved – but it was not true to how God willed it. In the purpose of God the elder son was the only begotten Son – the holy child of the eternal Spirit. The younger son is humanity in a far country, in sin and disgrace – any man who has been mastered by sin. The Father's heart is heavy and the home is changed. The blinds are drawn and disgrace has saddened the home. Then there comes a day in the long process of the purpose when the Father says to His Son: "We must seek and save that which is lost – the boy will not come home on his own – he has gone too far". The elder son squared his shoulders and said: "Father thy will be done – I will fetch him home, come what may". And so he went and sought the broken man, from place to place, from bad to worse. Stiffening his back to the wind, the biting wind; facing the storm and tempest – calling for the wandering boy. Over the mountains, through the barren desert, by the way of the valley of shadows he went. And then at last he found the boy in the very depths, in the mire, half naked and starving. He stooped, this elder son, and whispered a word of encouragement into the lad's ear, lifted him up and carried him on his broad shoulder – that shoulder upon which one day the government will rest. By faith and courage they turned towards home – out of the valley of the shadow, over the moor, across the torrent. The young one would have feigned turned back for fear but the elder one would not let him go and at last he brought him home. There was great joy in the house of the Father. They sang a song of salvation. That which was lost was found and that which was dead once, was made alive. Not a saved servant but a son. That is what really happened. Something the Pharisees resented – but something which God willed by His determinate counsel. "This man receiveth sinners" – he not only receives them but goes after them and recovers them.

There is a sense in which it happened once, on the green hill once for all. And there is a sense in which it still goes on every day – on this sabbath day – over the mountains through all the ways of men, and amid all the wrecks of human nature. The man who receives them is out, seeking them. And here is the thing to sing about – the prodigals are coming. Those who come to themselves and say: "Father, I have sinned against heaven and before thee".

Once embittered, once hot, restless, worldly, ill-tempered, paralysed, they came and found that the word uttered to condemn the Redeemer is wonderfully true – he does receive sinners. This we have come to celebrate. God grant that in this solemn moment of bread breaking when every third party is excluded and you are alone with the man of atonement, and you make your confession, you may feel it in your deepest heart to be true.

# 21

## THE PARABLE OF THE UNJUST STEWARD
### (LUKE 16)

THE Parable of the Unjust Steward (Luke 16:1-13) is at first sight quite perplexing. The problem is that it seems to commend something we ought to deplore. It holds up for admiration and imitation a man who is a bad example. It commends to us somebody who is dishonest. Add to this the problem presented in verse 9:

"Make to yourselves friends of the mammon of unrighteousness; that, when ye fail, they may receive you into everlasting habitations".

It exhorts us to engage in what on other occasions we are urged to avoid – friendship with the world and with unrighteousness. It seems that the very things we are concerned to shun as disciples of Christ, are the things this parable urges us to seek. There have been various explanations for this apparent contradiction and the one offered now forms the subject of this exhortation.

**Wasting His Master's Goods**

Let us look again at the parable. Evidently the steward or manager of the estate was being dismissed. Complaints had been made to the master about the steward. It looks as though "wasted his goods" means he had in some way been squandering the very things for which he was responsible and which he ought to have protected carefully. Whatever, he was under notice to go and he had to write up his final accounts without delay. He was in a fix; the future was black. He was used to being a steward which was a responsible job with good pay and high status. Now he would never be a steward again. The thing about stewards is that they must be dependable and trustworthy because they have to bear heavy responsibility. The master depends upon them. So to get a job you have to present good references and have sound credentials. This steward knew that when he wrote his accounts up and presented them to the master, it would mean the end of his reputation. The master's testimonial would be bad. Remember, the Apostle Paul says:

125

"It is required in stewards, that a man be found faithful." (1 Corinthians 4:2)

This steward was unfaithful. He knew his career was finished; the future looked bad.

As he ruminated on the future sadly, he realised that the only job he could get of labouring in the field, was one he could not do. The years in an office had made him soft. The alternative of begging when hitherto he had won respect and admiration was more than he could stomach. The shame of it – a high steward turned beggar. No, not that! So he faced the issue squarely and weighed it up realistically. He resolved upon a master plan to ensure the future was as bright as possible.

## The Steward's Plan

Notice verse 5 and the word "debtors". This needs explanation. They were debtors, but of a particular kind. They were tenants, farm tenants, and what they owed was farm rent. Now the method of their rent calculation is important. The rent was not fixed in advance. It was in fact calculated as a percentage of the value of the crops the tenant farmer produced. They did not pay the rent in money, but a proportion of their crop at a rate agreed was given to the landlord via the steward. So if a tenant farmer produced, say, a thousand measures of olive oil, his rent might be at ten per cent – one hundred measures of oil. Simple enough, but with one snag. Would there not be a strong temptation for the tenant farmer to give a low declaration of his total produce so that his rent would be lower? Well, human nature being what it is, of course there would.

About his thousand measures of oil, he would like to admit to only seven hundred, and pay seventy measures instead of a hundred. How could the master ensure that there was no such defrauding? How could he ensure a sound check on the tenants' returns? His faithful steward was entrusted with the task. He was the insurance against fraud of this kind. He and his staff checked the returns of the farmers and then agreed with them what the rent should be. He had to be a man of unimpeachable character, free from corruption and incapable of being bribed. Hence it was required in him that he should be found faithful. At the same time he had to be respected by the debtors for his fairness and honesty. Evidently he had agreed in this case what the rents were to be, but his plan involved a second scrutiny. He called the debtors together and said: 'Look I know we have fixed the rents for this year but I am going to do you a great favour. Because I appreciate your difficulties as farmers and how you are always losing money, I am going to give you a big discount this year. I am going to halve the rent for the oil farmers and give a twenty per cent reduction for the wheat farmers. So you can alter your rent accounts accordingly and I will alter my debtors' ledger'. And then this: 'When I leave this job next month and am looking around for some consolation, remember who helped you today'.

It was a bold plan, carefully thought out and diligently executed. When the master discovered it – perhaps when the steward had gone – ruefully and reluctantly he had to admit that his former steward was a prudent man. Remember it is the landlord who commends the steward, and it is for his foresight that he is commended. He had acted wisely – not honestly, not purely, not honourably – but wisely and diligently.

## The Key Lesson

It is this one thing that the parable seeks to focus on. We must not take everything in the parable and use it for an example, but only the one thing. This sometimes is the case with other parables. The Parable of the Labourers in the Vineyard who received the same wages, some after working for the whole day and some after just one hour only, was not intended to teach trade union practice or industrial relations, but something else. The lesson is this: be sure to fix on the one thing which is the issue of the parable, and rest with the drapery which enshrines it. So with the Parable of the Unjust Steward. There is one lesson to be learned from the diligence of the steward and it is in verse 8:

> "The children of this world are in their generation wiser than the children of light."

If we are to apply the teaching of the parable to ourselves it means asking this question: 'Do we put into our living and service to the Truth the same faithfulness and diligence that we put into our ordinary daily lives?' Now this is a very serious question and it can be very incisive and really uncomfortable. The point is – and I am going to be straight and explicit – there are I believe, three things that hinder progress in the service of the Truth and I will tell them clearly. Firstly jobs and careers; secondly homes and family; and thirdly geographical isolation. They need not be impediments but sometimes they are. When the claims of your job clash with the claims of the Truth, which has to give way? When they are the claims of home and family, which have to give way? Are you prepared to accept transport problems on behalf of the meeting as readily as you accept them for your work, family and anything else? In other words, what are you prepared to allow to interfere with your active participation in the services of the ecclesia and the Truth? Let me give you an example of what I mean. This memorial service: what do you allow to interfere with being here regularly? Here are some reasons I have met: 'We had to help the children with their homework'; 'We had friends call to see us'; 'We had to finish the decorating we began yesterday'; 'It looked very stormy'; 'We just had to have a lie-in'; 'We came last week, anyway'.

Now bearing in mind the lesson of the parable, that we should put into our religion the same diligence we put into the rest of our lives, would you be prepared to offer any of those reasons to your employer for not going to work tomorrow? Conversely, would anybody be willing to say to the boss: 'Overtime? Certainly sir whenever you want me, but never on a Wednesday, because then I have an appointment which I must keep at the Bible Class'. Life is really a list of priorities and somewhere on the list is the service of the Truth. In theory it is right at the top, but you and I know that in practice it has to take its place where it can and it has to compete with all kinds of important things jostling for our time, our energy and our love. Let me not misrepresent it. Of course there are some things in our life which just have to take priority over the service of the Truth. Sometimes there are things that must have the first preference both in the home and in the career. This is incontrovertible. What this parable is urging us to do is to take a long look at what our preferences really are, to make a careful scrutiny of our priorities, because Jesus says men tend very much to be more diligent about their own affairs than about the affairs of God: "The children of this world are in their generation wiser than the children of light". This is saying that the children of light are not as careful, diligent, and urgent about their important things as the children of the world are about theirs. If you feel grieved with me for putting it so bluntly then I must take it – but to tell you the truth, that honestly is the message of this problematical parable.

**Diligence Each Day**

Can I anticipate a reaction? You say to me and indeed I say to myself, 'When some great and vital issue comes I would always put the Truth first'. Indeed that may be true, but here is something to ponder. Great and vital issues rarely come. If you are going to wait for one in order to be counted, you will have to wait half a lifetime. I have been in the Truth many years and twice only have I had to take a stand and say: 'Here I stand and I will not be moved'. Only twice have I had to stand up and be counted. The issue, which the parable enforces, is realised in the infinitesimals of daily life. It is every day that we have to say whether we will or will not do this or that. Every week we have to decide upon the priorities – our decisions cause us to act wisely or unwisely. We are diligent every week about the ordinary things – the things we want and strive for. So every week we have to say how much we want to serve the Truth. We choose every time we make a decision one way or the other. If you think I have overstated it, then look at Luke 16:

"He that is faithful in that which is least is faithful also in much: and he that is unjust in the least is unjust also in much."                                                        (verse 10)

Hear it in modern English: "He that is cheating in little things is cheating in large things". That is the measurement of heaven. So it is in ordinary everyday living we have to learn the lesson of the parable. The exhortation is, seek to put into your service to the Truth the same diligence you put into the daily affairs of your life (homes, career, family, leisure). Neglect the responsibilities of neither – give to both all your strength, energy and faithfulness.

## "The mammon of unrighteousness"

Finally, verse 9: "Make to yourselves friends of the mammon of unrighteousness; that, when ye fail, they may receive you into everlasting habitations". The mammon of unrighteousness represents money and all the things which money and the world is able to provide us with. We have to handle these things; it is part of living in this world. The parable is saying, when you use them, do it in such a way that in the day of account they may have been your friends instead of your enemies. We have all been entrusted with money to varying degrees. I can so use it that in the Day of Judgement it will curse me and condemn me – that is, it will be my enemy. Or I can so use it rightly and faithfully, that in the Day of Judgement it will have the effect of laying up a good foundation – that is, it will be my friend. The steward did not know how long he had got. He felt there was no time to be lost and therefore he acted wisely and diligently. We are in the same position. We do not know how long we have got; the time may well be short and the issues are as urgent for us as they were for him. So let us be diligent; let us act with prudence; let us live wisely so that the things we have used and the ways we have used them may have the effect of ushering us into the final and glorious habitation of God.

Remember the exhortation of the New Testament writers. They teach that we have to respond in love to what God has done for us through Christ. The love of Christ ought to constrain us. The atonement ought to have a practical effect upon our daily living:

> "The grace of God that bringeth salvation hath appeared to all men, teaching us that, denying ungodliness and worldly lusts, we should live soberly, righteously, and godly, in this present world."
>
> (Titus 2:11,12)

Our giving at any level ought to be provoked by what Christ has given for us – not only money, but also time, talents, and energy. It is a call to generosity at all levels:

> "For ye know the grace of our Lord Jesus Christ, that, though he was rich, yet for your sakes he became poor, that ye through his poverty might be rich." (2 Corinthians 8:9)

So in the solemn moment of bread breaking, when we are alone with the Redeemer and we are faced with this question: 'Are we ready to put into his cause the same devotion we put into our own?'. God grant that reverently we may answer in the affirmative with dedication and resolve.

# 22

## THE AUTHORITY OF THE KING
### (LUKE 20)

"The chief priests and the scribes came upon him [Jesus] with the elders, and spake unto him, saying, Tell us, by what authority doest thou these things? or who is he that gave thee this authority?" (Luke 20:1,2)

IN these opening verses of Luke 20 we see something which is quite startling. The sworn enemies of Jesus are compelled to do something which was the very last thing they wanted to do – that is recognise his authority. It occurs in other places.

Recollect that incident in John 7 where the Pharisees sent their officers to arrest Jesus and eventually the officers returned without him. The Pharisees asked: "Why have ye not brought him?" And the officers replied: "Never man spake like this man" (verses 45,46). Ponder it carefully because it is worth it – it ought to do you good. Imagine some officers in this country being sent to arrest a suspicious person, someone against whom a charge is to be made, and the officers return to the police station and when the Superintendent asks them where the man is, they say: 'We did not arrest him because of the way he spoke to us'. Could there be a more unlikely story? yet this is what happened in Jerusalem. They were sent to arrest him and somehow he arrested them. I reckon there was laughter among the angels in heaven; holy, sanctified laughter. Men with swords and staves and a warrant to arrest the man from Nazareth, somehow were halted and sent away empty handed.

**"Never man spake like this man"**

What was it that arrested them? Well, their own words explain it – the authority of the King. "Never man spake like this man". At the end of the 7th chapter of Matthew you will read a strange thing, but it explains John chapter 7. Listen to this: "And it came to pass, when Jesus had ended these sayings, the people were astonished at his doctrine: for he taught them as one having authority, and not as the scribes" (7:28,29).

131

This is why it is strange. The scribes were the most authoritarian people in the nation. They were full of authority – critical, censorious, dogmatic. They held an official position which entitled them to lay down the law. Yet when the king spoke the people knew that here was an authority which transcended anything they had ever heard from the scribes. In the words of the gospel writer they were astonished. Like the officers in John 7 they were aware that this was something altogether new – strangely new and wonderful. Never man spake like this man. As we have seen in Luke 20 even his enemies were compelled to recognise it. They did not submit to it, but they could not escape it, and without willing it they confessed it.

Remember verse 2 – "Tell us, by what authority doest thou these things? or who is he that gave thee this authority?" Verse 26 says: "They marvelled at his answer, and held their peace".

## The King's Authority

So we come to the crucial question – what really was the nature of the King's authority, which the people of Israel were compelled to recognise? At the risk of wearying you I repeat that it was different from that to which the people were accustomed from the scribes and rulers. Trying to mark the difference may help us. The scribes' authority was interpretive. There is nothing wrong with that in itself; sometimes interpretation is of great value. But they interpreted other men's words. The King's authority was not merely the authority of interpretation, though he was able to make the prophets' words live with a new meaning, as he did on the Emmaus Road. The scribes' authority was dogmatic. The King was no mere dogmatist, though he taught without reference to other people and without fear or favour. The scribes, because of their position were able to wield authority and claim a right to be heard. The King, on the other hand, could claim no right to be heard by reason of any official position in the hierarchy of the church or government. Yet when he spake to the people they were astonished, soldiers were transfixed, priests and lawyers were compelled to confess, critics were silenced. What was it that constituted his authority? I put it to you as it appears to me.

It was the self-evident truth of what he said. As he spoke men were compelled to say: 'Yes – that is true, that is true'. It was the voice of supremacy, the voice of origination, the awe-inspiring authority of the final word; the voice of God. I say then, the self-evident truth of what he said, coupled with

132

the personality of the one who spoke, and confirmed by the wonderful signs he did – these constituted his authority. On a lower level, there is a sense in which even today when a voice speaks that which is clearly and honestly and incontrovertibly true, it carries its conviction deep into our hearts and we also are compelled to confess it, if we are honest men and women. So the gospel writer saw it superlatively in the man of Nazareth. "He taught them as one having authority". As you hear the voice are you not compelled to confess he is the King, the final voice, the voice of God? Here is the conviction of mastership.

Sometimes his words scorch us and at other times his words soothe us. As he speaks our reason is satisfied, our hearts are moved and so our wills are energised. I know you have heard it my comrades. His word places God in the position of absolute and final supremacy. "Seek ye first the kingdom of God ... and all these things shall be added unto you".

**Treasures in Heaven**

Do we not know in our deepest heart that this is the only perspective which can satisfy us? – that to have gained the world and be without him is to have lost all? These material things, good though they may be, are really empty things and worthless things if they are to be secured at the cost of losing his comradeship and his fellowship. Listen to his measurement of humanity: "Lay not up for yourselves treasures upon earth ... but lay up for yourselves treasures in heaven". He is telling us that man can realise his true destiny, not by satisfying his senses only, but by living on the plane and on the level of the spiritual. He is saying something which we must hold to firmly – that man is a spiritual creature, in some sense kin with God. By that I mean, according to the King, man is able to realise his life most fully in the possession of those things which are essentially part of the infinite life of God.

Notice that judgement he delivered on the relative claims of men and God in Luke chapter 20 which we read. He said: "Show me a penny" (verse 24). If he had produced one himself the issue would have been blunted. *They* must show the penny. They did and said he: "Whose image and superscription hath it?" And without a moment's hesitation they say "Caesar's". That was the moment when the answer was fashioned. The penny was theirs and the image was Caesar's. "Render therefore, to Caesar the things which be Caesar's and to God the things which be God's". The principle

is this – that for the true man, doing the second, will ensure
the first. Do God's will and you will serve men rightly. Later
on the New Testament writers will clearly develop the
principle so as to teach that obedience to the civil government
is a faithful part of doing the will of God, always with the
understanding that for men who are in the world to represent
the kingdom of God, their first loyalty is to its king. Their
best method is to seek to realise in the world the very values
of the kingdom which they represent, even love and joy and
peace, and to proclaim that ere long that kingdom will burst
forth upon the world in flaming glory. The King declares that
in all the forces of human life which might come to be called
Caesar's, his men must never forget that their final
allegiance is to the throne of God.

**The Ethic of the Gospel**

Think of something else. Mark how he looks upon the
restlessness of men. He does not say that anxiety is wrong.
He knows that it is part of human nature to care and to be
anxious. He knows that often anxiety is the inspiration of
endeavour and striving. But he draws our mind to what is
important about the things which cause anxiety and after
which we seek. To be anxious about the abiding things is the
ethic of the gospel. Seek ye first the kingdom of God. His view
of life is that it is full and free and wonderful, only when all
its varied ways and possibilities are related to the one centre
of life – the throne of God. That is the central passion of his
teaching. He declares that character is the vital thing. He
places no benediction on *having* or even on *doing*, but on
*being*. He is not saying: "Blessed is the man who has", nor
"Blessed is the man who does". By his measurement the great
man is the man of character more than the man of property
or of attainment. Now be honest – in this fundamental
estimate of the King is there not the ring of absolute truth?

Then think of this. To those who have accepted his
Lordship, he reveals the vital importance of influence and
marks the kind of influence that men need most. "Ye are the
salt of the earth ... Ye are the light of the world". Salt is
pungent, antiseptic – it hurts when it is in the vicinity of the
wound, but it heals and preserves and saves at last. It halts
the spread of corruption by its aseptic influence. Light
disperses the shadows and is not by any means welcome to
the man who has something to hide, but in the end it is the
only way to be led out of darkness and doom into the light of
liberty and freedom. Is not this the very science of life? There
are some things which hurt and pierce us through, but in the

end they heal us and succour us. We may hide the truth for a long time but in our deepest heart we know that the day we bring it out into the light and confess it and repudiate it; that is the day of freedom, restfulness and release.

## As a Man Thinketh

I said that sometimes his word scorches us. Do you remember this teaching? He who looks on sin with desire has committed it already in his heart. There are some who are held back from sin only by the lack of opportunity. They would if they could but circumstances make it that they cannot. Do we not know that the King's estimate of guilt is absolutely true? As a man "thinketh in his heart, so is he". His word cuts decisively like a knife through all our sophistry and our guile.

I know how it is, that we sometimes think to make wrong things right by trying to make them plausible. But in the presence of the King's measurement we are made to be openly what we are inwardly. Our inwardness is brought out, not to destroy us, but at last to save us from ourselves.

Again think of this. Notice his measurement of righteousness. The scribes and the Pharisees sought to do right in order to sustain their reputation. They said it was important to be seen to be right. They said that they had a standard to uphold, a law to fulfil. At its best it is not the ideal motive, because it is not strong enough to ensure righteousness when things are set against it. With this motive a man may keep straight whilst all is well and whilst the sun shines. But in times of adversity or ridicule or if some alluring self-advancement can be secured only if the standard is compromised, then this motive will break down. Mark therefore the wisdom of the King: "Except your righteousness shall exceed the righteousness of the scribes and Pharisees, ye shall in no case enter the kingdom of heaven". The righteousness which exceeds is that which acts in response to the love of God and for the glory of God. For love's sake is the only motive which will hold strong against all the slings of misfortune or against all the insidious temptations to compromise. You will remember the old proverb: 'Honesty is the best policy'. The truth is that a man who is honest as a matter of policy, is really at heart a rogue. I was once present when a man said: "My quarrel with Christ is that he is not practical. Confucius said: 'Be just to your enemies'. That is practical. Christ said: 'Love your enemies'. That is impractical, I cannot do that – it is beyond me". It was doubtless an honest criticism. But the man to whom it was directed said this: "But suppose you could be brought to love your enemies – what then?" And the critic said: "God help me – it would solve all the problems that curse humanity". I mention it just to stress this – it was a compulsive recognition of the authority of the King. That is all we need. Has he ever said a false thing? Has he ever said aught which we could overthrow? Where do we differ from his position? Where does our criticism commence? We know that all he says is designed to realise the glory of God, and he is doing it by securing the salvation of men. Was there anything nobler? Is he not Lord of the Universe; the high priest of humanity; the voice of God?

## Power to Forgive Sins

There is one last word. Though he spoke with the voice of divine authority, that was not the end of his work. We know he went forward to the cross-crowned hill, and in the unfathomed mystery of that hour, when he was bruised to death, he bore my sins and yours in his body on the tree. And out of that death he won a life which he will communicate at last to all such as put their trust in him.

As I stand at the gate today wanting to draw near into his fellowship, I know that in my deepest heart I am not fit to come. At the parting of the ways, too often I have taken the way which is wrong. I rose with consecration in my heart and ere noon had come I was enwrapped by dark sin. I know that somehow that which I hate, that I do. It is this that leads us to the noblest expression of his authority.

I read it lately in Luke 5: "Man, thy sins are forgiven thee" (verse 20). And in response to the complaint that only God can forgive sin, he justified it with these words: "That ye may know that the Son of man hath power [authority] upon earth to forgive sins". That is the triumph of the man with authority. It means we may come just as we are, with our weakness and failure, with our weariness and our restlessness, with our broken resolutions and our aborted reformation. We may come. Even though we are guilty we may come. And because of his authority, upon the guilty will be pronounced the verdict of the guiltless. Given open confession and true contrition you may be released from your burden. Not partially but completely. Not tardily but instantly. As swift as lightening is swift; as gentle as the first breaking of the sunlight; with no impediment allowed; with every voice of accusation silenced; notwithstanding your doubt; in spite of your recurring disability; upon the basis of infinite mercy you are declared forgiven and cleansed. The word of the King's authoritative voice says directly to you:

"Man, thy sins are forgiven". It is not my broken word; it is his unassailable word. May God in His infinite grace, at this moment of bread breaking, speak this word to us as no human voice can speak it; the voice of forgiving authority. God grant you may feel it to be true.

# 23

## "TAKE HEED TO YOURSELVES"
### (LUKE 21)

**N**O exhorting brother today, wherever he is, can lightly pass over this 21st chapter of Luke. We are always saying, consistently and conspicuously, that the return of Christ is near. Some people would say it could be the world's next great event. For those who are ready it will be a day of unutterable joy, but for all of us ready or not, it will be a day of awe. No man in his right mind can contemplate meeting the Son of God without a sense of awe. When I hear people talk about it lightly it makes me tremble.

So when we hear the voice of Jesus say to us today "Take heed to yourselves", spiritual common sense tells us to pause and understand what he is saying. Notice the words once again:

"And take heed to yourselves, lest at any time your hearts be overcharged with surfeiting, and drunkenness, and cares of this life, and so that day come upon you unawares. For as a snare shall it come on all them that dwell on the face of the whole earth. Watch ye therefore, and pray always ..." (Luke 21:34-36)

Let us try to get down to the nitty-gritty, if you will allow the expression. It is the opposite of vague generalisations. To tell you the truth, I am sick to death with vague generalisations. Let us look at the words carefully. I do not think it likely that your problem is surfeiting and drunkenness. I am not saying that is not a problem with some; I know it is – but not with you. To some extent it is the language of Wycliffe. In modern parlance it goes like this: 'with dissipation – with self-indulgence – with revelry – by debauchery – with gluttony.' This is how modern versions translate it. So as we say, not likely to be your problem.

But the next few words could be very applicable to all of us: "cares of this life". There is no question about this. Every day we are concerned with the cares of this life. Think of some words in the Sermon on the Mount as they stand in the Authorised Version: "Take therefore no thought for the morrow" (Matthew 6:34). If this is what Jesus meant as the words reveal it, then every day we disobey it. We have to take thought for the morrow else our lives would be chaotic. But those words do not describe what Jesus meant. This is one rare case where the Authorised Version has done the truth no favour. What Jesus meant was: 'Do not be over anxious about tomorrow. Do not fret about the future. Your heavenly father knows you have need of the things to sustain your daily existence – trust Him and do not worry'.

Come back then to Luke 21 and think of the cares of this life and one word in that sentence about taking heed. It is the word "overcharged". As a start let us just think of the meaning as we usually use the word. To be overcharged is to pay too much for something – to give too much for some article or service. That is not quite the old-fashioned meaning – Wycliffe's meaning. In his day it meant to be overburdened. But I am willing to accept the old and the new meaning. Jesus is not asking us to have nothing to do with the cares of this life. That would be impossible – we have to care about this life every day and if we did not then we should soon be in serious trouble. What Jesus is urging is that we shall not pay too much attention to the cares of this life; that we shall not be overburdened – not overloaded with such cares. In other words, that we shall get the cares of this life in perspective.

When all is said and done, the cares of this life are the transient things. That does not mean that they are not important but that in the end they are transient. And Jesus is telling us that in being ready for the fateful day of his coming we must take heed to strike the right balance between the things which are transient and the things which are eternal. We must be aware that it is possible to be so obsessed with the transient things that the eternal things are neglected – to be so taken up with the temporary things that we have little time and energy for the everlasting things. A proper balance is needed between the everyday things and the things of God – between the secular and the spiritual.

## Striking a Right Balance

This matter of striking a right balance is at the very heart of the life of faith. Let me give you an example. In John chapter 6 Jesus says: "Labour not for the meat which perisheth, but for that meat which endureth unto everlasting life" (verse 27). Now every day we are doing what Jesus says we should not do. We labour for the meat which perisheth. We do it because if we did not we should be left empty and bereft. But there is more – if we could and did not we should be breaking

139

another part of the word of God. In 2 Thessalonians 3:10 it says: "For even when we were with you we commanded you that if any would not work, neither should he eat". Now what we have to do is to strike a balance between one exhortation and the other. And we are doing it every day. We are working to earn a living and support ourselves and our loved ones, but at the same time trying not to let it become so obtrusive that spiritual things are diminished or neglected. The key is to get the temporal and the spiritual into the right perspective. Both things are right and important, but there is a right relationship between the one and the other, and the balance is a vital thing in the life of faith.

Today we have heard the voice of Jesus say that we must take care, take heed to strike the right balance – not to be so overburdened with the temporal that the spiritual is forgotten. Human nature being what it is, it stands to reason that the balance will not be the same for each disciple. Where the balance is struck will depend upon all sorts of forces which influence our attitude. Not least, what in the past has been taught us about what is reasonable. This I believe to be a very important factor – what we have regarded hitherto as reasonable and sensible. This can be seen in the New Testament. What was quite reasonable to the publicans would be an outrage to the Pharisee. Both points of view arose out of what they had been taught and how they had been nurtured.

Let me give you an up-to-date illustration. Suppose this ecclesia resolved to hold its Sunday morning meetings at 8 o'clock in the morning. Most people would say that was a very unreasonable decision. It would present great difficulties for a good many people. Some might say it was outrageous. But here is the point – I happen to know that Roman Catholics have been doing it for hundreds of years without thinking it outrageous. I did every Sunday for 18 years and never thought it strange. I heard a man say once that there are two kinds of people out early on Sundays – milkmen and Roman Catholics. To them it seems reasonable because over the years they have been taught it and they accept it. It does not mean that they are any better than people who meet at 11 o'clock, it simply means that they have been influenced in a different way. It may be that they have got the wrong balance – all I am saying is that this is a factor in striking the balance. What each has come to accept as reasonable is a variable thing affected by individual circumstances and influences which operate in each individual life.

So I think most of us would agree that when Jesus says to us today that we should take heed to ourselves about being overloaded with the transient things and the temporal items in our life, he is not saying that we should become indifferent to the provision of a proper way of life for ourselves and our families, but that in the claim which the ordinary life makes upon us, we must be sure that the claims of the life eternal are much more important; and in striking the balance it should be heavily biassed in favour of the things which are eternal.

The paradox is that when we speak of striking a balance it is not that each side is nicely balanced – about equal one over against the other as on a pair of scales. The right balance in this case is where the side of the eternal is heavily weighted and well down – that is the right balance. It is like that teaching of Christ to hate father, mother, houses, lands, etc. It means that the relationship with the King is far more important than any earthly relationship we may have, important as that may be.

The language is stark because the issues are incisive. The thing to emphasise now is that this need to strike a balance is not something reserved for the great crises of our lives, when some earth-shattering decision has to be made. The Truth is being assaulted and we have to stand up and be counted. We say: 'Here I stand and I will not be moved and I will take the consequences'. Such occasions are rare. So, if you wait for those circumstances to strike a balance, you will wait half a lifetime. No – it is something which is going on every day whether we like it or not in the ordinary and commonplace things of life. When the bags come round you have to strike a balance between how much to give  and how much to retain. This evening you have to strike a balance whether to come to the lecture or whether to stay at home. I am not passing any judgement on what we decide to do, I am simply stressing that it is something which goes on all the time. Striking a balance between the things which are earthly and the things which are heavenly – between the transient and the eternal. Jesus is saying to us today in Luke 21: "Take heed to yourselves" and make sure that the balance is heavily weighted in favour of the eternal. That is the way to be ready.

If you think about it, it very often amounts to this – what temporal things will you allow to interfere with eternal things? At what point is it justified that the transient can take priority over the spiritual? This is not a question on the very highest levels only; it arises in the ordinary involutions and convolutions of ecclesial life – the every day affairs of the life of faith.

Let me give you an example. This happened last year – I can assure you it is true. A brother and sister took their holiday in the spring and it so happened that the half-yearly business meeting of their ecclesia occurred two days before their holiday ended. Now the normal striking of the balance would mean that they would say to the Recording Brother: 'Sorry we shall not be at the business meeting this time as we shall be on holiday'. That would be regarded as perfectly reasonable. It would be axiomatic that the holiday would come first. In this case the brother and sister came back two days early from their holiday so as to be at the business meeting. Some people thought they were a little off beam; a bit eccentric. But measured by the voice of Jesus they were utterly concentric – dead on centre. They struck the balance so that his things came first – weighted in his favour. I use it as an illustration to show that it is in the commonplace things of our lives that this issue has to be faced and in these things we have to take heed to ourselves.

When in John chapter 6 Jesus said: "Labour not for the meat which perisheth, but for that meat which endureth unto eternal life", they asked: "What shall we do, that we may work the works of God?" Notice the words in reply: "This is the work of God, that ye believe on him whom he hath sent". Now this is crucial and it is a revelation. The great force which regulates where you strike the balance is the intensity of your belief in Jesus Christ and in his Kingdom. It is not just a frame of mind, a mental outlook, an assent to some doctrine only. What you believe in the end issues in activity, just as unbelief issues in inertia. Remember: "They could not enter in because of unbelief". Faith is the action of the will accompanying conviction. Abraham was utterly sure of the unknown land because he was utterly sure of the unseen God. The King is saying in John 6 – because you believe in him as Lord and King then you must abandon yourself to his cause. Because of what you believe about this man you behave in a certain way. It is inspirational – that is, you are inspired to do the things he wills. But it is not only inspirational, it is inclusive – that is it takes in all the things which make up life – low levels and high levels, crisis things and commonplace things. And in these things we strike the balance according to what we believe about him – we say he is the King, the living Lord, the high priest of the universe, the prince of life among the dead, the redeemer. We believe in him. I know we said it years ago. We said it when they put us under the water. We said: 'Yes, we believe in him'. When we were talking to the interested friend, we told them: 'Yes, we believe in him'. But what we have heard today in Luke 21 and John 6 may force us to consider saying it again, perhaps with more intensity and more resolution. Yes we believe in Him and therefore we will take heed to ourselves lest our hearts be overcharged with the cares of this life and that day come upon us unawares. It means bringing to bear eternal principles upon transient things, so that people of the dust may touch the forces of eternity. Faced with the temptation to rob God of some time or attention, to grasp some material advantage which may dishonour His cause, to neglect His business because it suits you better – flash upon it His most holy word. Measure it by the side of His Son's loved-mastered sacrifice which we now celebrate. Feel the searching fire of eternity in your little life. Give heed to yourselves as you remember – and you will get the balance right.

# 24

## "THE TRUTH SHALL MAKE YOU FREE"
### (JOHN 8)

WE have come today, as we do every Lord's day, to dwell upon the things which are at the centre of our faith. There are some things which are on the circumference about which we may disagree – but we have not come today to dwell on those things. We have come to think about the things which unite us. And so brethren and sisters I bring you no new message – for the things which are at the centre of our faith are old things. We have come then to renew our interpretation of the old things; to re-focus our vision of the fundamentals; to reaffirm our stand upon the foundation of our faith. And one of those fundamental articles of faith we have heard today from the lips of Jesus:

> "If ye continue in my word, then are ye my disciples indeed; and ye shall know the truth, and the truth shall make you free." (John 8:31)

We are here today because we believe that is true. If it is not true then the best man who ever lived has deceived us. We have come from all walks of life; we have left all kinds of religion; we have shed superstition and false doctrine because we believe that freedom can be gained only by knowing the Truth. To what extent you have felt that to be true in the long experience of discipleship or the beginning of the life of faith, of course I cannot tell, but this little exhortation invites you to consider it now. To so look at the words of Jesus as to be able to judge whether you are free with the freedom of the Son.

As a start think of the other ways which are supposed to bring freedom. There is freedom by force – but in this imperfect world that often means freedom from one thing and bondage in another, as we have seen in Europe since the war. There is freedom by legislation, but that sometimes means freedom from slavery into anarchy and lawlessness, as we have seen in Africa. Freedom by civilisation – but very often civilisation contains within itself the forces which bring a new servitude – a servitude to machines, luxury, conventions

144

and habits. Things designed to make life easier at last become the forces which enslave, as we see in Britain today.

Jesus did not choose any of these roads to freedom. He used no force – indeed part of his glory is that he did not requisition the power of the angels though he was their commander. He sought no conferences with Rome nor did he say that the hope of liberty depended upon the right division of wealth. He spoke not of the progress of civilisation nor of a climb to perfection through culture. None of these things did he choose but said: "Ye shall know the truth, and the truth shall make you free". What did he mean? There is no dispute about what it is that makes men captive. The Word of God and our own experience teach us that men are in bondage to sin. Jesus said it in John chapter 8: "Whosoever committeth sin is the servant of sin" (verse 34). Paul said it in Romans 6: "To whom ye yield yourselves slaves to obey, his servants ye are" (verse 16). It means seeing the right and then doing the wrong – a man curses himself for doing it but goes on doing it. Paul told it like this: "What I hate, that I do". That is slavery.

## Control of Appetite

What makes it happen? It is because human beings have natural appetites which must be satisfied at all costs! Think what sin is – it is the satisfying of the natural appetite outside the realm of God's law. It is not wrong to eat, but it is wrong to do it by robbing another man's larder. The desire for sexual relationship is not wrong, but it is wrong when it is satisfied by taking another man's wife. But it cannot be the appetite which is the cause of sin for we know a man who had all the natural appetites as we have them, yet he did not sin. He was tempted in all points as we are tempted – tempted to satisfy the appetites outside the realm of God's law – tempted to secure lawful ends by unlawful means – yet he did not sin. So it is not the appetite which is the real cause of sin, but the fact that man has lost that part of his nature which gives him proper control over the appetite. In other words he is dislocated and unbalanced – the spiritual part of his nature which could control his appetites has become lost. The flesh, the natural appetite, has taken charge and has dominion. So men and women are at the mercy of their own passions because the spiritual part of their nature is dead. By this means sin is on the throne.

Here is the difference between Jesus and ourselves. He had all the natural appetites as we have them and the temptation for him was just as real as for any other man, perhaps ever more real because he was more sensitive, but his character was not dislocated – he was a balanced man, because he was perpetually truth-governed; he had his appetites under control. The spiritual part of his nature was real and active. That explains why, he being tempted in the same way as we are, triumphed over it where we fail. His character was balanced – apart from the Truth, ours is not. By this method we can see the real purpose of the Truth. Its purpose is to restore in man that spiritual character he has lost, so that step by step he can control his appetites and resist his temptations – so that sin is dethroned and man is set free. This spiritual nature is called in the New Testament the new man, created in God's image in righteousness and true holiness. So the balance is achieved. Of course it is not magic and it does not happen overnight. A drunkard who comes to the Truth does not suddenly lose his craving for drink. The new man begins as a babe and grows by steps into manhood.

If this is the function of the Truth to create and sustain the truth-governed life, it must be evident that knowing the truth in the way Jesus means, is more than giving assent to a number of formulated doctrines. I uphold the Statement of Faith faithfully – let no man misrepresent what I say, but the word of Jesus in John chapter 8 proves my proposal. "If ye continue in my word, then are ye my disciples indeed; and ye shall know the truth, and the truth shall make you free" (verse 31). Notice carefully the word "continue". It creates a perpetual link between saying and doing. The Truth is not something to be speculated upon but to be done. Jesus said: "Then shall ye be my disciples indeed". Stress the "deed" part of "indeed". In deed as well as in word. A man is half false already who talks about the Truth but does not do it. A traitor is not one who fights the king from outside, but one, who being inside, assents to the king's words and then goes and asserts his own will. That is the teaching of John chapter 8 as it seems to me.

## Made Free from Sin

There is a very telling passage in Romans chapter 6 which shows that obedience to the Truth is the source of freedom – listen:

> "God be thanked, that ye were the servants of sin, but ye have obeyed from the heart that form of doctrine which was delivered unto you. Being then made free from sin, ye became the servants of righteousness."    (verses 17,18)

146

Could anything be plainer? The religion of the people to whom Jesus was speaking had become just a collection of formalities and empty traditions. Poor men trembled at its priestcraft and its threat of excommunication, wielded by men from whose hearts the real truth of God had drained away. They paid the penalty of those who, having speculated upon the truth and never doing it, found that the very truth itself by degrees became for them a falsehood. People who boasted in their descent from Abraham but did not share his faith. They therefore were never free with the freedom of the Son. Here is a revelation – the secret of discovering real spiritual truth is by spiritual obedience. Remember the word of the King in John 7:17: "If any man will do his will, he shall know of the doctrine, whether it be of God". This is what Jesus meant by knowing the Truth – the experience of the Truth which step by step creates victory over the power of sin, so that the shackles are broken from the will.

Think of it in another way. When we speak of the forgiveness of sins, what do we mean? Do we mean that the guilt is removed and that is all? Do we mean that the estrangement is cancelled – but we are still to continue as slaves to sin? If forgiveness meant that God says simply: "Never mind, pass it over and say no more about it", would that get to the heartache and the anguish of a person under the burden of being dominated by the flesh? The forgiveness of sin is equated with redemption, and redemption means being brought out of bondage. Forgiveness means that not only has God cancelled the guilt, but He has provided means whereby men can be rescued from the power of sin as well as its guilt. That power is revealed by Jesus. "Ye shall know the truth, and the truth shall make you free".

If you want to say that the theory does not work then you have an argument with Jesus. Freedom means that the carnal man is dethroned and the new spiritual man takes over the government. This is the freedom of the Son. I say to what extent it has happened in your life I cannot tell – but consider carefully what it means in practice. Freedom of the Son does not mean we are free from temptation, but it does mean we are free from that paralysis which makes defeat certain. Freedom of the Son does not mean that we shall never make mistakes when we exercise our spiritual judgement, but it does mean we need never exercise that judgement unaided. Freedom of the Son does not mean freedom from the sorrows and infirmities of life, but it does mean freedom from those curses which are the result of

147

wilful sin. Freedom of the Son does not mean freedom from faults and imperfections, but it is freedom from the unchanging necessity of wilful sinning.

In these things it is not the case of a man who would do good but cannot, but rather of a man who can do wrong but will not. It means that in the clear shining of two ways there is no necessity that the wrong way must be chosen instead of the right. Tempted we shall always be, as Jesus was, but always defeated we need not be. Some of the things we suffer arise from yielding to the flesh when we should master it. So freedom of the Son is freedom of the will, sustained by love, made firm by faith. Not magic – it takes time. It is sometimes imperceptible but it is real enough.

Measure your life then to see if you are free with the freedom of the Son. What is that free man like? He is frank, generous, and true. He may have many faults, but nevertheless his heart is mastered by love, and his mind is governed by the word of Christ. A man who acts rightly at the centre is therefore more likely to act rightly at the circumference. He is as a disciple who can sin, but will not. That is freedom.

**Freedom from Fear**

Consider now how the Truth brings freedom from fear. Let me illustrate. Two persons see a strange hideous shape in the darkness. One leaves it unexplained and so the mystery becomes for him a source of fear. The other examines it, learns what it is and so he knows the truth about it and the truth makes him free of fear about it.

So it is with life. Fear enslaves – courage liberates. Those who have felt the power of his resurrection do not fear death. Those who have seen the vision of his kingdom are not crushed by the tragedy of human failure. Those who have come to understand the meaning of true riches are not broken by the dread of poverty. Those who have felt the truth of real greatness are not dismayed by the loss of reputation. Those who have caught something of the divine goodness in the Son are not soured by the wretchedness of evil. Those who have been redeemed by the Son are conscious of the dignity of their great privilege, so they will not cringe, nor pollute themselves nor demean themselves. The Truth has made them free because they have continued in his word.

Consider the final conception of how the Truth makes us free; a conception which today is nearest to our hearts. It comes from a realisation of the price which has been paid for our redemption and our freedom. Some people know the price but are never able to measure the cost. Let me illustrate. Sometimes you hear the story of a drunken man who is saved by the faithfulness of his loving wife. She might have left him but she does not. She stays with him bearing the outcome of his wretched life – the evil temper, the polluted breath, the shame and degradation. So she clings to him until one day his torpid conscience is aroused, he realises his guilt and comes to repentance. What was it that energised that man's weak will? Was it the realisation of the evil consequences of his life upon himself? No – it was the realisation of the evil consequences of his life upon his loving wife. It was her sacrifice on his behalf – it was her unchanging love in spite of his awful predicament, and it touched his heart and when he realised it he was set free. So it is with the Lord Jesus and ourselves. He has come into our life and partaken of our nature and our weakness and endured our affliction. He has endured the onset of the world's hatred and sin's bitterness – endured it for you and for me so that we might be set free. He might have left us to perish, but he did not. He stayed with us and bore the shame and degradation.

The day we realise the cost of his sacrifice for us we are able to appropriate our freedom, shed the shackles, repudiate the things which enslave us. In the presence of these emblems we can thank God for the Truth which sets us free. So when this service is over and once more you enter into the common places of daily life, you can be conscious of the dignity of your life and have a lilt in your step, and a song in your heart. Your burden will be light, and you may lie down this night and not be afraid – encompassed by a joy which has eluded those in bondage. So you may face tomorrow with a heart garrisoned by the Truth, where every duty becomes a delight because you are free with the freedom of the Son.

So I say to all this day – in this moment of solemn remembrance – as free men and women, let us eat and drink and take courage. Amen.

# 25

## "I HAVE CALLED YOU FRIENDS"
### (JOHN 15)

"Henceforth I call you not servants; for the servant knoweth not what his lord doeth: but I have called you friends; for all things that I have heard from my Father I have made known unto you."          (John 15:15)

LET us begin by having another look at these well-known words from the Master to his disciples. Notice the words carefully. Quite evidently a change is taking place in the relationship. It suggests that these men were passing into something deeper and closer.

The King called them "disciples" at first, and surely a disciple if he be true, is in fellowship with his Lord. Later on he called them Apostles. An Apostle is one sent forth in the name of another with his authority. If they went forth in his name and with his authority then surely the fellowship is intensified. But now there is a change in the relationship; no longer servants, but friends. Let us not make a mistake here. It does not mean that in some sense they had not been his friends before. Nor does it mean that being friends, they had ceased to be disciples. Nor does it mean that they were no longer Apostles. As a matter of fact the greatest part of their apostleship was still future. Nor does it mean that they had ceased to be servants. Indeed one of the greatest Apostles later on loved to call himself the bondslave of Jesus Christ. All this being true, here it seems the King is distinctly and definitely making a change in his relationship with his disciples, apostles, servants.

'No longer' – the very words mean a change is taking place, because if it is to be no longer then something is in the process of alteration. No longer to be called slaves. Then the very character of the change is revealed in these words: "I have called you friends". At once we are taken onto a level which is different. Discipleship is one thing – it is essential and vital. Apostleship is one thing – it is central and authoritative. Servanthood is one thing – it is devoted and obedient. All these relationships express an idea of fellowship – but then "I have called you friends". And the sentence does

150

not one whit diminish or negate any other of the relationships, but instead takes their values and makes them intimate, beautiful, exciting. So here I draw a conclusion – that friendship is the highest form of fellowship.

## All Things Common

There are certain words used in the New Testament for the idea of fellowship and I want now to remind you of them: *fellowship, contribution, distribution communication, communion, partners, partakers, companions.* But to advance the enquiry I want to think of Acts chapter 4 and the picture of the infant church there presented. It tells us that in the days of the pure and uncorrupted faith, in the days when the disciples were impulsed by love and mastered by the Truth – that is in the days when fellowship came to its finest realisation – they had all things common. And the word which is translated "common" is the root word from which comes the word translated "fellowship". If we pursue this idea and ask what is fellowship with men, then it is having all things common with them. If we pursue it even further and ask what is fellowship with Christ, then though it may sound startling it is nevertheless valid – it is to have all things common with him.

Now here is the interesting thing. If we go back to John 15:15 we can notice the reason why the King was ceasing to call them servants and was now calling them his friends: "… for all things that I have heard of my Father I have made known unto you". That is to say, he was with them in having all things common. He was sharing with them the things he had received. And because of this they became his friends. A slave must give unquestioning obedience to his master – blind obedience. He did nothing on his own initiative. Unable to possess, unable to elect, he acted out of fear, without understanding. But in the changed relationship, the bondage is changed. When he elects, he does it under the loving compulsion of his friend's choice. When he possesses, he shares the good gifts which come from his friend's bounty. When he acts, he acts to advance the very cause in which he has himself become a partner, having become a fellow labourer with God. The master principle of slavery is unquestioning obedience and blind submission, but it is not the master principle of friendship with the King. The friends of Jesus are submissive but not unquestioning. The friends of Jesus are obedient but not blindly so. He has told them all things and they have asked him many things. When he had answered their doubts and when he had illuminated their minds and when he had shattered their blindness, then he said: "No longer do I call you servants … I have called you friends". Meaning, 'I have admitted you into the secret things; you are coming into the inner circle; you are my next of kin; I have told you all things; we have all things common'. So at last they gave him intelligent obedience and satisfied submission.

Of course in practice it did not happen overnight, in a flash, like magic. What is this? A man is asking: "Lord whither goest thou?" A man is asking: "Lord why cannot I follow thee now?" A man is requesting: "Lord show us the Father and it sufficeth us". Are these men slaves? Yes, slaves getting ready to be friends; beginning to have all things common, and by that he made them his friends. The action was not on their part. Remember: "Ye have not chosen me, but I have chosen you". He took their doubts and made them the bastions of faith. He took their weakness and made it the foundation of strength. And so as they came more fully into the relationship they were not slaves dragging themselves after him in misery and thinking that in the very misery there was some virtue – no never.

You never find the Apostle Paul for example saying: 'Brethren, this is a bad business, and I can offer you no amelioration. What cannot be cured I am afraid will have to be endured'. These men followed their friend gladly. Gladly they suffered in his cause, thinking themselves in some way privileged. They did it for the love of him because they were his friends, seeking his interests as he was theirs, putting all they had at his disposal, as he had put all he had at theirs. Having all things common, they were not slaves but friends – and yet in a sense slaves as never before.

I think I read your thoughts – it sounds attractive but when you get down to the nitty-gritty there is about it a touch of unreality. It is easy to say we are the friends of Jesus but to believe in it as a practical thing is another matter. So we need now to think in another way about friendship.

**Fiendship Defined**

Many years ago I came across a definition of friendship which I now want to communicate to you. I am going to read it. It was written by a lady named Mrs. D. M. Craik, an authoress of the nineteenth century who wrote several works. This is taken from a work called *A Life for a Life* and it is about friendship. Please listen carefully:

"Oh, the comfort – the inexpressible comfort of feeling *safe* with a person – having neither to weigh thoughts nor measure words, but pouring them all right out, just as they are, chaff and grain together; certain that a faithful hand will take and sift them, keep what is worth keeping, and then with the breath of kindness blow the rest away".

Now that makes friendship a very valuable thing. It is not every day that you have friends measured by that standard. With a true friend there is no need to wear a mask; no need for window dressing; no need to play the hypocrite; no need to make believe. You can be yourself without fear. You can feel safe. You can speak out of the honesty of your own heart, knowing that your friend will blow away the chaff and keep only the grain. If when you get home tonight you sit down quietly and make a list of friends like that, I do not think you will be late to bed, neither are you likely to get writers' cramp. You see with this kind of friendship you can think aloud. You are true to yourself. Such as you are, so you are. And because of the affinity between you, so is your friend. There is no fear and no apprehension and no panic.

Now here is the crucial point. I am proposing that it is not irreverent to put this measurement on your friendship with the Son of God. In Psalm 32 where the wonder and relief of pardon is being celebrated, David says: "Blessed is the man … in whose spirit there is no guile". Guile is putting on a performance. Guile is being outwardly what we are not inwardly. Guile is pretence. Sometimes we practice it with God. David did and his conscience gave him no rest. So here is the measurement. If there is some secret thing which ought to be acknowledged but is not; if there is some indulgence which ought to be repudiated but instead is nursed; if there is some room marked 'private' from which the king is excluded, then your fellowship is not this kind of friendship. You do not have all things common. With a friend you do not practice guile. With a friend you can be honest and open. In the fellowship of friendship you may confess your doubts, your fears, your griefs, your restlessness – perhaps about how God has dealt with you – and he will take out the grain and with the breath of gentle understanding, will blow the chaff away. "We know not what we should pray for as we ought: but the spirit maketh intercession for us with groanings which cannot be uttered" (Romans 8:26).

### Friends of Christ

Remember we are trying to understand how broken, failing men and women, can have true friendship with the Son of

God. It is possible – the Bible says so. Think of a sentence in Isaiah chapter 41 that ought to seal our conviction. "But thou, Israel art my servant, Jacob whom I have chosen, the seed of Abraham my friend" (verse 8). Recall the nature of that friendship as it is revealed in Genesis: "Fear not Abram: I am thy shield, and thy exceeding great reward" (15:1). Then: "And the LORD said, Shall I hide from Abraham that thing which I do?" (18:17).

Mark it well – exactly the same principle is revealed in John 15. "All things that I have received of my Father I have made known unto you". Compare that with: "Shall I hide from Abraham that thing which I do?" They had all things common – this great God and this faithful man. Abram was called to fellowship with God and as a result of the revelation he came into the inner circle of God's friendship.

The counterpart is in the invitation of the Master: "Take my yoke upon you, and learn of me; for I am meek and lowly in heart: and ye shall find rest unto your souls" (Matthew 11:29). We are exhorted by Paul not to be unequally yoked, but this yoking is unequal yet permitted. In this yoking the burden is cast upon him and we are rested. It is a picture of two yoked together, the strong and the weak and because of the strong one the yoke is easy and the burden is light for the weak. Bit by bit his step becomes our step, so slowly there is created a kind of harmony betwixt the two. "All things I have heard from my Father I have made known unto you". This speaks of having all things common. The same effort, the same purpose, the same direction. This is the highest and the sublimest law of life. This is friendship. So I make my submission again; the highest form of fellowship is friendship.

### Bearing Fruit

The final consideration takes us back to these words:

> "Ye have not chosen me, but I have chosen you, and ordained you, that ye should go and bring forth fruit, and that your fruit should remain: that whatsoever ye shall ask of the Father in my name, he may give it you."
>
> (John 15:16)

Notice a vital thing – they were not only the friends of Jesus, they were called to be the fruit-bearing friends of Jesus. The friendship was to produce definite and practical results. I mean there is nothing more real than fruit. These men had seen their God in the man of Nazareth – in his sinlessness they had seen the holiness of God and in his compassion they had seen the love of God. And living in the orbit of that revelation they were to bring forth the fruit of holiness and compassion. All this is of course connected in a vital way to the word of the King at the beginning of this discourse.

"I am the true vine". He did not mean to imply that all other vines were false, but that all the others were but replicas, patterned upon himself. Imagine it – God caused the vine to grow in the field as a figure of His own Son – growing and bearing fruit and then being crushed for the life of men. In a true vine the branch bears fruit and does so by gaining from the vine the very life which enables it to be fruitful. In a way the cluster of fruit is the branch's answer – the branch's response to the giving of the vine. He said "I am the vine, ye are the branches". As he was, so his friends are called to be. Somehow, by his friends, the values of his friendship are to be manifested in the world. They are the great master principles of the kingdom – truth and righteousness. Through the fellowship of those who are redeemed – the incorporation of those who are new-born – the ecclesia of Christ – the great master principles of the kingdom of God are to be revealed among men and proclaimed. Ye are a city set on a hill. Seeking men may come to itand find succour and sanctuary. Within its fellowship there is to be truth and compassion, warmth and love. Its citizens are to be impulsed by a master passion to reveal the person, the shining light, the Word made flesh. When you pass into the New Testament conception of fellowship and breathe its rare and spacious atmosphere, then the trivialities which divide us and occupy us seem utterly paltry.

The real issue is this – there is a person the world needs to see. If we are his fruit-bearing friends then his abundance can be repeated in us. It may mean sacrificing our sensibilities and our refinements and our preferences. It may mean pocketing our pride and confessing that we have been wrong sometimes. It may mean going on when saner people would say "spare thyself". It may mean getting closer to polluted humanity – if by God's grace we may save somebody. It may mean having infinite patience with God's other children in their foibles and their failings. Remember the fruit we bear is for them. If you mean business about this friendship there is one last thing to be said – the motivation, the driving force. It is fixed in one sentence , written for us by the finger of God: "Greater love hath no man than this, that a man lay down his life for his friends" (John 15:13). I can say no more. In this solemn moment of bread breaking I must leave it with you.

155

# 26

## KEEPING BACK PART OF THE PRICE
### (ACTS 5)

W HEN I read in advance the readings for today in preparation for this duty, I knew at once what I ought to choose by way of a subject for this exhortation. I knew it, but I wanted to avoid it. It was Acts chapter 5 and the case of Ananias and Sapphira. There is something here for all disciples, but it is hard to speak of and harder to receive. It has to do with keeping back part of the price. You will not love me for this investigation, but I shall have to risk that notwithstanding.

Keeping back part of the price. First of all we shall need to look again at those circumstances to which these words have a peculiar and original reference. That is to say we shall need to think of that infant and ideal realisation of the ecclesia of Christ as it is revealed in Acts chapter 4. There emerged from the upper room a company of men and women no longer geographically near to their Lord. He was absent as far as human appearance and human presence was concerned. They were no longer one with him sentimentally – 'knowing him after the flesh' as Paul put it afterwards. Yet they were one with him very much by the tie of spiritual life. The invisible spirit of Jesus Christ was in the midst of the ecclesia and so the ecclesia came to be. They were an elect race, a company of people called out, blood-sprinkled and chosen, unified by a common hope and a common faith, whose real destiny was to begin in the age to come in the Kingdom of God, and who therefore even now were mastered by the principles of that kingdom and where even now, to some extent, the values of that kingdom were being realised – even love, joy and peace. They were a company of people, through whom the principles of that kingdom were manifested to the world and by whom the facts of God's kingdom were being proclaimed, so that in the truest sense they were witnesses of the gospel.

Jesus once said to the Jewish rulers: "The kingdom of God shall be taken from you, and given to a nation bringing forth the fruits thereof" (Matthew 21:43). The ecclesia was that nation – a holy nation, a royal priesthood, a peculiar people,

156

underlying whose life were the master principles of that kingdom and by whose way of living were the fruits being manifested. Observe how they did it. They had all things common. Acts 4 says:"Neither was there any among them that lacked" (verse 34). This common sharing was the voluntary act of regenerated men and women, with a new conception of life, a new scale of values and a new vision of their destiny. The record says they "were of one heart and of one soul". That means they were selfless. Mastered by one impulse, they expressed it by having all things common. It was part of bringing forth the fruit of the kingdom. There were no rules, no compulsion, no pledges. They held with light hands the things of this world, because every disciple's need was met.

There was a man named Joseph, the uncle of Mark, who having a field sold it and laid the proceeds at the Apostles' feet for the common good. It was his investment in the new life. It was a venture of faith – its impulse was love. Others did it too. They were not compelled to do it by any rules, but by the very nature of the life they shared with the rest.

All this lays emphasis upon two important features in the infant ecclesia – its purity and the reality of its fellowship. It was pure because it was unsullied by selfishness – its fellowship was fair and fragrant because it was mastered by love. Notice the word which begins Acts chapter 5 – 'But'. It may be a little word but sometimes big consequences follow it. In this case the word introduces a dark and disastrous contrast.

Into the purity and holiness of the infant ecclesia came two disciples with a lie on their lips and in their life. The story is well known to us and we have just refreshed our memory of it in the readings. Let us be sure we understand what the sin of Ananias and Sapphira really was. It was not that having sold the possession they did not give all the proceeds to the ecclesia. There was no compulsion to give any. They were perfectly free to keep the whole or give whatever proportion they wished. The sin lay in the fact that having committed themselves to give all, they represented the part as the whole. They pretended, and they lied to support the pretension. They attempted to appear what they really were not. They were half-hearted and wanted to appear wholehearted. In an ecclesia impulsed by love they were impulsed by self. They secretly preferred to retain some earthly possession for themselves – quietly and furtively for themselves – rather than enter into the spacious life of love and truth which governed the ecclesia. Outwardly they had given their all – inwardly they had made a secret reservation about how far they would go and how much they would give. The Old Testament says: "When thou vowest a vow to God, defer not to pay it" (Ecclesiastes 5:4). This they had violated. Peter called it lying to the Holy Spirit.

If you think the judgement was too severe, remember it was not the judgement of Peter; it was the judgement of God. It had to do with the peculiar circumstances of that particular situation. Many a man or woman has lied to God since then and many a time kept back part of the price and no judgement fell from heaven. But this judgement was related to the unique conditions of the infant ecclesia. That is why I began by asking you to recall what the infant ecclesia was like – its purity and its love. The awful purity of the ecclesia then compelled Ananias and his wife to be excluded.

It would have been an awful violation of the truth for disciples, lying to the Holy Spirit and living that lie daily, to have sojourned in the spirit-filled ecclesia, whose members were truth-governed and love-mastered. At that time a pollution of the ecclesia's purity would have paralysed its power. As a result of the judgement a great fear came upon the whole ecclesia. And so its awful purity is revealed. The Lord of the ecclesia will not have His holy things to be profaned. Long ago He said: "I will be sanctified in them that come nigh me" (Leviticus 10:3). No man in his right mind can ponder this thing without a sense of awe. Here for a moment the folly of man impinged upon the holiness of God.

### Applying the Principles

We have to face the fact – the Lord's government is not manifested in the ecclesia now like it was then. Consequently there is not so much fear nor is there so much purity, nor is there so much absolute abandonment to the cause of the King. What we have to do is to try to take the principles of this solemn event and apply them to our own circumstances as far as we can and as far as is proper – to lay something of this measurement upon our own lives. Remember these failing disciples sought to evade their commitment by pretence. So it seems reasonable to suggest that we have to think about our own commitment. In Acts 5:32 there is the record of the Apostle Peter standing before the High Priest and saying: "We are his witnesses of these things". Be sure he did not mean just: 'We saw them happen', though that was true. He meant rather: 'We men as you see us to be, we are the proof that these things are true. We ourselves are the

158

credentials. We prove the truth of this gospel by the transformation our our lives'.

Now from this we can draw an important conclusion – it is the duty of the ecclesia to confront the world with living witnesses, else we have been deceived by this holy word of God. Unless behind the testimony of our lips is the testimony of our life, then our witness is diminished and might even be a sham. A life transformed is the proof of the risen, living, exalted, working Christ. It means that every disciple is a witness in one form or another, but always by the evidence of a transformed life.

## Living Witnesses

I once heard a story about a lady in a very remote part of the world telling some children about the man of Nazareth and she was reading from the gospel of Matthew about his way of life, his compassion, his service, his goodness. They had never heard it before and one child became restless and almost agitated. The teacher stopped and said: 'Mary what is the matter?' The child said: 'Miss, Miss, I know that man about who you are speaking – he lives in our street'. The humblest and the simplest of men and women in New Testament times who heard the gospel and by it were being changed became a force in its propagation – that is a witness. "We are witnesses of these things". Of course we know what witnesses ought to be like – they ought to be men and women with burning hearts and shining faces – instant, strong, bold and faithful. They ought to be people of unreserved commitment and unfettered resolution. But we also know that in practice the ideal is often missed because there are forces in our lives which cause us to keep back part of the price.

My comrades, I know about the disability of human nature which makes us fail too often. I see the clear shining of two ways and then take the way which is easiest and wrong. How easy it is to creep back and try to rebuild the bridges we said we had burned when we came into the Truth. How easy it is to sing the song of the cross and then be reluctant to be ever so slightly crucified. How easy it is to have one room which is secretly marked private where the Lord is not welcome – one part of the day which is not submitted to his will and which consequently makes his presence impossible. How easy it is to wear the livery of a witness, but live a life which in some way is a melancholy contradiction, so that in some sense we are compelled to represent the outward part of our discipleship as a whole, and secretly keep back some part for ourselves. My comrades, I am half ashamed to tell you – I know it so well. But not for one moment do I suggest that you are like this – I draw attention to it by way of warning. How easy it is, human nature being what it is.

There is something else. Sometimes the price is held back by pessimism – consecrated pessimism. A kind of fainting through disappointment. It may come through putting what seems to be dead seed into cold ground and never seeing the emerald sheen of fruitfulness. The Truth has not proved to be as exciting and rewarding as it at first promised. The cry of the psalmist is repeated: "Who will show us any good?" So disappointment is a weight which holds back the witness and cramps the energy once so devoted.

Or ponder this – sometimes disciples are tempted to hold back some part of their commitment, because to give the whole would mean the losing of some reputation, the relinquishing of some material advantage, the passing out of their life of some worldly benefit which they cannot bring themselves to surrender. But I must be realistic – I do not suppose that you are likely to be wooed away from your commitment to Christ by some indulgence of the flesh, or the love of money, or for some paltry worldly advantage. I am going to suggest to you that your peril is something else – something which arises from within and perhaps therefore more subtle. Here it is – the peril of weariness.

The Apostle Paul said: "Let us not be weary in well doing: for in due season we shall reap, if we faint not" (Galatians 6:9) To all that we understand by reaping – fainting is antagonistic. Notice what the peril is – it is not being tired. Tiredness is a blessing which makes us rest after we have worked so that we shall be fit and ready to work again. Weariness is a peril and it means losing heart and at last not caring. The result in the final issue is that witnessing will become but a mask worn sadly to hide the fact that we have lost interest and that our lives are in the past tense. At all costs we must strive to avoid this. As witnesses it is our business to uphold the King's standard in a world which is dying and degenerating. How we live will either advance or devalue the gospel.

It will happen in the highways and in the closets. In the place of work, in the place of recreation. So I exhort you – we must be diligent, instant, urgent to give what we have committed. Remember this – God never keeps back His part of the price. That means you are not left defenceless, you are not bereft. If that is not true then we are of all men most pitiable. The cause for our confidence is the fact of Christ himself. To those who were beset and facing the foe he said: "Be of good cheer; I have overcome the world". "He hath said, I will never leave thee, nor forsake thee". Let us rest on that and take courage.

On the practical level therefore I make now some suggestions whereby we make sure of the bulwark and appropriate the safeguard offered by the Redeemer. Keep close to this blessed Word of God – make it the master passion of your daily life of discipleship. Never neglect commerce with heaven through prayer. Keep the windows open. Men ought always to pray and not to faint. The meaning of that is inexorable – if men faint it will be because they have stopped praying. Enter with warm hearts into the fellowship of the ecclesia. Be patient, tender, seeking to restore, to build, to strengthen the things that remain.

Finally in this solemn moment of bread breaking, let its loving influence affect your lives. Always in the New Testament the great act of atonement is presented as having a practical effect upon our lives. The love of Christ ought to constrain us. How can we keep back part of the price if he has given his part to the uttermost? "For ye know the grace of our Lord Jesus Christ, that, though he was rich, yet for your sakes became he poor, that ye through his poverty might be rich" (2 Corinthians 8:9).

May God grant that in this solemn moment you may feel it to be true.

161

# 27

## THE SUFFERINGS OF PAUL
### (ACTS 20)

THE emblems on the table speak to us eloquently of the sufferings and death of Jesus Christ. And we have come primarily to recall once again the way in which Christ sacrificed himself for us. I used the word "sufferings" deliberately because we say that the broken bread is a reminder of the broken body of the Lord and the pouring out of the wine is a reminder of the shedding of his blood. These things tell us that he was a man of sorrows and acquainted with grief and by his stripes we are healed. Unmistakably the purpose of this service is to recall the sufferings and death of our Lord.

But whilst the emblems speak of the sufferings of Christ, our reading today from the Scripture speaks of the suffering of another. Acts 20 verse 23 is prophetic of the trials and afflictions that were to befall the Apostle. "The Holy Spirit witnesseth in every city, saying that bonds and afflictions abide me". During the course of this week we shall be reading of the fulfilment of the Holy Spirit's witness. We shall learn how the Apostle Paul for the Gospel's sake became a victim of the hate and spite of the enemies of the Gospel and suffered at their hands. The sufferings of Christ and the sufferings of Paul are before us today together and it is in one verse in the scriptures where they are joined in a strange way: "I Paul am made a minister; who now rejoice in my sufferings for you, and fill up that which is behind of the sufferings of Christ ..." (Colossians 1:23,24). This is a strange saying. We most certainly believe that the sacrifice of Christ is all sufficient. There was nothing left undone by him that might have been done. He "was once offered to bear the sins of many", "For by one offering he hath perfected for ever them that are sanctified". Christ's ministry of atonement is perfect and complete. In one commanding sacrifice for sin, Calvary leaves nothing behind to be done. And yet Paul, having been made a minister of the Gospel, now rejoiced in his sufferings and filled up that which was behind (lacking) of the sufferings of Christ, in his flesh, for his body's sake, which is the church.

**Imputed Righteousness**

What does it mean? We speak some times of "imputed righteousness". Often we refer to it in our lectures. We explain simply to our friends that as we have no righteousness of our own, upon the expression of our trust in Him, God regards us as being righteous. That is putting it very simply and sometimes those who have heard it thus have thought that it was a kind of fictitious righteousness, a kind of figment, a self-deception in the mind of God – a kind of pretended righteousness.

The truth is that the doctrine of imputed righteousness has more substance than that. The truth is that when God looks at Jesus Christ he sees perfection. God sees in His Son the Divine idea of man completed – the archetypal man. Christ is the realized ideal of God manifest in flesh. When God looks at Christ He looks also at those who are in Him. When he looks at us, He looks at us through Christ and sees the perfection of Christ upon those who, though imperfect, have in themselves the desire, the spirit to become like him. God gazes on the imperfection of such men and sees in it through Christ the perfection which men desire. "By one offering he hath perfected forever them which are sanctified".

As an illustration – the man who lives in the arctic regions sees only the vegetable world in stunted and weak plants and trees. If he has been to the tropics he knows the magnificence to which the vegetable world can attain given the rich soil and the genial climate. But as he looks at the weak and stunted plants of the arctic, he fills up by his conception of what he knows is possible, the miserable facts which are presented to him by the stunted plants. He attributes to them, that is imputes to them if you like, the magnificence which he has seen elsewhere.

We are feeble, dwarfish, stunted things in the sight of God – but to His infinite eye who sees in the perfect one the assurance of what is possible, this dwindled humanity of ours, becomes glorious and acceptable. So the New Testament speaks in this way. It says that in Christ many wonderful things are regarded by God as having happened to us. We have been raised from the dead and are sitting with Christ in the heavenly places (see Ephesians 2:6).

We are called, justified, glorified – if we are in him. The things that have happened to him have, in prospect, happened to us. We are accepted in the beloved. His victory is our victory. On the same principle this is also true that when Christ died, God saw in him each one of us dying also.

When he saw Christ submitting to the law of self-sacrifice, he saw our humanity submitting to the same law. That is what we mean when we say Christ is our representative. That is what the Apostle Paul means when he says:

"For the love of Christ constraineth us; because we thus judge, that if one died for all, then were all dead; and that he died for all, that they which live should not live to themselves, but unto him which died for them, and rose again."　　　　　　　　　　　　　　(2 Corinthians 5:14,15)

He doesn't mean that because one died for all, then all must have been already dead in sin – though that is true. He means that as Christ died for all, then all died with him at the same time. All this is meant by being in Christ.

I say then that when Christ submitted to the law of self-sacrifice, God saw all those who were in him submitting to the same law so that real life in Christ is a perpetual completion – a repetition of the same sacrifice. It then becomes true that the sacrifice of Christ although it is sufficient in every degree, only becomes efficacious for us when the same spirit is worked out in our own lives. That is what Jesus meant when he visualised a great line of Christ's men following him carrying their crosses. That is what we ought to mean when we speak of walking in his footsteps.

### Christ's Ambassador

All this we have said to bring us back to the sufferings of Paul which, he says, fill up the sufferings of Christ. It follows the pattern which the New Testament describes. But more than this. Paul was called especially – a chosen vessel – he says he is an ambassador of Christ. Now although a king may speak, he must repeat himself through his ambassadors.

A Gospel requires an evangelist. In his own sphere and in his own degree Paul must be Christ repeated. "Christ liveth in me". As a minister of Christ in Greece and Asia Minor, Paul must reincarnate the sacrificial spirit which Jesus had in Jerusalem and Galilee. He must "fill up that which is behind (lacking) of the sufferings of Christ". He must fill up that which remains to be filled up. It seems therefore that all true ministry for the Master must be possessed by the same sacrificial spirit of the Master. It means that what Jesus did on the Calvary Road, Paul must do on the road to Rome. The spirit of Calvary is to be reincarnated in Ephesus and Athens, and Rome.

Let us just think for a moment how this saying of Paul became true in his own life. Of Jesus it is written: "He ...

164

offered up prayers and supplications with strong crying and tears". So for the Master. Paul says to his children: "I would have you know how greatly I agonize for you". So for the Apostle. The Saviour prayed with strong crying and tears. His Apostle agonized in intercession. Did not the agony at Rome fill up the strong cryings at Jerusalem? Again it is said of the Master: "He shall see of the travail of his soul, and shall be satisfied". Paul says "Ye remember, brethren, our labour and travail"; or again: "My little children, of whom I travail in birth again until Christ be formed in you". Was not this the echo of a stronger word spoken of him who was acquainted with grief: "He shall see of the travail of his soul".

Here is another association. The Jews once said to Jesus: "Master, the Jews of late sought to stone thee; and goest thou thither again?" Jesus steadfastly went back to the place of danger. In the Acts we read of Paul: "And, having stoned Paul, [they] drew him out of the city [Lystra], supposing he had been dead" (Acts 14:19). But it is later we read: "And ... they [Paul and Barnabas] returned again to Lystra" (verse 21). He went back to the stones. Is not the Apostle the complement of the Master? Is he not doing in Lystra what his Master did in Judea? Is he not filling up that which is behind of the sufferings of Christ? When we think of this, some well known words of Paul have a way of taking on a new glory: "That I may know him, and the power of his resurrection, and the fellowship of his sufferings, being made conformable unto his death" (Philippians 3:10). "If we suffer, we shall also reign with him" (2 Timothy 2:12). "As the sufferings of Christ abound in us, so our consolation also aboundeth by Christ" (2 Corinthians 1:5). This is the sacrificial spirit of the Master – the man who set his face steadfastly to go to Jerusalem – to suffering and to glory.

## The Spirit of Self-Sacrifice

It would seem that if Christian service is to be fully fruitful the servant must be baptized into the spirit of self-sacrifice. It is more blessed to give than to receive. We are baptised into his death; we are crucified with him. Perhaps after all it was not intended that there should be only fourteen men on the Calvary Road.

These emblems speak to us of shame and glory – of suffering and shame and sacrifice and spitting. We have come to the communion of his body and blood. Communion means oneness – What fellowship hath light with darkness? But let us face it – our lives are nothing like that of Jesus or Paul – it seems hardly worth saying that we are filling up that which is behind of the sufferings of Christ. And these are hard doctrines and seem impossible. Self-denial – self-sacrifice – self-surrender. Perhaps in our more honest moments we sceptically ask – Is it possible? Is it natural? Has God sent me here for misery and not happiness? Is this the way of sonship after all – a way of sorrow and hardness and shame? And so our spirits are weighed down with the honest contemplation of the greatness of Christ and Paul and the weakness of ourselves. Yet introduce into this idea one word upon which the New Testament dwells, and the dark doctrine becomes illuminated: "the love of Christ constraineth us". Self-denial for the sake of self-denial does no good. Self-sacrifice for its own sake is no religion at all. It is self-culture and you are as much in the circle of self as ever before. But to do it for the sake of Christ is very different – his love constraining us – turning our compulsory task into a privilege and a joy – as  the virtue of Christ changed the task of Simon of Cyrene, from that which was hateful to that which was glorious.

This service is to help us – to know his love which passes human understanding, and knowing it to follow in his steps for his sake. And if your life be not like Christ's or Paul's – be not dismayed. Christ may be your model or he may be your example – and we must distinguish between the two. You might copy the life of Christ, making him a model in every act. You might wash the feet of poor fishermen, as he did; live a wandering life with nowhere to lay your head; go about teaching and only use words which he used; have no home and mix only with publicans and harlots. Then Christ would have been your model. You would have copied his life like a picture – line for line, shadow for shadow and yet with all that, you might not be one whit more a Christian than you were before – unless the spirit of his sacrifice is the motive of your work.

On the other hand you might not do one single act which he did. You might be rich whereas he was poor; you might never teach publicly whereas he was teaching always; you might live in comparative comfort whereas he had not where to lay his head; you might lead a life in all outward particulars very  different from his and yet the spirit of his self-devotion might have penetrated into every thought and act.

And the difference is this. In the first place Christ would have been your model. You have come to know him intellectually but without him entering into your heart. In

166

the second case Christ is your example. You know him as a sheep knows his shepherd – not by outward appearances, but by that spiritual intuition and the sound of his voice that is constrained by his love. It is when a man begins to understand the love of Christ for him personally that he follows in the same way with joy. We have seen today of the faithful and almost unimaginable loyalty of Paul through great tribulation and adversity – and the secret, I suggest, is revealed in one saying of the Apostle: "Christ liveth in me: and the life which I now live in the flesh I live by the faith of the Son of God, who loved me, and gave himself for me" (Galatians 2:20).

And so it could very well be true that the measure in which you are able to participate truly in this celebration today and the measure in which you are able to hold fast to the faith in the face of difficulty, adversity and suffering – or in joy and prosperity – will be regulated by the measure in which you have been able to realise and feel that personal love which Christ has for you. In this way you may also be constrained by his love to loyalty and endurance with joy. Remember that gratitude like guilt is a personal thing. It is true that all men are sinners and when we are so accused we do not feel angry or resentful. But let someone accuse us personally of some sin to our face and we shall feel it much more deeply and may resent it more strongly. When a thing becomes personal it becomes real. So it is with gratitude. If we can feel that in some way it was for us – nay for me, he died; that he loved me and gave himself for me; that in some way my sin contributed to his death – then we shall be constrained like Paul.

In this solemn moment as we are alone with the King, may God help us to feel it to be true. Amen

# 28

## "PRESENT YOUR BODIES A LIVING SACRIFICE"
### (ROMANS 12)

TODAY brethren we have reached the crucial point in the letter to the Romans. Up to the end of chapter 11 the Apostle Paul has been preaching the gospel. He has been speaking of universal guilt and sin, of human failure and the need for Divine mercy; of human inability and of Divine power; of acquittal and justification and forgiveness and peace; of faith and atonement; of justice and love; of sin and grace; of flesh and spirit; of baptism and resurrection; of predestination and election; of the wholeness and the fulness and the completeness of redemption in Jesus Christ. And at the end of chapter 11 – gathering together in his mind all the wonder of the ultimate purpose of God in Jesus Christ – he is constrained to cry out in a paean of joy and thanksgiving:

"O the depth of the riches both of the wisdom and knowledge of God! how unsearchable are his judgments and his ways past finding out! For who hath known the mind of the Lord? or who hath been his counsellor? or who hath first given to him, and it shall be recompensed unto him again? For of him, and through him, and to him, are all things: to whom be glory for ever. Amen. I beseech you therefore, brethren, by the mercies of God, that ye present your bodies a living sacrifice, holy, acceptable unto God, which is your reasonable service." (Romans 11:33–12:1)

The word "therefore" is the crucial word because it connects what he is saying now and will say, with all he has said before. 'Therefore because these things are true – present your bodies a living sacrifice'. He is making a practical application of all that has gone before. The gospel, if it is not in action, is not a gospel at all.

We shall all agree no doubt that Paul is always at pains to preserve the orthodoxy of the faith – but remember that it is because it must issue in orthodoxy of conduct if it is to be real. A false gospel will lead at last to a false life. Speculation without action is a mere husk – an empty thing. The truth of our theology is to be seen in the transformation of our lives. The rightness of our belief is to be certified by the kind of men

168

we are. That is what Peter meant when he said: "We are witnesses of these things". He did not mean: "We have come to argue with you only", but: "We men as you see us to be, we are the witness that these things are true". So with the Apostle Paul: "Because all these things are true which I have sought to expose before you – therefore present your bodies a living sacrifice to God – holy and acceptable". The one ought to be the outcome of the other, and so he goes on in the rest of the letter to speak to us on the practical issues of the life of faith.

## "Present your Bodies a Living Sacrifice"

In the terms of the old law, a living sacrifice would be a contradiction with one exception. All the sacrifices were slain, with the exception of one of the goats on the day of atonement – one was sent away alive – as was also one of the birds in the cleansing from leprosy. But these exceptions apart, all the sacrifices were dead sacrifices. But though there is a distinction between the dead sacrifices of the old law and the living sacrifice which Paul enjoins – underlying both there is the same idea.

Notice brethren the word "holy". "Present your bodies a living sacrifice, *holy*, acceptable unto God". In the Bible the word 'holy' is very often interchangeable with the word 'sanctified' – it means, as you know, set apart for the use of God – free from blemish. But I want to bring you to a deeper meaning if I can, and so will ask you to reflect upon the history of the idea in the history of Israel.

Recall how when the eldest born of every Hebrew house was saved from the destroying angel in Egypt at the first passover – that firstborn was thereafter viewed in a peculiar light by God. He was reckoned as a thing strangely devoted to the Lord. In the fullest and noblest sense he belonged to God. He was redeemed and therefore set apart. The Lord said unto Moses: "Sanctify unto me all the firstborn ...". That firstborn became consecrated – sanctified. Later on instead of one son in each family, it was one tribe set apart for God. The tribe of Levi was said to be sanctified to God. Notice the ceremony of the Levite's sanctification. The priest touched, with the typical blood of the animal, the Levite's right hand, right foot, and right ear. It devoted every faculty and every power to the service of God – all seeing, all walking, all doing – the best and the choicest – all were consecrated to God's peculiar service. He was sanctified, made holy – devoted to God. As the firstborn was the representative of the family consecrated to God, so the tribe of Levi was the

169

representative of the nation consecrated to God. "If the firstfruit be holy, the lump is also holy" (Romans 11:16).

## Consecrated to the Service of God

Come now to a scene in the upper room on the eve of a great sacrifice. In John 17:19 the words of Jesus are recorded: "And for their sakes I sanctify myself, that they also might be sanctified through the truth". The word is taking on a deeper meaning still. Jesus was already holy, in the plain meaning of the word. He was already set apart – already without blemish. But now he consecrates himself in a peculiar sense – he is facing the cross-crowned hill and he resolves upon an act of self-sacrifice for others. He steels himself unflinchingly against the sacrifice – he nerves himself against the things which are to come. It is an act of inward resolve, of absolute self-devotion to the will of God for the sake of others in spite of what that might mean in terms of sacrifice. It was not that Jesus chose suffering for the sake of suffering. There is no virtue in that. He chose the will of God – and in so doing it led him through the way of loneliness, pain and death. So then we see the deepest and noblest meaning of a holy sacrifice. A consecration without reserve to the service of God, come what may, for the sake of others.

It was against the background of his own life that Jesus called men to be his disciples. "Follow me", he said and spoke of the disciple taking up the cross. The real cross was borne by him and he became a dead sacrifice. The disciple is free from execution on a real cross – but instead is a living sacrifice, bearing a cross indeed and the shame and the offence which arises from it. That is what we *say*, brethren, but when we go back to Romans 12 and read the words again, most of us are deeply conscious that we have not yet come to this kind of consecration. The word 'holy' makes us feel uncomfortable. Living we may be – but holy in our estimation we are not.

The absolute consecration of Jesus is expressed by the gospel writer in these words: "He stedfastly set his face to go to Jerusalem" (Luke 9:51). He knew what it meant but he would not be deterred. The word that counts is 'stedfastly'. On the way to Jerusalem for the final act of consecration, Jesus met three men at different points on the journey and had a conversation with each. One man said: "I will follow thee whithersoever thou goest". Perhaps it was a sincere intention" but impulsive. Jesus replied: "Foxes have holes, and the birds of the air have nests but the Son of man hath not where to lay his head" (verse 58).

## Looking Back

Another man received a call from Jesus: "Follow me". The man replied: "Lord, suffer me first to go and bury my father" (verse 59). The man did not mean that he was on his way to his father's funeral. His father was probably hale and hearty. The man meant – 'Wait until my father is dead and buried and my share of the inheritance has come to me and everything is settled and then I will come and follow thee'. Jesus said: "Let the dead bury their dead: but go thou and preach the kingdom of God" (verse 60). The third man said: "I will follow thee; but let me first go bid them farewell, which are at my house" (verse 61). To him Jesus said: "No man, having put his hand to the plough, and looking back, is fit for the kingdom of God" (verse 62).

Christ in speaking to those men unveiled his own mind at that time. Mark the answers: "The Son of man hath not where to lay his head". It means detachment from every comfort and every earthly thing which would prevent progress towards Jerusalem. All personal property is abandoned in the interests of making the final act of holy sacrifice. Mark the answer again: "Let the dead bury their dead". It speaks of giving up of the nearest and dearest earthly tie in pursuit of the realest and noblest devotion to the will of God. Hear his word again: "No man, having put his hand to the plough, and looking back, is fit for the kingdom of God". "Looking back" speaks of that passion in all of us to cling to the things which are hardest to leave – but which will in the final issue lead us to destruction. Remember Lot's wife – she looked back. Brethren, the answers of Jesus reveal his own heart on the road to Jerusalem – they reveal his attitude on the way to make the holy sacrifice. They speak of detachment from everything which would hinder or set back the absolute consecration to the service of God for the sake of others. "I sanctify myself, that they also might be sanctified". Is it not true, brethren, that those three men on the way are enlargements of ourselves? Is it not true that the third man is a concentration of a good many of us? "I will follow thee, Lord, but …". Is there not some reservation we would make when we in our more honest moments consider our consecration to his call? Is it not that thing which follows the word but – whatever it is – which is making the presenting of our bodies as living sacrifices less holy than they ought to be? It is the thing which comes after the word but which needs to be resolutely put out of our life. It is against that thing that we have to throw every ounce of our strength – our faith must be laid squarely in opposition to that thing which comes after the word 'but'.

Very often there is one thing which most easily besets us. Habits, practices, friendships – "weights" as the writer of the letter to the Hebrews calls them – things which if we were wholly devoted to Jesus Christ we would not carry any further. 'I will follow thee Lord – but'. Somebody may say this is a hard doctrine. Yet brethren, we know it must be true. In the name of God give us five minutes of honesty. Is there a person in this house today who would seek to justify anything in life which they know is coming between them and Jesus Christ? Is it not better to be the comrade of the Jesus who has no comfort and no friendship, than to be housed and homed in luxury  without him? Is it not better to die with him and share his disgrace than to win any passing triumph just for the present?

## "Our reasonable service"

I have been trying to make you think of that thing in your life which might make it difficult to present your body a living sacrifice, 'holy', acceptable unto God. 'I will follow thee Lord – but'. But what? You know the answer and you must deal with it. When the Apostle speaks of this being "our reasonable service", he does not mean that it is to be just that which is reasonable and fair and convenient and no more. He means "our rational service" – that is to say service given freely as an act of the mind and the will — not like the dumb animals which were offered in the Old Testament time and which could not reason and offer themselves as sacrifices. It is a solemn responsibility. The blemished and the torn and the lame were not acceptable to the Lord as a sacrifice. We are to present our bodies holy, and therefore acceptable to the Lord.

I would say that many of us are deeply conscious that our holiness is tarnished. But let us not be cast down. The Truth is so hopeful. Paul says it is "by the mercies of God" that we shall accomplish this. Because of His mercy we are accepted. It is not our holiness which makes us perfect – listen to the Apostles' words:

> "[He is able] to present you holy, and unblameable and unreproveable in his sight: if ye continue in the faith grounded and settled, and be not moved away from the hope of the gospel which ye have heard."

(Colossians 1:22,23)

172

"Christ also loved the church, and gave himself for it; that he might sanctify and cleanse it with the washing of water by the word, that he might present it to himself a glorious church, not having spot, or wrinkle, or any such thing; but that it should be holy and without blemish."

(Ephesians 5:25–27)

"Wherefore, beloved, seeing that ye look for such things, be diligent that ye may be found of him in peace, without spot, and blameless." (2 Peter 3:14)

He is able "to present you holy and unblameable and unreproveable …". Brethren there is reason for solemn confidence.

I know we must face the facts. We are feeble, dwarfish, stunted specimens of holiness. Our best resolves are sometimes but withered branches, our holiest deeds are in the end but blighted fruit. The word 'sacrifice' in us scarcely deserves the name – and yet, and yet my brethren, the infinite eye of the great God looking at our impoverishment, sees in us a willingness and a desire to submit ourselves to the law of self-sacrifice. And presenting our bodies as living sacrifices, in the light of that endeavour, be it ever so weak, seeking to be like His holy child Jesus, God sees us through Christ's perfection. He sees not what we are, but what we would wish to be, and is satisfied. This is what the Apostle meant when he spoke of the imperfect, yet in these terms: "By one offering he hath perfected for ever them that are sanctified".

"I beseech you therefore, by the mercies of God, that ye present your bodies a living sacrifice, holy, acceptable unto God, which is your reasonable service". Brethren – let us eat and drink and take courage.

173

# 29

## SACRIFICIAL SERVICE
### (ROMANS 12)

A T the end of Romans 11 we have come to a turning point in this great letter. Proof is in the words which begin chapter 12. "I beseech you therefore ...". The word 'therefore' means 'in the light of all that has gone before – because of what I have written so far'. Think what has gone before. All the world is guilty in the sight of God; both Jews and Gentiles, both pagans and believers. But there is hope – one man long ago trusted God and His promises and was counted righteous. Abraham the faithful, believed and gave glory to God. Just as all men have been included in the failure of Adam and shared the outcome of sin and death, so now all who are willing may share in the victory of Christ and find righteousness and life. Standing by ourselves we are mastered by sin, but by faith and grace there is the possibility of reformation and renewal. So even now there is a remnant elected by grace – a once wild olive now grafted into the good olive tree – which means for us life from the dead, and mercy for all. In the light of all this Paul now says: "I beseech you therefore, brethren, by the mercies of God, that ye present your bodies a living sacrifice, holy, acceptable unto God, which is your reasonable service". In other words, Paul is moving from theory to practice.

The word 'reasonable' is important because a misuse of it will spoil the whole application of the exhortation Paul is making. Sometimes 'reasonable' means that which is sane and sensible, especially to include that which is convenient and certainly to exclude that which is extreme. That is not its meaning here, although it means sensible in that it has to do with the senses. It means 'rational'. The word is the Greek word *logikos* which occurs in only one other place in the New Testament. When Peter says "desire the sincere milk of the word that ye may grow thereby" (1 Peter 2:2), the phrase "of the word" is *logikos*. It does mean 'logical' so you can see why it is sometimes translated in Romans 12 as "rational". So the point is this. In the light of all that has been said in this letter up to now, it is logical, and rational and spiritual, that the disciple's service which should follow ought to be sacrificial –

174

that is in the nature of a living sacrifice. The idea of sacrifice involves the idea of a readiness to lose something or give up something or suffer in some way for the sake of some other person or some other cause. It is the surrender of something for the sake of others. Now Paul is saying that action of this kind is logical, rational and proper because of the nature of the gospel and the calling we have to it in Christ. So in this context to say: 'I will not do this service because it will need me to sacrifice time, money, convenience or comfort', is in the mind of the Apostle Paul, illogical. Measured by the wisdom of the world of course it would be sensible to take this view. When fidelity brings hardship or sacrifice, the wisdom of the unregenerate mind would say: "Enough – spare thyself". That is what Peter was really saying to Christ when he set his face to the cross. 'No, Lord – spare thyself'. It was spoken in love, but it was illogical if Christ was to accomplish God's will. Jesus said that Peter was speaking as a man who minded the things of men, not the things of God. It was, at that time, a mind mastered by the wisdom of the earth. To the mind of the earth, he spoke sensibly – to the mind of heaven it was satanic.

So in Romans chapter 12 verse 1, sacrificial service is only logical and rational to the mind which is mastered by the principles of the Truth. That is why Paul goes on in verse 2: "and be not conformed [fashioned] to this world". The word "conformed" has in it the idea of material which is malleable and which takes the form of a mould when pressed upon it. It may be soft metal or it may be soft food, but the mould determines the shape. Paul says the world is a mould and we are the material. Be careful he says or you will be moulded. The alternative is to be transformed by the renewing of the mind, so that you may be able to determine what is the good, acceptable and perfect will of God. With this transformed mind a new perspective is realised. Things which to the natural mind appear unreasonable, to the transformed mind become spiritually rational. Sacrificial service to the King's cause becomes desirable instead of illogical. Things become satisfying instead of a nuisance. Surrendering convenience and time become spiritually sane instead of carnally foolish. It is, of course, a matter of perspective, a matter of values. Our lives consist of a list of things we serve or are served by – things which call for time, money, service, loyalty. How important we regard any particular subject is regulated by how we are inside – that is by our state of mind. Somewhere on the list is the Truth. It might be on the top or it might not.

I am speaking now from the point of view of practical service. I know that the Truth is at the top of the list for all of you in one sense, that it is the most important thing in your lives. But forces, transient and eternal, have valid claims upon our lives. It is easy for me to form theories, even scriptural ones, but it is a lot harder to put the theories into practice in the framework of daily living in a form-moulding world. The point I am wanting to stress in the light of Romans chapter 12 is that in these circumstances it is certain that it will involve the making of some form of sacrifice for the Truth's sake. It may not be a very great sacrifice – perhaps some loss of time, making a special effort to come, adjusting your mealtime, giving up some usual arrangement, foregoing some enjoyable pursuit, postponing some relaxation you always insist on.

If you think this sounds very ordinary, I agree, but this is usually how it is. In the normal run of things, living the Truth does not involve some earth-shattering sacrifice which lays bare the soul and pierces the mind and spirit to the very depths. When the voice says: "Go"; that is: "Who will go for us?", it may not mean going very far. It may mean going to visit the sick member, the lonely soul, the isolated, the over-burdened, the bereft. 'Going' may may mean only 'coming' – coming when the ecclesia needs your support and needs it badly. Can I therefore exhort you, my comrades whom I love in the faith, in the light of Romans 12:1, and the call to sacrificial service, when this week you hear the voice which says 'Man, spare thyself', that you resist it at all costs. There are one or two sentences in the chapter which ought to make an especial appeal to us in this context.

**Being Fervent**

Look at verse 11: "Not slothful in business: fervent in spirit: serving the Lord". Are you fervent in your service? Let me just remind you what "fervent" means in the New Testament. It means two things and they are both related to verse 1. First of all it means 'to be stretched out, to be extended, to be fully committed'. Then it means to be 'on the boil' – ardent, intense. God loves people who are on the boil. Jesus said so. He does not like cold people, but what he dislikes most of all are lukewarm people. If you want to argue, the argument is not with me – it is with the man of Nazareth. He said it. We sometimes pray: "O Lord, help us to be well-pleasing in Thy sight". Well, here is the answer – this is the way to please God – He loves it. Be fervent, melt, get hot – not under the collar, but in the heart. Get heartburn. "Did not our heart

176

burn within us while he talked with us?", they said. Get burning hearts in this place for Christ's sake and his cause.

## Giving Liberally

Verse 8 is interesting: "He that giveth, let him do it with simplicity". This is old English – this is William Tyndale. In the RV it says "with liberality". There is no doubt that Paul is not calling you to be simple, but to be bountiful. It does apply to money, of course, but now I want to apply it to all giving – the giving of time, energy, effort, talents. Be prodigal with your giving in service. Be a prodigal son or daughter. Do it gladly, not grudgingly. Do it joyfully, not miserably. Our Recording Brother has put a reminder about this on our notice-board lest we forget it: "The Lord loveth a cheerful giver".

Notice verse 10: "Be kindly affectioned one to another with brotherly love; in honour preferring one another". Or verse 13: "Distributing to the necessity of saints; given to hospitality". Or verse 15: "Rejoice with them that do rejoice, and weep with them that weep". Or verse 16: "Be of the same mind one toward another ...". Part of discharging the debt of sacrificial service is the healing of all wounds, and the ending of all antagonism. Compassion is at the heart of reasonable, rational, spiritual service. And it takes time. Can we make time to be given to hospitality – distributing to our comrades necessities?

I know that life being what it is, sacrificial service is not likely to fail because you do not believe in it, nor because you are indifferent to it, nor because you are self-satisfied, nor because you are flesh-mastered. It will fail through none of those things. Your chief problem is time. I believe never in the history of our community was this so true as today. I honestly believe that if you and I are to be influenced by Romans 12:1 and if we mean business, you and I may well have to take another look at our timetables. The reasons for that cannot now be investigated, but the need for it may well be unassailable.

## Positive Action

One thing I would like to add. One of the ways in which sacrificial service can fail is by our neutrality. It is not that we do anything consciously to hinder the Truth, or against it – but we do not positively do anything to further it. It is by a kind of gentle neglect that the cause can be set back. Please do not be offended, but be willing to ask yourself – are you willing to take some positive action about sacrificial service

177

as a result of the confrontation of this day's consideration forced upon us by the Roman letter?

Let me be open and frank. There are things about our ecclesia which could do with some improvement. I am not being hyper-critical – there are many good things here, and I thank God for them, but we all know that there are some aspects of ecclesial life where improvement is highly desirable. This exhortation is concerned to stress that it can happen, but it will mean some sacrifice. Not earth-shattering, not volcanic, but some small sacrifices may be entailed if we mean business. What Romans 12 is stressing is that this is divinely right. The service of Christ's cause will entail making sacrifices. It is not unnatural; it is what God asks for. It is rational and reasonable. "I beseech you therefore, brethren, by the mercies of God, that ye present your bodies a living sacrifice ... which is your reasonable service."

**Invigorated Endeavour**

Supposing that word took hold of us and inspired us to new endeavour for Christ's cause in this place. You could imagine it – meetings full of all those who are able to come in spite of difficulty. Fervent services, especially on Bible Class nights and Sunday evenings – eager, dedicated, seeking. The giving of talents, time, energy, and effort liberally for love's sake in the service of the ecclesia; whether it be pastoral, preaching, or protecting Christ's cause. Exercising the blessed gift of brotherly kindness, spreading care and dispelling loneliness. More fellowship and increasing hospitality for love's sake. The ecclesia impulsed by love and mastered by the Word of God.

Is this the foolish dream of an old disciple? No, I think not. The Apostle Paul did not think it a foolish dream. He surely was not knowingly calling them to the impossible; nor does his word today. There could be a transformation with sacrificial service. In this solemn time of bread-breaking when we dwell intensively upon the sacrifice of our saviour, there is not a better moment to resolve upon a new act of dedication – a new intention to make our service full-hearted and love-mastered. Let us be done with any neutrality. Let us rewrite the list of priorities; let us look penetratingly at the timetable. Let our lives be spiritually logical in the truest sense. The New Testament writers are continually saying that we ought to be influenced in our discipleship by the realisation of what Christ has done for us. His love ought to have a practical effect upon our lives. Since he gave everything, can we be partial and tardy? I must leave it with you now:

"Ye know the grace of our Lord Jesus Christ, that, though he was rich, yet for your sakes he became poor."

God grant you may feel it to be true.

# 30

## "ALL THINGS ARE LAWFUL"
### (1 CORINTHIANS 6)

THERE is a statement by Paul in this letter to Corinth that raises some very practical issues. The thoughts for our exhortation are based on having a look at this passage:

"All things are lawful unto me, but all things are not expedient: all things are lawful for me, but I will not be brought under the power of any." (1 Corinthians 6:12)

It is clear what Paul is saying. There are some things which are perfectly legal or lawful, that do not violate the law of Christ and we are free to do them lawfully, but that freedom must be qualified by the question, 'Are they expedient?' That word 'expedient' has changed its meaning since the days of Queen Elisabeth I. Today it means the thing that pays respect to practicalities without too much reference to principle. In the days of Tyndale and Wycliffe it meant something different. It meant making progress on a journey. It was a word taken from the King's highway. It was a word used by travellers. You will notice in the centre of the word a syllable *ped* – ex-*ped*-ient and you will know that *ped* has to do with the feet. A pedal is a lever moved by the foot. A pedestrian is someone who moves on their feet. Pedicure is cosmetic treatment of the feet. So expedient means going forward on the feet – making progress on the journey. Paul is saying when you exercise your Christian liberty you have always to ask whether it will make for progress or hinder progress. There is one other reference we must make to illuminate this passage. It is in 1 Corinthians 10:23: "All things are lawful for me, but not all things are expedient: all things are lawful for me, but all things edify not".

To "edify" is a word from the vocabulary of the master builder. Mark the resemblance between "edify" and "edifice". So Paul is saying that not all things build up. Here then is the complete qualification of liberty – will the things we do make progress and build up? The point I want now to stress is this – that whilst this principle has an individual and personal application, that is, the things we do should always

180

help our own progress and build up our own character, it so happens that in 1 Corinthians 10 the context is pre-eminently to do with our relationship with the ecclesia. The very next verse goes like this: "Let no man seek his own, but every man another's wealth". This is the test of ecclesial relationship. We must always ask ourselves how what we do and how we act will affect our brethren and sisters. But notice something particularly. Romans 14:15 says: "Destroy not him [thy brother] with thy meat, for whom Christ died". That says simply to be careful not to destroy your brother with the exercise of your liberty; but the Corinthian passage goes beyond this. In the first Corinthian letter Paul is saying that the thing which is lawful becomes unlawful if it does not actually build up my brother. When you ponder the application of this principle it becomes very solemn indeed. Put simply it means that when we act and when we speak and when we serve, the predominating motive ought to be that it will actually enable others to make progress in the faith and build up strength and faithfulness in the life of the ecclesia.

Can I just detain you for a moment on another word? "All things are lawful ..." – "all things". The word the Apostle used is the Greek word *panta* and it is simply the plural form of the Greek word for "all". But it is very inclusive. It really means all things. Remember another place where he uses the word like this: "All things are yours; whether Paul, or Apollos, or Cephas, or the world, or life, or death, or things present, or things to come" (1 Corinthians 3:21,22). All the forces of the world, or the forces of life are yours – all things.

Then the word "lawful". The best way to understand it is to say that it is the very opposite of being in prison. It means to be free and unfettered. There are no limitations, no constrictions. But of course it is not the last word, for he goes on: "And ye are Christ's; and Christ is God's" (verse 23). It means that the law and love of Christ is over the freedom of man to use all things. The last word is the Christ who reigns over all things. Then there is something else.

In 1 Corinthians 2:15 we read this: "He that is spiritual judgeth all things". This tells us that he who is pursuing the spiritual life has to use his discernment about all things. That is, he does not take them promiscuously but with discernment. In the margin it says: "with close examination".

So with these ideas in mind we come back to our first reference in 1 Corinthians 6. It means that whilst all things in the universe of God are lawful for the disciple, he must use them discerningly with one certain motivation – that their use must never harm the ecclesia of Christ. Rather, they must, wherever possible, build it up and enable it to progress towards perfection. And by the ecclesia of Christ we mean God's other children, sharing the same hope and having a common faith.

Your reaction I think, if you told it openly, is that it is asking too much. Some people would say it is outrageous. A good theory – but in practice not practicable. To have to apply this test for all things we do and say, is far too involved. So this is what the remainder of this exhortation is about – to examine how we can best apply the principle on a reasonable and sensible level.

## Applying the Principle

For help I now turn to Paul's letter to the Ephesians: "Giving thanks always for all things unto God and the Father in the name of our Lord Jesus Christ; submitting yourselves one to another in the fear of God" (5:20,21). You may be interested to know that Brother John Carter in his book on the Ephesian letter argues that, taking it as it stands, it is impossible for everyone to be subject to everyone else. That is the concept does need interpretation. Think of the word "subject". It means "submit to". So being subject to one another on a sensible level means placing ourselves at the disposal of our brethren and sisters in order that they may be helped forward and encouraged in the faith – for love's sake.

The same thought is found in Hebrews 10:24: "And let us consider one another to provoke unto love and to good works". In the New English Bible it goes: "We ought to see how each of us may best arouse others to love and active goodness". Every disciple is an individual and in a certain sense unique. What provokes one may not provoke another. What is a help to one may not be a help to another. So we ought to see, said the Hebrew man, how best to accomplish the right provocation in each case. It means bringing our time and energy into subjection to the particular and peculiar needs of our brethren and sisters. Accommodating our skill, our effort and our compassion to their need and their character. Being subject to the problems, burdens and hardships of our comrades in the faith. Making ourselves available and amenable. And an important thing is to seek to create in others that confidence that we are available and we are amenable. Let me illustrate.

The other day I was in difficulty – suddenly I needed help. As it happened those who I would not have hesitated to ask were all away on holiday. I went down the list but I was too reluctant to ask anyone else – I felt I could not put them to the trouble. You may say that was my fault and you are right; it was lack of loving confidence in my brethren and sisters. But perhaps it is your fault to some extent that I lack that confidence.

The spirit of this attempt to be in subjection to the needs of others is revealed in a sentence as we saw earlier: "Let no man seek his own but each his neighbour's good". Is there anything more outrageous than that? Not to seek our own good, not to be preoccupied with that – forget that – seek the good of others. It is expanded at the end of the chapter like this: "Even as I please all men in all things, not seeking mine own profit, but the profit of many, that they may be saved" (1 Corinthians 10:33).

I was looking here so that I could make the principle more reasonable and it seems that I am making it more difficult. "Not seeking mine own profit". That is what most of us are doing most of the time. It looks as though, if we mean business, it is not likely to be easy. It is fairly easy to subject our compassion to the needs of those whom we like and who we relate to, but the essential issue of the exhortation is that it is one to another without distinction. This is what the Lord meant perhaps by the word "least" when he spoke of "The least of these my brethren".

Think what it means on another level. It may mean the submerging of our personal preferences for the sake of the common good. They may be lawful but not expedient. Strong opinions which to us are valuable and right – but we cannot enforce them on others if they do not share them.

Most of us have them, but it is no good saying – 'This is what I feel and if you do not agree then I shall not come'. Or, 'If you do not submit to my view I shall go elsewhere'. Unless it is something of serious principle then I think such an attitude would not be in harmony with 1 Corinthians 6 and Ephesians 5. In a right and loving way we are entitled to seek to bring others to our point of view. The accepted means are persuasion and experiment – never in hobnail boots. Being in subjection to one another calls for humility, and a spirit of self-abnegation. It requires a recognition that, at our best, we are unprofitable servants and that, anyway, what matters is the commonwealth – the profit of the many, not the exaltation of the few. Self-interest is a powerful force but in the Christian life it has a low place. Think of those 300 souls in Judges chapter 7 who lapped from the stream and were chosen by God to defeat the oppression of the Midianites. God chose them because at the lapping at the water they revealed that they drank not just for themselves but for the common good – ready for battle at any moment. Put simply, some 9,700 drank for themselves; the others, the 300, drank for the commonwealth. They subjected themselves to the discipline for the good of all, the profit of the many.

The one word which perhaps expresses the spirit of it best is the word "cooperation". I know it sounds old hat, but notwithstanding it is true. Cooperation in love. Of course sometimes confrontation is necessary. When evil assaults the ecclesia it has to be confronted, defied and overcome. But in the normal duty of Christian life, mostly the work of Christ in the ecclesia is done by cooperation in love. The spirit of subjection in the ecclesia is the spirit which holds together in balance and in proportion all the varying and multifarious forces which are manifest in the saints and which by subjection are concentrated into three great qualities of the Truth – namely: *faith*, *fervour* and *fidelity*. I commend these words to you at the end of this exhortation and urge you to make them the master principles of your discipleship.

So on a practical level then, here are some thoughts on how to operate the principle that all things are lawful but not all things are expedient, and how to bring ourselves into subjection one to another. If you have been overbearing, then give it up and make your self subject to the commonwealth. If you have been opting out of service, then give it up and get into harness and do your solemn duty for love's sake. If you have been uncaring for the needs and feelings of your brethren and sisters, then give it up and put yourself at the disposal of your comrades in the faith. If you have been proud and touchy then give it up and seek to be humble and meek. Pardon me for speaking frankly but this subject has no place for vague generalities.

One last thing – notice that the Apostle adds a phrase to his exhortation for subjection one to another in these words: "in the fear of God". Why did he do that – he does not mention it with other commands? This, I think, is the reason. This matter of mutual subjection has to do with the development of the ecclesia. Ultimately he will present it without spot and without blemish. Those who impede and harm that process must be under his censure. In this very letter to Corinth these words are there in chapter 3. "If any man destroy the temple of God, him shall God destroy; for the temple of God is holy, which temple ye are" (verse 17). Those words should teach us that this matter of subjection is a very solemn thing and one of the awful duties of discipleship.

So in this solemn moment of bread breaking let us resolve that we shall do all we can to advance his ecclesia along the path of progress. And is there a better moment to think on it than when we remember what he has done for us for love's sake?

# 31

## THE EFFECT OF THE ATONEMENT
## ON BELIEVERS
### (TITUS 2)

THE subject of this little exhortation has been provoked by one sentence in Titus chapter 2:

"For the grace of God that bringeth salvation hath appeared to all men, teaching us that, denying ungodliness and worldly lusts, we should live soberly, righteously, and godly, in this present world." (verse 1)

Notice what it is saying – that the atonement, that is the sacrifice of Christ for our redemption, ought to have a practical effect upon our lives. "The grace of God that bringeth salvation hath appeared". That is what we have come to remember. The grace has been manifested to teach us how to live in this present age. So the recollection of the sacrifice of the redeemer ought to have a practical effect upon our lives.

Almost always when the New Testament writers refer to the atonement, it is in the context of changing our way of life. Of course here and there we find a theological reference to it (e.g. Romans 3:23) – but mainly it is associated with this idea of teaching us how to live. Let me give you two other examples:

"Forasmuch then as Christ has suffered for us in the flesh, arm yourselves with the same mind ... that he [we] should no longer live the rest of his [our] time in the flesh to the lusts of men, but to the will of God." (1 Peter 4:1,2)

"For the love of Christ constraineth us; because we thus judge, that if one died for all, then were all dead. And that he died for all, that they which live should not henceforth live unto themselves, but unto him which died for them, and rose again." (2 Corinthians 5:14,15)

In a modern version it is even clearer:

"It is the love of Christ which compels us ... and his purpose in dying for all, was that men while still in life, should cease to live for themselves and should live for him, who for their sakes died and was raised to life".

186

This is just a selection, but it is all through the New Testament. The cross of Christ ought to have a practical effect upon our lives. Of course you would expect this to be true, in the great and important things about the faith – in times when the faith is being assaulted and believers have to take a stand and hold the line and be counted.

## Application in Everyday Things

But here is a startling thing. The New Testament writers apply this principle in the ordinary and commonplace things of life. In the everyday things the love of Christ and his sacrifice ought to have an effect upon how we live; and even in the commonplace things. Listen:

"Husbands, love your wives, even as Christ also loved the church, and gave himself for it."     (Ephesians 5:25)

The love of a married couple is excellent, but face it – commonplace – yet Paul says it is fashioned by the cross.

Take industrial relations:

"Masters ... forbear threatening: knowing that your Master also is in heaven."     (Ephesians 6:9)

"Servants to be obedient unto their own masters ... in all things that they may adorn the doctrine of God our saviour."     (Titus 2:9,10)

Here is a wonderful thing – the fact that Christ died on the cross and now sits on the throne of universal empire in heaven justifies Paul in giving a word of advice to employers and employees about industrial relations.

Of course one of the best examples is in 2 Corinthians 8. This is about one of the most commonplace things possible – money: the matter of a collection for the poor saints in Jerusalem. Some people think money must be outside the realm of the spiritual, but notice this:

"As ye abound in every thing, in faith, and utterance, and knowledge, and in all diligence, and in your love to us, see that ye abound in this grace also."     (verse 7)

"This grace" is giving money; "this grace" is being generous with your substance. Now let us be careful to notice the reason why the Corinthians should be generous with their money.

"For ye know the grace of our Lord Jesus Christ, that though he was rich, yet for your sakes he became poor, that ye through his poverty might be rich."     (verse 9)

So there it is — the ordinary things of daily life of discipleship are related to the noblest doctrines of the faith.

187

It means that our daily lives can be influenced by that life which was won out of death by the sacrifice of the Son of God. Another example is in 1 Corinthians 15, the famous chapter on resurrection. Remember how it ends:

"O death, where is thy sting? O grave, where is thy victory? The sting of death is sin; and the strength of sin is the law. But thanks be to God, which giveth us the victory through our Lord Jesus Christ. Therefore, my beloved brethren, be ye stedfast, unmoveable, always abounding in the work of the Lord, forasmuch as ye know that your labour is not in vain in the Lord. Now concerning the collection for the saints ... "  (15:55–16:1)

The ordinary thing like a collection is related purposely to one of the great doctrines of salvation. At the risk of wearying you I stress again, that the love of Christ in the one great atoning act of redemption ought to be changing us daily and in the things which are commonplace and ordinary. Your home life, your working life, your leisure and your marriage, your career, should all be affected by the sacrifice of this one lonely man for those who are sin-stricken and death-bound. The love of Christ constraineth us ...

## Remembering the Crucifixion

Now then, the question which confronts us all is – How can we ensure that this becomes true for us personally? For instance – this service of remembrance which we engage in each Sunday – to what extent is it having an effect upon our daily lives? Are we more like Christ today than say this time last year? Is there anything we can do which will advance the effect of this remembrance upon our characters? It is the most graphic method we have of remembering the cross and its victim. How can we ensure that doing it so regularly and being so familiar with it week after week, it does not become just a performance but rather has an incisive effect upon us? I heard the case once of a girl of seventeen who read the gospel of Matthew for the first time and when shc came to the part which described the arrest and crucifixion of Jesus she broke down and wept. That could not happen to us today. I am not criticising you – it is a matter of fact. We have become so familiar with it that the first dramatic impact has been lost. The familiarity has to some extent dulled our sensitivity. We know it so well, we have heard it so often. It cannot be helped.

But I have a theory which I want to put to you which may help us to recapture something of the first impact which we have lost and thereby increase the power of its effect upon us.

The idea is fixed in one short sentence of the Apostle Paul in Galatians:

"I live by the faith of the Son of God, who loved me, and gave himself for me." (2:20)

The thing to notice is the personal appreciation of Paul – that in some way Christ died for him personally. It is easy to say this but difficult to believe, because it means acknowledging that it was because of my sin that this man died. My sin condemned him. My sin crushed him and bruised him. Immediately there is a strong tendency to say that if we had been there it would not have happened. We had no hand in it. It was the Pharisees who sought to kill him. It was Caiaphas who condemned him; it was Pilate who was weak and allowed him to be executed. Some unknown Roman soldier drove in the nails. Peter denied him; the apostles forsook him and fled. We cannot be involved in the complicity of guilt for this man's suffering and death.

Yet the Bible insists that in some way it was the sins of the world which brought this man to his death. In some way he felt the weight of all sins as he was dying. "Behold the Lamb of God, which taketh away the sin of the world". How did he feel the weight of the world's sin? There is a theory to explain this and it goes thus. That when he was dying on the cross there passed before his consciousness all the sins of the world in a moment of time. Every crime of every criminal, every white lie of every little child; every unholy thought that ever passed through a human heart – they all passed before him as he was gasping out his life an the tree. If you find that a satisfying explanation of how he bore the world's sin – so be it. But it does not satisfy me.

**Sin became Exceedingly Sinful**

There is another thought to ponder. These men who were involved in the great drama – the scribes, the Pharisees, the priests, Caiphas, Pilate, the Romans – they were simply representatives of the race. Really the forces that crushed him were envy, jealousy, selfishness, pride. It was sin in all its forms which came against him. Sin became exceedingly sinful. These men were but enlargements of all men, insofar that we have all been jealous, envious, selfish, willing to countenance the downfall of another to save ourselves. To that extent we have partaken of the forces which came against him. In their envy was our envy; in their jealousy was our jealousy; in their pride was our pride. This is how he felt the weight of our sins – yours and mine. If all other men had been perfect except us, he would have had to die for our

189

sakes; so we cannot claim to be exempt from the responsibility.

Of course our first reaction is to say we never wanted him to die. But when we sin, whether we wanted him to die or not, we have made it unavoidable. It was sin that did it and we are part of it. This is how the Apostle John sees it. Sin for him is one connected world principle, of which all have partaken. If only we can come to conceive that our sin caused his death, the appreciation will be intensified. But it is not easy. When things become personal they become real. Let me illustrate. If tonight in the address I say that all men are sinners and that includes you – you will not be offended, you will not feel that I have insulted you. You will accept it without turning a hair. But suppose when the meeting is over I come up to one of you and accuse you of a specific sin – then the situation will be quite different. You may well be offended and may feel inclined to tell me to mind my own business. Do you see the difference? If you are a sinner amongst a few million other sinners it means very little at all, but if you are a lone sinner, a real sinner, then the situation is quite different. It has moved from the universal to the personal, and it becomes real. So it is with the death of the Son of God. To say he bore the sins of the world we can accept and not be worried; but to say and admit that it was my sin which condemned him and brought about his death is very different.

If we can only face it – *we* bear a responsibility for his death. I know what we want to do because I want to do it myself. We want to say that it is unreal. We were not there and we had nothing to do with it. It is 2,000 years ago and it was not we who did it. That is true, but think of this: in Matthew 23 in response to the accusations of Jesus, the scribes and Pharisees said: "If we had been in the days of our fathers, we would not have been partakers with them in the blood of the prophets" (verse 30). And Jesus said that nevertheless they were guilty because they manifested the same spirit as their fathers. I use it only as an illustration to prove that distance and time cannot invalidate the principle.

I repeat, these men were but enlargements of all men. He came to fight sin and master it and it was sin that fought against him. Whether it was their's or ours – it was sin that rose up to oppose him. As the New Testament says: "He put away sin by the sacrifice of himself". So there it is – if only we can think of it in this personal way. In some way he did it for me. He bore my sin. By his stripes I have been healed. He loved me and gave himself for me. I am saying if we can only feel it in this personal way it must intensify the effect upon our lives. The love will be even more constraining.

So let us draw near with a true heart in full assurance of faith and let us thank God solemnly that the provision has been made for our cleansing from sin. The guilt can be removed altogether, the accusation is cancelled.

In a moment, in the twinkling of an eye, as swift as lightning and even swifter – upon the repentant soul is pronounced the verdict of the guiltless. Is there anything better than this? The relief, the burden lifted, the slate clean; the old sin obliterated; the iniquity covered.

What the New Testament writers are saying is this. When it happens it ought to have an effect upon us; it ought to be changing us; it ought to work an amendment in our living.

So I leave you where we started, in Titus 2:

"For the grace of God that bringeth salvation hath appeared to all men, teaching us that, denying ungodliness and worldly lusts, we should live soberly, righteously, and godly, in this present world ..."

He gave himself for us that he might redeem us from all iniquity and purify unto himself a peculiar people, zealous of good works. God grant that in this solemn moment of bread breaking you feel it to be true.

# 32

## THE PRIESTHOOD OF JESUS CHRIST
### (HEBREWS 3–10)

THINK what a priest is. According to the Bible the priest is a mediator, one who stands in between; to use an old Bible word – a daysman. The Bible reveals that the priestly office is therefore mediatorial, and that its function is twofold. First of all intercessory and then benedictory. As an intercessor, the priest stands in the presence of God pleading the cause of men and then in the presence of men pleading the cause of God. Then in the function of benediction the priest stands in the presence of men pronouncing the blessings from God and then in the presence of God offering the praises of men.

We can observe this in practice in the ritual of Hebrew religious life. A Hebrew man or woman conscious of sin, comes to the priest with an offering of an animal to make an atonement and to find pardon. The sin of the person is in symbol transferred to the animal and the animal is slain.

In the slaying there is a recognition that this is what the sin deserves – the price is paid and the sinner is set free. The animal, the representative has borne the penalty. Upon this the priest in the name of God is able to pronounce the blessing and the pardon. Of course it is highly symbolic but in a very real way figures the facts. Men are sinners; in their sinful condition they cannot come into the presence of a righteous God who is pure and undefiled. To overcome this impediment God set up the system of the priesthood, where specially appointed men act as intermediaries – as intercessors. Because God is holy, they must be holy, and in the Hebrew ritual the emblems of their ceremonial holiness was strictly enforced. They must come in the way prescribed, properly cleansed, in the correct vestments, in careful obedience to the pattern revealed. All these things intend to stress the holiness of the God in Whose presence they ministered, and on Whose behalf they pronounced judgement and blessing.

We must stress that this system of mediating priesthood was right at the centre of Hebrew national life. It represented as its final responsibility the utter necessity of the strictest observance of the law of God. The priest is the final exemplar of holiness. He is the measurement of faithfulness to the Lord of Israel and the abandonment of individual souls to the will of God. Putting it succinctly, the priesthood was created for the nation. It was, so to speak, the fount of honour, the centre of purity, the aggregation of holiness. Just how important this was may be gathered from a chapter in the Old Testament. I bring you to Leviticus chapter 10:

> "And Nadab and Abihu, the sons of Aaron, took either of them his censer, and put fire therein, and put incense thereon, and offered strange fire before the LORD, which he commanded them not. And there went out fire from the LORD, and devoured them, and they died before the LORD. Then Moses said unto Aaron, This is it that the LORD spake, saying, I will be sanctified in them that come nigh me and before all people I will be glorified. And Aaron held his peace." (verses 1–3)

If anyone should think it shocking that the judgement of God fell so summarily upon two disobedient priests, remember what I have said already about the position of the priesthood in the life of the Hebrew people. A disobedient priesthood means a corrupted nation. Historically this is what happened. Eventually the priesthood was corrupted and the nation as a consequence degenerated, issuing finally in the rejection of its Messiah – the death of that Messiah being engineered and enforced by the priests.

Exactly what these two priests did is not clear. The record says they offered strange fire. In Leviticus 16 there are clear directions about entering into the holy place to burn incense:

> "And Aaron ... shall take a censer full of burning coals of fire from off the altar before the LORD, and his hands full of sweet incense beaten small, and bring it within the veil." (verses 11,12)

It looks as though Nadab and Abihu placed in their censer fire from some other source than the altar of the Lord. If it be asked: "Why on earth did they do it?", then there is in the story a dark hint. Immediately after this act of disobedience it says: "The LORD spake unto Aaron, saying, Do not drink wine nor strong drink, thou, nor thy sons with thee, when ye go into the tabernacle of the congregation, lest ye die; it shall be a statute for ever" (Leviticus 10:8,9). It looks as though when these two priests went into the holy place they were drunk. Whatever the cause, the holiness of God was violated, His being was not sanctified, His will was ignored, God was dethroned. It shows how important and how significant was the priesthood in the life of the Hebrew people and it reveals how God regarded it. The priest is essential in the relationship between men and God.

## Two Functions of the Priest

Earlier we mentioned the two functions of the priest – as an intercessor and then as a pronouncer of blessing. A good example of this is to be found in Numbers 6. The early part of the chapter, indeed most of it, is about the offering of sacrifice. It is true that it is about a special kind of person. It applies to the Nazarite, who dedicated himself to God in a very special way, but the principles are true of all Hebrews.

"This is the law of the Nazarite, when the days of his separation are fulfilled ... he shall offer his offering unto the LORD ... And the priest shall bring them before the LORD, and shall offer his sin offering, and his burnt offering: and he shall offer the ram for a sacrifice of peace offerings unto the LORD." ( verse 13–17)

Now notice that once the sacrifice had been made, once the offerings had been presented, there followed the benediction by Aaron:

"The LORD bless thee, and keep thee: the LORD make his face to shine upon thee, and be gracious unto thee: the LORD lift up his countenance upon thee, and give thee peace." (verse 24)

I stress again this was a distinct part of Hebrew worship through the priesthood. In Leviticus chapter 9 verse 22 we read: "And Aaron lifted up his hand toward the people, and blessed them, and came down from offering of the sin offering, and the burnt offering, and peace offerings". This was the process – benediction followed the presentation of the offerings. So it was in Numbers chapter 6. This was the Hebrew priesthood. Intercessory and benedictory. The mediator, the daysman, the advocate – instituted by God for His people.

## Replacing a Failed Priesthood

Now we come to the issue. The day came when the Hebrew priesthood ended. It ended because, as I said before, it became corrupt, and ultimately rejected and executed the Messiah. The judgement of God came upon the nation, the people were captured by the Romans in AD 70, the temple was destroyed, and eventually the Jews were scattered through the world. This is exactly as the Messiah predicted and forecast. I bring you to Matthew chapter 21. Notice verse

23. Jesus is speaking to the chief priests and the elders of the nation:

"And when he [Jesus] was come into the temple, the chief priests and the elders of the people came unto him as he was teaching."

Next look at verse 42:

"Jesus saith unto them [the chief priests and the elders], Did ye never read in the scriptures, The stone which the builders rejected, the same is become the head of the corner: this is the Lord's doing, and it is marvellous in our eyes? Therefore say I unto you, The kingdom of God shall be taken from you, and given to a nation bringing forth the fruits thereof".

That is precisely what happened. The kingdom of God focussed in the Hebrew nation was to be taken from them and given to another nation that was living in accordance with the kingdom principles.

If it be asked who and what was that new nation, the Apostle Peter gives the answer. Writing to some of his friends, he said:

"But ye are a chosen generation, a royal priesthood, an holy nation, a peculiar people; that ye should show forth the praises of him who hath called you out of darkness into his marvellous light."                    (1 Peter 2:9)

There is no need for any bush-beating. Believers in the gospel of Jesus Christ are the new nation. They are the new people of God. They were those who formed the church of the New Testament, for it was those to whom Peter sent his word. But here is something to understand for sure. The principles of approach to God have not changed. He still will be sanctified in them that draw near to Him. That is to say there is still need for a daysman, a mediator, an advocate. Listen to this from the Apostle Paul to Timothy: "For there is one God, and one mediator between God and men, the man Christ Jesus" (1 Timothy 2:5).

One of the weaknesses of the Hebrew priesthood was that it was made of mortal and corruptible human beings. They died, they were imperfect, they were capable of failure. The writer of the Hebrew letter is stressing this very point – let us drop in on his argument in Hebrews chapter 7:

"And they truly were many priests, because they were not suffered to continue by reason of death: but this man, because he continueth ever, hath an unchangeable priesthood. Wherefore he is able to save them to the

195

uttermost that come unto God by him, seeing he ever
liveth to make intercession for them." (verses 23–25)

Notice how the Hebrew man goes on:

"'For such an high priest became us, who is holy,
harmless, undefiled, separate from sinners, and made
higher than the heavens; who needeth not daily, as those
high priests, to offer up sacrifice first for his own sins, and
then for the people's: for this he did once, when he offered
up himself. For the law maketh men high priests which
have infirmity; but the word of the oath, which was since
the law, maketh the Son, who is consecrated for ever
more." (verses 26–28)

Yes, I know the old English of Tyndale here is not easy, but
in modern parlance the Hebrew man is saying that the new
high priest, Jesus Christ himself, does not have the
weaknesses of the high priests of Israel. First he is
essentially holy without any fear of pollution at all; then he
is undefiled with no possibility of corruption of any kind; then
he is immortal with no possibility of death interfering with
his priestly ministry; then he does not have to offer daily
some animal sacrifice as they did, but he offered himself once
for all time. As the great sacrifice in the fight against sin, he
met it face to face and front to front. He met it and overcame
it and destroyed it in himself. To use words from Hebrews 9:
He "put away sin by the sacrifice of himself".

Those animal sacrifices that we have seen in the Old
Testament were but types and shadows of the one great
sacrifice which was to be made eventually by the Son of God
himself in the one great atoning act of love. There is a
sentence in this Hebrew letter which enforces this point
strongly:

"For if the blood of bulls and of goats, and the ashes of
an heifer sprinkling the unclean, sanctifieth to the
purifying of the flesh: how much more shall the blood of
Christ, who through the eternal spirit offered himself
without spot to God, purge your conscience from dead
works to serve the living God?" (9:13,14)

The Hebrew man is telling us just how much greater is the
high priest in Jesus Christ the Saviour. Through that great
redeeming sacrifice, he now mediates on the light-girdled
throne of his Father in heaven, on behalf of all who come to
him in faith. He is the high priest of the universe. This is
what the Hebrew man means by "made higher than the
heavens". God is saying to all men everywhere that in this

196

one man alone – His beloved Son, there is salvation. The Son's exaltation proclaims that.

What I invite you to do now is to return to a sentence in Hebrews chapter 7 because there we have in the priesthood of Christ the very essence of the gospel:

"But this man, because he continueth ever, hath an unchangeable priesthood. Wherefore he is able to save them to the uttermost that come unto God by him, seeing he ever liveth to make intercession for them."

(verses 24,25)

Please dwell with me on the word "uttermost". I want to stress that it does not refer to the quality of the salvation. There are no degrees in being saved. It is one thing or the other – you are either saved or not saved. If you will forgive the analogy, it is like being pregnant. You are either pregnant or not. You cannot be a little bit pregnant. So is salvation. No – the word uttermost refers to the condition out of which the sinner is being saved. It means to the very farthest range of isolation and separation. It means there is no failure so deep, no sin so dark, no pollution so awful, no rebellion so strident – but if we will turn to God through the high priest then He will save to the uttermost. It means we may come as we are with the pollution upon us, with the corruption about us, in the very midst of our failure – we may come and find grace and pardon and healing and at last salvation and the kingdom of God.

## The LORD Bless Thee

Come back to Numbers chapter 6, and the priestly benediction. Let us think of it again in the light of what we have discovered about the priesthood of Jesus Christ. Remember the first stanza: "The LORD bless thee and keep thee". When the Apostle Paul came to write his great Ephesian letter he opened it with this doxology: "Blessed be the God and Father of our Lord Jesus Christ, who hath blessed us with all spiritual blessings". The man of Nazareth once said: "Come unto me, all ye that labour and are heavy laden, and I will give you rest". Those words have affected profoundly many thousands of disciples because they are profound words. Many a weary head has found rest, many a troubled heart has found succour, many a broken soul has found healing, from resting on that promise. It is the counterpart of the priestly benediction: "The LORD bless thee and keep thee". Remember it goes on: "The LORD make his face to shine upon thee: and be gracious unto thee".

197

The next of kin of the man of Nazareth once said about him after they had companied with him for three-and-a-half years that he was "full of grace and truth". They wondered at the gracious words that proceeded out of his mouth. The face of God became luminous through Jesus Christ for those who have lost their sense of His nearness and His compassion. In the face of the Son we have the clear shining of the face of the Father. Then this: "The LORD lift up his countenance upon thee, and give thee peace". Turn to the word of Jesus and remember some of the final words to those who were his friends and his servants: "'Peace I leave with you, my peace I give unto you". He means: 'My peace is your peace'. It means he stands between his disciples and all the forces which assault peace and security.

The promise of his coming and his kingdom give peace to the soul in the day of frightfulness. A man may lay himself down to rest and not be afraid. Death is but a quiet sleeping-chamber awaiting the day of awakening at the resurrection. A man may rise and take his breakfast and do his duty and know he is under the providential care of God. So he is at peace. This Hebrew man in the 13th chapter of this great letter has recorded it for our satisfaction.

God has said: "I will never leave thee, nor forsake thee, so that we may boldly say, The Lord is my helper, and I will not fear what man shall do unto me" (Hebrews 13:5,6). That is the source of peace, and it can give us abiding quietness and unruffled calm if we trust in its promise.

So let us not mistake it – the noblest meaning of the priestly benediction of Numbers chapter 6 is fulfilled superlatively in this man of the seamless robe, the Lord Jesus Christ. There is one last thing to be said about the priesthood of Jesus Christ and it is perhaps the noblest thing of all. The passage is in Hebrews chapter 4:

> "Seeing then that we have a great high priest, that is passed into the heavens, Jesus the Son of God, let us hold fast our profession. For we have not a high priest which cannot be touched with the feeling of our infirmities; but was in all points tempted like as we are, yet without sin. Let us therefore come boldly unto the throne of grace, that we may obtain mercy, and find grace to help in time of need." (verse 14–16)

Notice this – he has been touched with the feeling of our infirmities. It means he is susceptible; he know our plight; he is aware of our predicament; he feels for our weakness; he knows the meaning of temptation. I leave it with you. Is there a better reason now for trusting in his mediation? So wherever we are, let us come with our failure and our wounds and our bruises and our doubts. Let us believe his gospel and let us worship at his altar; let us find succour at the place of mediation. Amid the restlessness of this fretful age let us find peace and rest. Let the high priest's promise become our experience.

# 33

## THE ONE OFFERING
### (HEBREWS 10)

As a beginning today think of a great sentence at the start of this Hebrew letter: "God, who who at sundry times and in divers manners spake in times past unto the fathers by the prophets, hath in these last days spoken unto us by his Son" (Hebrews 1:1,2).

Part of the revelation to the fathers was to make known to the people of God the means He had devised to heal the breach between man and his Creator. Here was revealed the way to restore fellowship, to enable men to fulfil the responsibility of co-operating with God in His great purpose with the world.

It means that the first and the final message of God's revelation is redemption. The Bible has been written, not for the perfect, but for sinning men. The Bible has been written because the birthright has been lost and the presence of the Almighty One has been denied through sin. We must know in our deepest heart that what God did was the best and only way for the breach to be healed. And it means that what God has devised He has revealed to us in His word.

The first stage of the revelation was to the fathers – the final stage is to us. The first stage was by suggestion, prediction, illustration – all in the splendid ritual of the Hebrew people: especially in the offerings as they foreshadowed the way of approach to God by sinning men. This foreshadowing revealed a way of complete dedication by a method of sacrifice and propitiation – which resulted in a gift from God, that is pardon and atonement.

Now as you know well, in that pictorial system there were five offerings – the burnt offering, the meal offering, the peace offering, the sin offering and the trespass offering.

Those five offerings can be divided into two groups. The first includes three offerings – the burnt offering, the meal offering, and the peace offering. The burnt offering portrayed the dedication of the entire life to God; the meal offering symbolised the dedication of service to God, and the peace offering revealed the possibility of true fellowship with God resulting from the dedication of life and service portrayed in the burnt offering and the meal offering.

The second group comprises the sin and trespass offerings. The sin offering revealed the necessity for and the method of putting away sin so that man can be brought back into fellowship with God, the birthright restored and intercourse resumed, resulting in co-operation in His great purpose. The trespass offering recognises that sin is damaging, and sinners must seek to repay.

Now you know that the writer of this Hebrew letter declares that these offerings in themselves were not sufficient. By themselves they were not truly efficacious. They had no value in themselves but pointed forward to something profound. They were adumbrations of something magnificently greater. They were but shadows demonstrating as far as they could the reality. In the chapter we have read today there was this sentence: "The law having a shadow of good things to come, and not the very image of the things ..." (Hebrews 10:1). The writer recognised that there can be no dynamic, no saving power in the shadow itself and also that there can be no shadow apart from the substance. Let us not make a mistake – these things of the shadow were infinitely more than just acts of feasting and fasting. They were eloquent evidences of the power and purpose of Yahweh the God of the Hebrews, to be yet more perfectly manifested. You know that the whole argument of this Hebrew writer is that, wonderful as these ancient rituals were, they were fulfilled as far as their deepest and profoundest meaning is concerned in human history in the person and work of the Son of God. We read it today: "For by one offering he hath perfected for ever them that are sanctified" (verse 14). All the five offerings of the shadow were fulfilled in the one offering of the reality. This is the means which God has devised so that he who is banished does not become an outcast from Him.

This exhortation invites you on the basis of what we have read in Hebrews chapter 10 to think once more of the one offering. We are not left to any speculation – notice verses 9 and 10.

"He taketh away the first, that he may establish the second. By the which will we are sanctified through the offering of the body of Jesus Christ once for all."

Then go back a little further and notice that quotation from Psalm 40:

"Sacrifice and offering thou wouldest not, but a body hast thou prepared me: in burnt offerings and sacrifices for sin thou hast had no pleasure." (verses 5,6)

The quotation of the psalm here by the Hebrew man is from the Septuagint version of the Bible, not from the Hebrew version. In the Hebrew version it reads (verse 5): "Sacrifice and offerings thou wouldest not, but mine ears hast thou opened". Did the translators of the Septuagint think that the Hebrew text was wrong? I doubt it because when you think about it carefully, the vital underlying teaching is the same in each case. However, the teaching is not clear if you give to the words "mine ears hast thou opened" the meaning of that ancient rite whereby the servant coming to the doorpost had his ear pierced to demonstrate his fidelity. I believe that in this particular case the underlying thought is to make the ear absolutely attentive in order that the soul may be mastered by the divine will. And I believe that is why the Septuagint version reads "a body didst thou prepare me".

**The Opened Ear**

In that ancient ceremony referred to in Exodus 21:6 when a Hebrew servant refused to leave his master, his master brought him to the doorpost and bored his ear through with an awl and thereafter he was bound to him for good. The point to notice is that the act was performed on a single ear. This is absolutely clear from Exodus 21 and Deuteronomy 15 and it is evident that a single ear was sufficient.

Now the thing to mark is that in Psalm 40 the words are precise:

"Sacrifice and offering thou didst not desire; mine ears hast thou opened; burnt offering and sin offering hast thou not required. Then said I, Lo, I come: in the volume of the book it is written of me; I delight to do thy will, O my God: yea, thy law is within my heart." (verses 6–8)

Without doubt the words are plural: "mine *ears* hast thou opened". So I believe that we are to understand from this, not the piercing of the single ear by the awl, but the opening of the ears to the word and will of God in absolute dedication. The influence of God, so working in the life of Jesus through the opened ears, enabled him to share all that was essentially human while at the same time being separate from sin and from all things which have ruined and spoiled humanity. It means that his body became the instrument of the spirit, yet by reason of his humanity he is infinitely close to us.

By reason of his perfect life he is distanced from us – the man of the centuries – isolated by virtue of his purity and his perfection. His body with all its appetites was never mastered by the appetites. His vision of God was never clouded by any illicit answer to the cry of the body. He was never deflected from the way of rightness by the allurements of the body. He, the child of the eternal spirit, having his ears opened by God to the voice of the spirit, made uninterrupted adjustment of his life to the purity, holiness and righteousness of God. We can be sure that the Septuagint is right, for the Hebrew writer quoted it by the power of the spirit – but it is in harmony with the Hebrew version rightly understood: "A body hast thou prepared ... Mine ears hast thou opened". Part of the prepared body was the opened ears.

## A Living Sacrifice

Come back then to the argument that the one offering fulfilled all the meaning of the offerings of the shadow. Think of the burnt offering – symbolic of the dedication of the entire life to God – the whole devoted to and consumed for one purpose. Think of the meal offering – symbolic of the dedication of service to God, for in that offering men brought that which they themselves had produced, the outcome of their own toil. Think of the peace offering – the symbol of unbroken fellowship with God – resulting from the dedication of life and service to God. As we ponder it we can see that the kindergarten of the old economy found its noblest realisation in the man of Nazareth. On the long pathway of his pilgrimage, the dominant note was that of the dedication of his whole life to God.

Paul says, "present your bodies a living sacrifice" to God. This was the story of Jesus' life. Because his spirit was always yielded to God, his body perpetually expressed the attitude of his spirit. Every journey the body took was a journey God-mastered – every activity the hands undertook was God-inspired; every onlooking of the eye was the outlooking of the divine will.

The body of the Lord was the clear declaration of his spirit – the medium of dedicated and devoted service to his Father. Everything was under the divine authority: "I do nothing of myself ... I speak nothing of my self. What my father gives me that I do; what my Father gives me that I speak". We can see him acting with the divine impulse in the midst of humanity broken and bereft. "Come unto me all ye that labour and are heavy laden, and I will give you rest". We can see him again under the divine impulse on another day looking into the eyes of the false rulers of his people and saying: "Woe unto you, scribes, hypocrites, whited sepulchres, full of dead men's bones".

That was not a spasm of passing human passion – it was the voice of God speaking out of His holiness and His wrath to men who oppressed other men. So he realised the meaning of the peace offering. He was always at peace with God and always in fellowship with God. He linked God with the things of earth – with flowers, with sparrows, with children, and felt that no sanctity was violated and no reverence impaired. So here was the body, prepared in infinite mystery by the power of the Holy Spirit through the womb of the virgin of Nazareth; the perfected and unharmed instrument of the spirit wonderfully adjusted to God at every level. In all the long story of human history has there been anything like it – before or since? "Earth was waiting spent and restless, moved with mingled hope and fear".

## A Man of Sorrows

Think next of the idea of offering. Think of it as a verb. The intention of the offering was symbolised in the sin offering and the trespass offering. Its method was cooperation with God and its purpose, reconciliation of man with God – making peace, or to take the great word of the Old Testament – making atonement. As we look at his life we see the element of sacrifice at every level. He was a man of sorrows and acquainted with grief. I heard a man say once: 'With consummate ease Christ healed the sick'. It is not true – all his life is touched with sacrifice. After the healing of the sick, Matthew adds that it might be fulfilled which was spoken by Isaiah the prophet saying: "Himself took our infirmities and bare our diseases". He felt the continual restlessness of humanity and in his heart a perpetual protest against the things which offend the purpose of God.

Because he was good and pure and true he awakened against himself the forces which were false, polluted and evil. Take sin out of the world and Christ would have known no sorrow. He could have lived a life of perfect peace untroubled by sorrow, undesolated by agony. But here is the mystery – the measure of his perfection was the measure of his pain. All through his life there was this element of sacrifice and finally it was gathered up in the awe-inspiring mystery of the body prepared by God, offered on the tree. All the purpose of God was centred in him and focussed in his life and death. The body prepared by the mystery of the spirit in the maiden's womb – of our very nature, with all our appetites – was the central instrument through which the life of the spirit was manifested. Dare we say it – God was manifested in spite of the flesh. In the light of these facts which defy our full understanding, we have read today: "For by one offering he hath perfected for ever them that are sanctified".

We must remember today that the one offering excludes all human activity because it is insufficient. It excludes all human merit because it is worthless as far as redemption is concerned. It excludes all human intervention because it is impotent. We rejoice today in this memorial when we remember again that the one offering means the restoration of all that is lost. Through it we have cleansing, through it we have access, through it we have reconciliation, through it we have fellowship, through it we have hope of eternal life. It means we need no longer blunder our way through the darkness, we need no longer have to admit the certainty of defeat; it means that we need no longer nurse our fears and succumb to our passions. He will direct; he will energize; he will succour. If this is not true then we have been grossly deceived. We believe it is true; that is why we have come.

**Sanctification**

The condition prescribed for appropriating the promise is sanctification. Sanctification is separation to the will of God. It is made possible by the ministry of the Son. It is to be adjusted to the purpose of God – desiring that His will shall be done in our life, come what may. The perfection begins now – perfect in relationship to God – yet to be perfected in experience of God. The realisation is incomplete but even in its incompleteness it is wonderful. The dwelling of the saints is in the holy place (see Hebrews 10:19). They sit at the table of shewbread and have communion with God. They trim the golden lightstand and stand before the golden altar. They pass into the holiest of all and have fellowship unafraid – because on the mercy seat are the tokens of the one offering whereby the redeemer "hath perfected for ever them that are sanctified". It is amazing and wonderful but let us not presume upon it. Let us not repose our confidence in anything else. Not in our service, though it ought to be even more devoted; not in our preaching, though it ought never to diminish; not in our wisdom, though it be faithful to God's word; not in our cleverness, be it ever so nimble. Only in this one offering is our salvation. Let us perfectly trust it.

Let us answer its demands so that we may realise its promise. Let there be lurking in our heart not one scrap of doubt about its power. Today we have read this "Their sins and their iniquities will I remember no more". So:

"Let us draw near with a true heart in full assurance of faith ... let us hold fast the profession of our faith without wavering; (for he is faithful that promised)".

God grant that in this solemn moment of bread breaking we may feel it to be true.

# 34

## THE WISDOM FROM ABOVE
## (THE TRIAL OF FAITH)
### (JAMES 3,4)

IF we had to select one verse in the epistle of James which pinpointed the character and mission of the writer – which gathered together the salient points of the epistle which is in a sense a microcosm of the whole letter – I think we have read that verse today in James 3:13. "Who is a wise man and endued with knowledge among you? let him shew out of a good conversation his works with meekness of wisdom". It seems evident that certain writers in the Bible were called to specialise in a certain aspect of Christian truth. It was given to John to be peculiarly the Apostle of love. It was given to Paul to reveal that justification by faith is the great active principle by which men are acquited in the sight ot God. And so to James was given a peculiar office – to proclaim the realities of true religion. James' task is to remind us time and time again of the necessity for moral uprightness – the need for spiritual integrity. He speaks to us as a man singularly honest, earnest, real. That is the key word – *real*. No wonder he is called emphatically: "James the Just". So in his letter he is protesting against men having the mere semblances of religion instead of the realities. He is saying in effect – all this talk, talk, talk of religion – in the name of God give us the realities.

### Martin Luther

I heard it said once that you can sometimes discover what a person is really like by taking a good look at those who are his enemies. And within limits this is true. If you take certain characters in the Bible and then look at their enemies, it does throw light on the kind of people they were themselves. It would of course be especially true in the case of Jesus. What is true of people is also in a certain sense true of the Bible – and particular parts of the Bible. It happens to be especially true of this letter of James. It is true in this case that there was one person who was particularly disparaging and antagonistic towards this letter and that person was Martin Luther. He called it an epistle of straw. When we know why, it throws light on the nature of James' letter. Martin Luther was a man who suffered from a guilt complex. In the early days of his life when he was an undergraduate at Erfurt University and later on, when he became a Catholic priest, he was constantly falling into fits of depression and despair because of his failure to keep the rules and commandments which his particular way of life demanded. He was very deeply conscious of his continual failure until it became for him a great burden which crushed him and mastered him. The more he tried to do good works the more conscious he was that they were inadequate and impoverished in the sight of God. The more he tried to measure up to the standard he saw in Christ Jesus, the more his puny efforts mocked his impotence. He strove and worked and failed and so despaired. Until in the course of time he went to Rome and saw the Catholic church at close quarters in its own capital and realised more and more how much of it depended on the performance of works of holiness – observing this thing and that. This fired him to make another great effort to resolve his difficulties and he set about making a study of the letter to the Romans because he was convinced that there lay the real solution. I do not want to drag out this little narrative but the outcome was his discovery of the great doctrine of justification by faith. This was like a great shaft of light, illuminating all the dark recesses of his life and mind. He saw that men are saved through faith – that their works are never capable of commending them to God. Imagine how fervently he believed in this – it answered all his problems. He held the doctrine of justification so passionately that in a sense he added a word to the New Testament – to the letter to the Romans chapter 3 verse 28. Therefore we conclude that a man is justified by faith *alone* without the deeds of the law. 'Alone' may be permissible properly understood, but Martin Luther from then on came to despise and reject any idea of works as being neccessary for salvation. Works represented to him so much the possibility of failure that he turned from the idea with revulsion. He held a true doctrine out of perspective – he over emphasised it and so it became itself dislocated and unbalanced. To him faith was everything and all else was nothing.

You can now understand why Martin Luther rejected the Epistle of James. It throws light on what James is seeking to teach. It marks the great purpose of his letter: that faith is good but without works it is dead; that faith untried is faith unreal. That is why this exhortation is sub-titled – 'The Trial of Faith'. The word 'trial' in this context means *test* - the test of faith. Faith untested has robbed faith of its real quality. It is like a piece of great music – composed but never performed. In reality it is only some black dots on white paper. It is like a Stradavarius violin, made but never used – hung on the wall. In reality it is only a piece of polished timber. It is like the seed of a rare plant which is never planted. In fact it remains a dry ball of inert chemicals. James has a vital message and to reject it or ignore it may result in dislocation of other things. It tells us again of the need to take the whole Bible. The whole is not in each part, but the whole is taking all together. Each writer has his peculiar office and therefore each one is important and essential.

### Tests that Try Faith

So James reminds us of the tests which try our faith and so make it real. The test of obedience. The test of brotherly love. The test of endurance. Yet there is another test he brings us to, which perhaps is the most severe of all – the test of the tongue. He says "The tongue is an unruly evil full of deadly poison". James is telling us that of all the forces of life the tongue is the most difficult to bridle. "The tongue can no man tame". Think of the harm which gossip does. Sometimes half truths are more deadly than full falsehoods. Hearts are inflamed, feelings are fevered, the mischief is done and our fellowship is poisoned. "If any man offend not in word, the same is a perfect man able also to bridle the whole body". If we would bless God we must learn also to bless men. James reminds of the contradiction of the fountain which out of the same source gives water which is pure and impure. That contradiction in terms of our life would be where men company around the Lord's table on Sunday and speak together of love and then later on the week change their overcoat and the language of love is forgotten. Hard and bitter things are spoken; the Lord's other children are hurt and the church is not edified. The test of faith about words is expressed like this: "Let no corrupt communication proceed out of your mouth, but that which is good to the use of edifying, that it may minister grace unto the hearers ... Let all bitterness, and wrath, and anger, and clamour, and evil speaking, be put away from you, with all malice: and be ye kind one to another, tenderhearted, forgiving one another, even as God for Christ's sake hath forgiven you" (Ephesians 4:29,31,32)

Language which is good to the use of edifying may sometimes mean having to speak plainly and un-compromisingly if the situation requires it. Not to speak like

209

that would be faithless and craven. But always and most of all then, it should be with grace seasoned with salt – "speaking the truth in love" – spoken in love to heal and to restore.

Our speech should be therefore not only free from corruption but in a positive way wholesome and healthful. And then the solemn thing about our speech is that in the final account we shall be judged by our own words: "By thy words shalt thou be justified and by thy words shalt thou be condemned". We shall be judged by the standard we have set up for others. This is just, but it is solemn. No man has a right to impose that which he is not prepared to accept himself.

The measure we have meted to others will be measured to us again. The merciful will obtain mercy and those who have hurt and harmed God's children with bitter words will discover that the tongue is a fire which scorches and burns ourselves as well as others. So then true faith is tested by the tongue – and it demands a tongue which speaks love and never hate – blessing and never cursing – healing and never harming.

**Faithful Prayer**

Finally he brings us to the test of prayer. For a man to speak of faith and never to pray is a contradiction so fundamental as to be unimaginable. The very essence of faith is trust, and trust is expressed in praying to God: praising, thanking, asking. James calls it "the prayer of faith". And the example he uses to reinforce his argument is the case of Elijah – the prophet of power. Elijah was a man inspired by faith to pray daringly. His great victory was done in the open but if we could know all the story we should find that it had been prepared in secret – praying and trusting.

Elijah may have appeared suddenly but he was not made in a day. Remember how James describes it. The effectual, fervent prayer of a righteous man availleth much. There was no frenzy in Elijah but there was fervour. He did not pray in cold blood – it was a cry of daring faith. He took his life in his hands. If the prayer had been unanswered he would have died instead of the prophets of Baal. It was a tremendous risk – but he was not afraid. He knew God and trusted in Him. It was the great test of his faith.

James tells us he was a righteous man. He was not praying for self but for the name and glory of God. Sometimes a wrong motive paralyses our praying – indeed James has warned us of this already in his letter. "Ye ask, and receive not, because ye ask amiss". James has also told us this about praying. "Ask in faith nothing wavering". These two principles were exemplified in Elijah – he did not ask amiss and he did not waver. So then, Elijah was a wonderful example, but James is careful to remind us that he was a man subject to like passions as we are. He was not fundamentally different. How *we* pray is a test of our faith. For the right things, with the right motives and in the right faith, and the outcome will be the right answer. Perhaps if we could pray with the faith and fervour of Elijah we should be able to abandon the things which are sapping our courage, or step out of the way of life which is full of worldly expectation but also full of spiritual danger – and our lives could be transformed – working and serving and not minding whether it means sacrifice and shame. This is the test of our faith, praying that God's will may be done in us – whatever it may mean, by way of change or reformation.

So then the trial of faith is not something to be feared or avoided or shed. Without it faith is emaciated, devitalised, dying and doomed. The trial of faith is a blessing. "My brethren, count it all joy when ye fall into divers trials. Knowing this that the trying of your faith worketh endurance. But let endurance have her perfect work that ye may be complete and entire, wanting nothing".

James' great principle is embodied in men of true faith all down the ages. God said to Noah – 'I am going to destroy this civilisation with a flood – build an ark and be saved'. Noah said: 'That is very interesting and I can believe it …', but if he had left it there it would have been useless. Instead he was moved with fear and worked. Abraham heard God say: 'I will bring you to a land of my choosing and give it to you for ever'. He said 'Thank you – I believe it', but he would never have received it without leaving Chaldea and working his way to Canaan. The walls of Jericho fell down but only because they were encompassed in faith for seven days. The principle is inexorable and timeless. "Faith without works is dead". To those who would dispute it, James has this word: "O vain man". "Therefore to him that knoweth to do good, and doeth it not, to him it is sin" (4:17).

My brethren, at this moment of bread breaking let us acknowledge that well-doing is an essential part of the discipline of Christ, "and let us not be weary in well-doing: for in due season we shall reap, if we faint not (Galatians 6:9).

211

# 35

## WORLDLINESS
### (1 JOHN 1 & 2)

THE words of the Apostle John about worldliness are so incisive and so trenchant that for an exhorting brother today to pass them over is not easy. Actually it was impossible for me because it is such a fascinating subject – so here we are – the exhortation is about worldliness.

Let us just recollect what John has written:

"Love not the world, neither the things that are in the world. If any man love the world, the love of the Father is not in him. For all that is in the world, the lust of the flesh, and the lust of the eyes, and the pride of life, is not of the Father, but is of the world. And the world passeth away, and the lust thereof: but he that doeth the will of God abideth for ever."                    (1 John 2:15,16)

One little digression – the word "lust" here in John is the same Greek word as in James 1:14: "Every man is tempted, when he is drawn away of his own lust, and enticed". The actual word means "desire" and whether it is good or bad desire has to be determined by the context. Obviously the desire in John is harmful. "The lust of the flesh, and the lust of the eyes and the pride of life". The desire is over-desire. What makes the subject so fascinating but difficult, is that whilst the principles about worldliness or perhaps I should say the principles about unworldliness are permanent, the application of them changes. Or put another way, whilst the principles are timeless, the maxims are variable.

### Standards of the Age

To give an illustration – it has been used before but it can be used again – if Brother Robert Roberts came into this meeting this morning, he would be utterly shocked and outraged – because of the manner of our dress. The ladies' legs actually visible, the colours, the style would be to him immodest and shameless. But our brother president is not shocked – to him it is perfectly normal and acceptable. Why is that? Because the measurement of worldliness is regulated to some extent by the standards of the age in which you live.

You do not have to go back 100 years to prove it – go back 50 years and hear my testimony.

When I came into the Truth worldliness was measured in our community by things like this – smoking, drinking, cinema-going and theatre-going, gambling, dancing. By most, these things were shunned. Today the measurement has changed. It is no good thundering about the cinema when every day and night it is in the corner of the room. When I came into the Truth Christadelphians did not enter public houses. Two weeks ago I went into a public house to celebrate my birthday – for a meal. Fifty years ago pubs were just drinking houses – today they are restaurants, usually very good restaurants. I should know – remember I was in the drink trade when I heard the Truth.

In those days people felt it was wrong. I recall many years ago Sister Ruth and I saw a couple of Christadelphians coming out of a public house – they were embarrassed and they said to us "The child was thirsty". So there you are – it is something to be borne in mind – worldliness has to be measured dispensationally to some extent, but the principles are timeless. In the case of Brother Roberts and the clothing – the principle is modesty and it is timeless, but what constitutes modesty may be regulated by the age in which you live. The maxims are variable.

**Creation the Evidence of Thought**

Let us give a little time now to looking at principles. Consider this. Behind every material thing, animal, vegetable, mineral, there is a thought, a conception, and intention. It is true of this glass – it was seen before it was made, it was intended before it was constructed. The principle is true all through life, be it sun, things, birds or trees. At the back of the material is a thought and behind the thought a thinker, behind the conception a conceiver. At the back of the world there is God – He is the Creator. Now this being true, the rational and reasonable process in the presence of the material things is to pass through them to the thought behind them, and so to the thinker, and in the presence of the thinker, to recognise Him and worship Him – to see the spiritual behind the natural.

Now this is my theory. A man of the world is a man who sees only the material and nothing else; who is prepared to deal with the material but never to recognise the spiritual of which the material is an expression; who lives in the realm of things seen and never passes through them to the reality of the unseen. This I believe is the fundamental idea of what

213

the Bible means by a worldly man. And I find confirmation of it in Romans 1:25 where the Apostle Paul speaks of some who "worshipped and served the creature more than the Creator". It is in this way that the world becomes an opposing force to the religion of God. Conversely an unworldly man, who seeing the world and using it, sees God behind it and worships the Creator instead of the creature. Watch the life of Jesus and you will see this to be true. He looked at flowers and enjoyed them and said that your heavenly Father clothes them. He heard the birds singing and said that God cares for them. He loved children and spoke of their angels beholding the face of God in heaven. He saw the shepherd on the hillside and said the shepherd-work of God will never cease until all the straying ones are brought home. He handled a common loaf and said that there is a bread which men may eat and live for ever. He looked at the vine in the fields and saw the life of God flowing out over the life of man. He held a penny and spake of rendering to God the things which are God's. He looked through the material and saw through it to the spiritual. In that sense he was not a man of this world.

**God and Mammon**

Jesus laid down an important principle about how to deal with the material. He said: "Ye cannot serve God and mammon" (Matthew 6:24). Jesus did not mean to teach that God and Mammon are fundamentally antagonistic. Mammon simply means the material world. God *provides* His children with Mammon. "Seek ye first the kingdom of God, and his righteousness; and all these things shall be added unto you". The whole matter turns on the word "serve". "Ye cannot *serve* God and mammon". No man can serve two masters. The service of one excludes the service of the other, whichever way it is. Behind the word "serve" is the idea of being mastered, of yielding full obedience. If a man is mastered by Mammon he will never serve God nor worship him. Let a man see through Mammon to God and he will serve God and worship Him, and Mammon will be in subjection. Notice then that Mammon is not evil in itself but it is how it is used which determines whether it is an opposing force or not. Worldliness, then, is being dominated by that which simply is material, transient, passing. It does not mean that worldly people are evil, or vulgar, or coarse or overtly fleshly. It could well be that their choices are highly respectable in every sense – their standards fastidious, their honesty meticulous. It is just that they live as though this were the only world, so that deep down the material is king. Here is an interesting thing. Jesus says to his disciples: "If the world hate you, ye know that it hated me before it hated you" (John 15:18). The world that hated Jesus and eventually slew him was embodied in some of the strictest men of his day.

They could argue about the length of a sabbath day's journey; they would never eat with unwashed hands – but they would leave a man to die in the ditch. These men hated Jesus – and why did they hate him? Because he challenged them in the midst of their material thinking with his conception of the spiritual. Although they were strict in some things they were worldly in the real sense of the word. They were men from whose hearts the real life of God had drained away. In spite of all their religion, they were dominated by material interests. So you see, it is how you regard the material, the transient, the transitory  that determines worldliness. The man of God gets the world in its right place and lays upon it the measurement of the spiritual.

Now did you notice this is exactly what John said today in our reading:

"If any man love the world, the love of the Father is not in him. For all that is in the world, the lust of the flesh, and the lust of the eyes, and the pride of life, is not of the Father, but is of the world. And the world passeth away, and the lust thereof: but he that doeth the will of God abideth for ever." (1 John 2:15)

Notice carefully that worldliness is not determined by the actual objects with which men have to do, but by the spirit in which those objects are used. It is not the flesh, nor the eye, nor the life which is wrong, but it is the lust of the flesh, and the lust of the eye and the pride of life. Lust of the flesh is the love of that which is purely sensual – an affection for that which is outward. The lust of the eye is the love of that which is transient; form and colour, which at best pass away. Pride of life is the love of that which is unreal – a view of life which depends upon possessions, wealth, advancement, rank and human opinion. Love of the outward, love of the transitory, love of the unreal. Mark that it is exactly in accordance with what Jesus said about worldliness – emphasis on the material to the exclusion of the spiritual. And John reveals something else – you cannot love the world and love God at the same time – one or the other but not both. The two loves are mutually exclusive. The love of the one expels the love of the other. Exactly the same as revealed by Jesus – no man can serve two masters. You cannot worship the creature and the Creator at the same time. And observe this – John takes it for granted that we shall love something – he does not seem to provide for any middle course. It is a case of love misplaced or love rightly placed; love of this world or love of God's world.

## The Secret of Unworldliness

One last witness – the Apostle Paul. He knew that the men and women of Christ were living out their lives in the midst of the facts of life and were in danger of being moulded by the world – so he said: "be not conformed [moulded] to this world, but be ye transformed by the renewing of your mind". So his advice is this: "Use this world, as not abusing it: for the fashion of this world passeth away" (1 Corinthians 7:31). What he means is this. If you use the world never think it is the end in itself – it is only the means. So notice this especially – men of the world and men of God do not use different things but what they do is this – they use the same things differently. This is the secret of unworldliness.

If you accept that measurement, then think what it means for ourselves living in this material age and on the margin of the Kingdom of God. It brings us back to something we are often facing in this house in our speaking and in our discussions – the need to strike a right balance between the transient and the eternal – between the material and the spiritual. There are some searching questions which come leaping at us from the teaching of Jesus, John and Paul – does our involvement with the world intrude into the life of faith and stop us being faithful and constant? Do we have to set aside our service of the spiritual in order to serve the material? Is our timetable right? In these days time is so vital. It determines how we live. We have so many good intentions but they are lost through lack of time – so have we got the timetable right?

And when we speak of striking a right balance, remember something important. With a pair of scales a right balance is where the two sides are just about equal – but in this equation there is a paradox. The right balance means being weighted heavily to one side, the side of the the spiritual, of the eternal, of the way of faith. Jesus gave the priority. He said: "Seek ye first the kingdom of God ... and all these things shall be added unto you". "Seek ye first ...". We do not believe that the world is number one – of course not. But the problem is, it is easy to get inveigled into having to live as though it is. So here are some suggestions that may be of help in the spiritual audit which John's words ought to make us face. In our present use of the world ask these questions:

- Is it hindering my spiritual progress – am I having to neglect the things of the Truth in order to pursue the things of the moment?
- Will it get a hold over me so that things being what they are I may wish to break away but somehow I cannot?
- Is it doing any harm to those close to me and is it hindering my brethren and sisters?
- There are some aspects of the Truth which just now are crying out for helpers and workers – could I be such a helper but my involvement with the world and with the transitory prevents me – I just have no time?

These are questions for you and for me and there is one last sentence I want to recall for you – the words of John: "This is the victory which overcometh the world, even our faith" (1 John 5:4). So the best protection and the best bulwark against worldliness is to get closer and closer to the things of our faith. Read the word of God more faithfully, get closer to the regular fellowship of the ecclesia, enter into the work which needs doing, let the spiritual become dominant in a practical way. Let prayer be more than two minutes of the lay-me-down-to-sleep kind – men ought always to pray and not to faint. That means if men pray, they will not faint under the burden of worldliness.

In case somebody may be thinking I have been unfair in this little exhortation and have shut my eyes to the facts of life – yes I do know that you are compelled to be in the world, work in it, and wrest a living from it. Yes, I know that very well and know also that exercising your proper liberty and using the world's legitimate forces, you are striving not to be moulded by it. It is not easy, indeed it can be very hard – so is there a better time to try to make some adjustments or to resolve to make them? At this moment of memorial as we break the bread and sip the wine – remember this man is the very best ally in the contest. In the most poignant prayer he ever prayed he said this: "I pray not that thou shouldest take them out of the world, but that thou shouldest keep them from the evil".

By faith we must believe that his prayer is a perpetual intercession, and seek to say Amen and make it our own petition. The love of the world is unlearned by the love of him. This is what I mean. You want to be a great success – the cross is failure. You want to win the world's approbation – the cross is infamy. You want to be prosperous and happy – the cross is pain and sharpness. Learn that lesson truly and the power of the world is gone. Then there will be no need to bid you, in denunciation or invitation, not to love the world. In this solemn moment of memorial I must leave it with you.

# 36

## "WALKING IN TRUTH"
### (2 JOHN & 3 JOHN)

THOSE two little letters of John, so short and concise, could be written on two sheets of notepaper. But notice how often he refers to "the Truth". This word "Truth" seems to be the predominating idea in these letters: "Whom I love in the truth" (2 John :1; 3 John :1); "They that have known the truth" (2 John :1); "For the truth's sake" (verse 2); "In truth and love" (verse 3); "Walking in truth" (verse 4); "Walkest in the truth" (3 John :3); "My children walk in truth" (verse 4); "Fellowhelpers to the truth" (verse 8); "Of the truth itself" (verse 12).

This phrase "walking in the truth" occurs in both letters and today I am concerned to know what exactly he means – to know it for our soul's sake: Walking in the Truth. Sometimes when we refer to the Truth we mean our community. We ask about someone: "Was he ever in the Truth?" We mean is: "Was he a Christadelphian?" It is not so much an enquiry about the quality of his spiritual life – but principally whether he was a member of our community.

Now when John says "walking in the truth" he is not using the word "truth" in this sense. The word which John uses is not a noun, like "truth" is a noun. It is an adverb and it means 'truly'. So what he is really saying in verse 4 of 2 John is this: "I rejoiced greatly that I found of thy children walking truly, even as we have received a commandment from the Father". The declaration is telling us something which is scattered all through the Bible – that in the final analysis truth is not just a matter of words, or just a matter of knowledge, but in the real sense it is a matter of character. Our Lord did not say: "I speak the Truth", though he certainly did. What he said was: "*I am* the Truth". We know well enough that it is possible to know the truth intellectually and at the same time to lead a false life. There may be perfect theology and yet the deeds may be heresy.

Sometimes in our community you meet people who want to move heaven and earth to preserve the right understanding of say the Apocalypse, and yet forget the right application of

219

love. In other words they hate those who disagree with them. We must try to see the inconsistency of being true only in one way. You sometimes meet people who would be horrified at the thought of actually telling a lie and yet their whole life is a tissue of small untruths. A collection of lies lived out – pretence, outward show, careless misrepresentation.

So, that is the first thing to remember – that truth believed ought to result in truth in action, else in a way it becomes false. Our Lord's enemies were people in this category. They were instant upon the theory – but forgot to do the real things which made the theory true.

## Walking with Integrity

There is no doubt, that the way in which John is using the word truth, involves very much the idea of integrity. By integrity we do not mean just being honest, though of course it includes that. From its derivation the word integrity means wholeness, entireness, soundness. We speak of something being an integral part of something else. We mean it is central – essentially the same in the fundamental sense. Entireness is a good central meaning. That which Jesus meant when he said: "If thine eye be single [or sound], thy whole body shall be full of light". In other words, integrity means extending through the whole of character. It is against the idea of a divided personality. It outlaws the idea of the split mind – that is being true in some ways but not true in others.

For example, people are often very careful never to break a rule which is laid down precisely in words – but constantly violate principles which need to be discerned and applied. Sometimes we think we hate falsehood and are gratified that we do, when really we are hating only the consequences of falsehood. Sometimes lies and hypocrisy are hated, not so much because they are untrue, but more because they harm us. We can test ourselves. We hate the false unpleasant things which are said about us – and are quick to have them denied for the sake of truth. But what about when somebody says something about us which is very nice – but untrue. Are we as anxious then to have the truth established? Are we not half-pleased with the false praise? Walking in the Truth means striving to be true in every department of life.

It is easy to think that standing up for the truth means holding fast in some great crisis – standing up and being counted. But walking in the Truth means being true in the everyday things of discipleship. The commonplace things – the infinitesimal details of daily life. The ordinary things of

220

the ecclesia, the home, the family, the career and recreation. These disparate things are integrated by the truth. Notice the verb that John uses – he says "*walking* in the truth". Just occasionally the Bible urges us to fight – fight the good fight of faith. Just occasionally we are urged to run – run the race. Just occasionally we are urged to bear the burden and not to give up. But regularly we are urged to walk – this is the verb which most often describes the way of the disciple. The Bible is full of it – walk in the light; walk in newness of life; walk honestly as in the day; walk by faith; walk in the spirit; walk worthy of the vocation wherewith ye are called. So it could go on. The shortest biography in the Bible is in Genesis 5 – it says: "Enoch walked with God".

Now the thing about walking is that it is an everyday thing. It enters into the commonplace things of life. It is the first thing we do as we leave our beds – it is the last thing we do as we go to our beds. And in between we are doing it all through the day. So walking in the Truth is letting truth influence all the commonplace things of life. Being true at every level. It is not easy. What is easy – and I know it to my cost – is to utter lofty sentiments of truth and then to exclude them from the everyday things. Just an example. We say that this word is the Word of God. The Voice of God – a light in the darkness – the Word of Life; an oasis in the desert; a covert from the tempest; a guide over the dark waters; a rock in the shifting sand; without it life is cold, and empty and without hope. That is the truth about the Word of God. The question is, do we walk as though it were true? How have we been this week? Were we using it every day? Did we seek to know it better – were we there when it was on the agenda?

## Ecclesial Life

The ecclesia – what is the truth about it? It is the ecclesia of Christ; it is the family of God; it is the assembly of the saints; it is the congregation of those who are called, blood-sprinkled, and chosen; it is the church of the firstborn; it is the place of fellowship; it is the body of Christ; it is the Temple of God. That is the truth about the ecclesia. How do we walk in the light of that truth? Do we love the ecclesia? Are we concerned to keep it pure and true? Is it the centre of our life? Do we give it top priority? Is our contact with it regular, faithful and supportive? Are we sad when it is criticised, knocked and despised? Think of the truth about the family. It is a family in the truest sense of the word. They are not just called your brethren and sisters – they *are* your brethren and sisters. Since the flesh is subservient to the

221

spirit, the spiritual affinity of the family of God is at least as important as your natural family. That is the truth about the family of God. How do we walk in the light of that truth? Are we interested? Do we care? Is there a loving anxiety for the welfare of God's other children? Would we consider being as generous to them as we are to our own children? What limitation do we put upon our pastoral work? Walking in the Truth means living in such a way as to make these things a reality every day.

**Fellowship**

Let us get another view of walking in the Truth. John in his first epistle says: "But if we walk in the light, as he is in the light, we have fellowship one with another, and the blood of Jesus Christ his Son cleanseth us from all sin" (1:7). Here is a masterpiece. John is insisting that the reality of a disciple's fellowship with God is to be measured by the reality of his fellowship with his brethren. In other words that which comes as a barrier between one disciple and another might at the same time be a barrier between that disciple and God. Barriers can become brick walls – on earth and between earth and heaven. Notice John's words: "If we walk in the light, as he is in the light". Ephesians 5:13 says: "Whatsoever doth make manifest is light". The conclusion is simple. Light reveals – darkness hides. When we are outwardly what we are inwardly, when we are willing to be open, honest, reproved, willing to be seen truly – that is light. When we are secretive, pretending, excusing ourselves, window dressing, filling our mouths with other people's faults, hiding what we really are – that is darkness.

John calls it walking in darkness. Walking truly is therefore walking in the light; to know the truth about ourselves; to be willing to hold the light to our motives and our methods; to stop using guile; to give things their right names. It means pocketing our pride; risking our reputation for the sake of being open and honest; being ready to say we might have been wrong; ready to abandon the wrong feeling; ready to cherish a loving spirit to those we might have neglected; ready to urge every defence for our brother which we claim for ourselves. Of course it is not easy. If anybody tells you it is you can be sure they have misunderstood it. It will be humbling, but if it is followed, the Truth will be lived on an altogether higher level. This is walking in the Truth to some purpose – in the spirit of honesty, integrity and openness. When the barriers are down and the masks are off then the Truth dominates men and women in fellowship and they walk truly for love's sake.

Where there is walking in Truth there is peace of mind and hearts. There is nothing to hide about which we have to manoeuvre. There is no fear of being exposed; no secret rooms where our brother is excluded; no feelings of being a fraud; no fears that others may be having hard thoughts about us which they are keeping to themselves. A loving confession or a loving challenge will bring peace to hearts which might otherwise be fevered with fear or disturbed by deceit.

Ponder these things and I believe we shall get nearer to what John meant by walking in the Truth – things of daily intercourse with the Truth and which prove to be at the very centre of our faith. As the spokes of a wheel get nearer to the centre, so they get nearer to each other. It is the truth at all its levels and in all its varied ways which brings us closer to each other. Men and women, sharing a common faith and partaking of a common hope; impulsed by one force – the force of love – all of one family and having one Father.

Here is another great truth. The Kingdom of God. It is the one thing which we long for. It is the centre of our hope. It is the focus of our expectation. It means our real vocation is not here at all, it is in the age to come. The Bible says that here we have no continuing city – we are strangers and pilgrims in this world. How do we walk in the light of that Truth? Do we lead a pilgrim life? Are we detached from the affairs of the world? Are we indifferent to its glittering prizes? Are we careful to ensure that our worldly business does not encroach upon our duties and our life in the Truth? Are we willing to draw the line on God's side? This is walking in the Truth about the Kingdom of God.

The final application of this principle has to do with the thing we have come to celebrate. Our redeemer sacrificed himself to the uttermost for our sakes. He held back nothing for love's sake. In your readings last Sunday you heard the Apostle Peter say that he is our example that we should follow his steps (see 1 Peter 2:21). It means that his love ought to constrain us. Because he spared not himself, we are urged not to spare ourselves in his cause. How do we walk in the light of that Truth? When the Truth claims our loyalty and our allegiance, when the service of the Truth claims our time and substance and energy. How do we walk in the Truth? We ought to have another look at our reasons for sparing ourselves. I know that when I do it for myself sometimes the reasons are paltry. Confronted with the cross, the reasons make us ashamed.

Remember, I said at the beginning I wanted to find out what John meant by walking in the Truth. Now at the end, evidently it was a little phrase full of awful significance.

Properly applied it could turn us inside out. Of course we could ignore it – but let us not do that. Give it a fair run in your mind and in your conscience. There is not a better time to do it than now – confronted by the one who walked in the Truth superbly for love's sake. When all is said and done, it is by this our lives will be measured.

# 37

## "THEY SHALL WALK WITH ME IN WHITE"
### (REVELATION 3 AND 7)

WHEN you think of the white-robed, spirit-filled, life-mastered multitude – those who are elect, blood-sprinkled, chosen and at last glorified – notice the conditions which preceded their exaltation. It is revealed in Revelation chapter 7. They came out of great tribulation; they had hungered and they had suffered thirst; they had wandered in the desert without protection and they had wept for sorrow in their adversity. The contrast is startling but it ought not to surprise us because it is in this way that the Bible presents to us the Kingdom of God. The possibilities are so wonderful and its realisation so glorious, that the only way it can be presented to our finite minds is by contrast with our earthly experience. The hope of the Truth is by its very nature the expectation of something desired but not yet attained. It is not the expectation of something we do not understand, else it would provoke no genuine hope. It shines brightest in the darkness and is strongest in conditions which would otherwise make for despair. What it promises therefore, is related to what we now lack.

What it provokes us to hope for is the very opposite of the things which we now suffer and which make us sad. So then, inevitably, we form our conception of life to come and all it means, out of the needs and experience of our present life. This is how the Bible presents the coming of the new day to the people of God. It is presented to us as satisfying our needs, healing our wounds and answering the cry of our hearts for life in all its divine variety.

Let me illustrate. The paralysed man was promised: "They shall mount up with wings as eagles ..." (Isaiah 40:31). The deaf and dumb girl learned: "The ears of the deaf shall be unstopped ... and the tongue of the dumb shall sing" (Isaiah 35:5,6). Some people call this superficial, and if they must they must, but this is how the Bible presents to us the picture of the morning without clouds: when the clouds of danger, distress and fear are banished. "Comfort ye, comfort ye my people ... the Lord GOD will come with strong hand ... behold, his reward is with him" (Isaiah 40:1,10). Remember this: "He

225

shall feed his flock like a shepherd: he shall gather the lambs with his arm, and carry them in his bosom" (verse 11). The King once said: "For the elect's sake those days shall be shortened" (Matthew 24:22). Included in those words is the same idea. All the powers and forces gathered in that phrase "those days" are to be ended for the sake of the elect – the white-robed multitude. All the things which are antagonistic and which seek to wear out the saints of the Most High, are to be vanquished in the light of the new day.

Once again our conception of that day is related to our present experience. Listen to God's promises: "They shall hunger no more, neither thirst any more; neither shall the sun light on them, nor any heat. For the Lamb which is in the midst of the throne shall feed them [be their shepherd, RV], and shall lead them unto living fountains of waters: and God shall wipe away all tears from their eyes" (Revelation 7:16,17). What a startling idea, a lamb leading the flock, a lamb protecting the sheep. Recollect the harmony between Isaiah 40 and Revelation 7. "He shall feed his flock like a shepherd: he shall gather the lambs with his arm, and carry them in his bosom, and shall gently lead those that are with young" (Isaiah 40:11).

This is the Bible method. In terms of human weakness you may gather hope for divine perfection. Within the limitation of human experience you may catch the infinite possibilities of the divine abundance. Following this method then, how do you conceive it? What does it mean for you as you ponder the words of Revelation 7 about the white-robed multitude?

### New Heavens and a New Earth

There was a broken-hearted man once who looked forward and onward out of his own experience to the day when that body of people will be revealed. He once wept bitterly and thought he was lost and finished – and as he looked forward he saw the end of all weeping, and loneliness and despair and weakness. All the things which once beset his path were to be swallowed up by the grace of the coming day. He wrote this to his friends: "We … look for new heavens and a new earth, wherein dwelleth righteousness" (2 Peter 3:13). Perhaps when you look onward to the day when the Lamb shall spread his tent over the flock, your conception of it is related to your present needs. I cannot tell, but you will know; some hope perhaps springing out of your present adversity or failure; the ending of some disability which has beset your path and which only the Lamb can deal with; the alleviation of some pain or the healing of some wound over which no

226

human physician has any power; the shedding of some burden which cannot be laid aside until the Lord bear it away; the ending of some weariness which no human sympathy can ameliorate; the realisation of some ideal which this mortality can do nothing to satisfy. So you are looking for the day when the white- robed multitude will be manifested and you long for it out of the deep recesses of your own experience.

I know this may sound too dreary to be real. I know that human life can be wonderful, but when the sun is westering, and the powers are failing and the zest is ebbing and the strength is waning – there is a sadness about the corruptibility of human life which we cannot escape feeling. It is the sadness of the autumn leaf falling and decaying. When the shadows are long and the flesh cries for comfort – life is too much limitation. Out of this condition there is only one real encouragement – the pole star of our faith; the master passion of all our striving, that one day we may walk with the Lamb in white. Let us make no mistake, my comrades, the assurance of all the wonderful things we may conceive, rests wholly and completely upon the Lamb. He is our confidence. He it is who spreads the tent, just as once he pitched it amid the Galilean fishermen. So one day he will spread it over the white-robed multitude. The man of the seamless robe, who alone and superbly is able to fill the world with divine government and cause God's will to be done on earth: the Wonderful Counsellor, the God of Battles, the Begetter of Eternity, the Prince of Peace. Immanuel – the Mystery of God.

Let us be sure of one thing. The Lamb is able to wield authority because he first submitted to authority. He exercises power because he first submitted to it. It is an old principle – he who holds the sceptre at last is he who kissed it at first. The influence you exert is the influence of the throne to which you have bowed – good or bad. The Lamb is in the midst of the throne because he first yielded to it. He is able to exercise perfect government because he first submitted to it. Remember Philippians chapter 2: "[He] took upon him the form of a servant ... and became obedient unto death, even the death of the cross. Wherefore God also hath highly exalted him". The Lamb in the midst of the throne is able to lead and feed and succour with unassailable power. He is there on the throne of universal empire. He lives in the spacious ages of eternity, because once he came into the littleness of human time and for love's sake bowed himself to

God's government and left nothing unremitted to God's authority. Between the submission and the authority there is a perfect inter-relationship. Paul wrote to the Ephesians: "He raised him from the dead, and set him at his own right hand in the heavenly places" (1:20). The right hand of God is the place of unfading and infinite glory. He is there on the light-girdled throne of the Ancient of Days as the shepherd and the file leader and the life-giver.

Brother Thomas says in *Eureka* that the white-robed saints have palms in their hands to indicate the great celebration of the feast of tabernacles. He says:

"This great national celebration of the Feast of Tabernacles, then, argues the previous cessation of judgment; and consequently, the resting of the Saints from their labours in the execution of it."

(Chapter VII, Part 12 – *Feast of Tabernacles*)

The king of love my shepherd is. For love's sake he is determined to end the forces which hurt and harm his flock. He is the shepherd and the lawgiver. He utters the final word on each man's probation. It is utterly dependable. We need have no anxiety about his power. In all the feverish fussiness of this neurotic age he is Lord of all. Twenty centuries have passed since men heard his voice, but his word is living and abiding. This very day it is searching our hearts and compelling us to be outwardly what we are inwardly. This is the one who walks with his friends in white, who brings his shepherd care to the aid of those who have washed their robes in his blood. That is why they are clothed in white. No fuller can whiten like the blood of the Lamb. By his judgement they are purified and succoured. Think what his judgement is. It is absolute rectitude. It is the holding of the balances. It is the re-adjustment of that which is wrong. Judgement is heaven's work of love, ending the sighing and the sobbing and the sadness once for all. He will make no truce with the forces which are bent on evil – the cowardly forces which maim and destroy God's world. He will avenge the blood of his saints. Thank God that on his garment and on his thigh there is a name written: "King of kings and Lord of lords". The Lamb with the Lion Heart.

**Heavenly Jerusalem**

Think of another great vision that John saw as it is revealed in Revelation chapter 21. He saw that great city, the holy Jerusalem, descending out of heaven from God. Flashing with jasper, beautiful with divine beauty, clear as crystal: Jerusalem the golden, where there is everlasting day and unsullied glory. Remember that it is a city of exclusion and a city of inclusion. These things are excluded – tears and mourning and crying and pain. Those who are fearful and unbelieving and abominable. Murderers, fornicators, sorcerers, idolaters and all liars. Night is excluded – night that provides opportunity for evil. The unclean is excluded – the occasion of evil. That which makes a lie is excluded – the occupation of evil. The curse is excluded – the outcome of evil. So all the things are excluded which corrupt and harm; the things which falsify and dislocate; the things which degrade and disgrace; the things which bring sorrow and doom. All conditions and character and conduct which are in opposition to the final and perfect social order are excluded from the city, the holy Jerusalem.

Mark the things which are included. Light and life and love and order and beauty; everlasting day and peace and strength. Purity is the master force of the city and truth is the government. The water of life – the fountains of living water, as clear as crystal. The Lamb is there and they which are written in the Lamb's book of life – the unnumbered white-robed fellowship of the redeemed – of the firstborn. So, included are all the things which succour and save, the things which ennoble and empower. The forces of goodness and grace which are set on the healing of wounds, the ending of strife, the drying of tears, and for the bringing of the final victory. For these reasons, the promise is utterly dependable. "They shall walk with me in white" (Revelation 3:4).

Come back to the word of that man who once said: "We … look for new heavens and a new earth, wherein dwelleth righteousness". In a few incisive syllables he gave us a vision of the new day and the new life. He called it: "an inheritance incorruptible, and undefiled, that fadeth not away" (1 Peter 1:4). "Incorruptible", he said, and you can measure it only by your present experience.

Think of the numbness in the hearts of those two sisters at Bethany when they looked on the dead face of their brother. Think of the agony in the heart of the widow of Nain as she walked alongside the bier upon which her only boy lay cold in death. Or bring it to our own day. Think of the breadwinner taken, the children orphaned, the promise of life cut short. With soft footfall and hushed spirits we take our stand in the midst of death-stricken humanity to confess the awfulness of the corruption which has spoiled the race. Or think of the defilement of sin. Think of life tarnished by ruthless temptation. Think of the constant struggle which has to be

229

waged against the allurements of the flesh. Think of self which comes every day demanding preference and seeking to grasp the place of government in a human life. Think of all the insidious ways in which good men and women are ensnared and sometimes degraded by the power of the flesh. Think of that warfare where there is never a discharge and where the best may be polluted. Think of these things – the awfulness of death and the shame of pollution – and then note well these words: "an inheritance incorruptible, and undefiled, that fadeth not away". They describe a condition where there is no more sin, and no more weeping over failure and no more festering corruption, and nothing to hamper the development of divine life – where at last there is perfection and purity. Here is revealed the moment of emancipation – life not just of endless continuity but of unsurpassed quality: the wandering ceased; the weariness ended; the tears halted; the robes pure white. It is outside our grasp – we have to measure it out of present experience.

## We Shall Be Like Him

The Bible does not lead us where it is impossible for us to go, but there are great whispers in the word of God giving us a gleam of personality beyond the horizon. Think of the great whisper of John: "We shall be like him". John knew what he meant for he had seen the risen Lord, the ever-living had touched him, spoken with him and eaten breakfast with him. That is the wonder of it – men of our kith and kin handled the immortal flesh of God's lamb – knew him to be the same man who had walked the streets and hills of Galilee; who laughed at Cana and wept at Bethany; who sweat blood in the garden of spices and who first called them by name. "We shall be like him".

The last word has not been spoken about that life which was won out of death by the bruising of the holy child, even the death of the cross. The Lamb has broken in pieces the gates of brass – he has cut the bars of iron asunder. Apart from him all life is emaciated – our hope is forlorn. Our path is cold and wasted. Our garments are filthy and wretched. We stumble and fall. Let us not mistake it. The claimant cry for life is satisfied in him and in no other. He is the river, the refuge and the rock.

As you think finally of the majestic walking in white with the man of the seamless robe, think sympathetically what it means for the world. It means that all the pain and groaning of the world is answered in the things for which the redeemed saints are made whole. As we meet here today London is groaning, New York is groaning, Moscow is groaning, Peking is groaning. Soon there will be an epidemic of fear. All the burdened multitudes of the world are waiting for deliverance – for the dawning of the new day.

The world travails waiting for the manifestation of the sons of God. That includes you. Say it not boastfully but tenderly, reverently, gladly. You for whom the white robe has been woven without seam by the Lamb's striving. For you it is rousing, invigorating, and exciting. It is the realisation of all your longing, the issue of all your striving. You are coming to the morning without clouds, to the city where no night is; where tears are wiped away and all harm is excluded.

So in the solemn moment of bread breaking in memory of his life-giving sacrifice, when we have the opportunity to open our hearts in private to God, let us give thanks with hushed spirits for this man of Nazareth, the virgin-born, the ever-living, the guarantor of our redemption.